Also by Steve McKee:

The Call of the Game

COACH

Steve McKee

STACKPOLE
BOOKS

Library of Congress Cataloging-in-Publication Data

McKee, Steve.
    Coach / Steve McKee. — 1st ed.
      p.   cm.
    ISBN 0-8117-2537-5
    1. Coaching (Athletics)   2. Coaches (Athletics)—United States—
Interviews.   I. Title.
GV711.M38   1994
796'.07'7—dc20   93-27901
                                                                 CIP

*This book is dedicated to my sister, Kathy,
and her husband, Jon, true believers both,
who have always encouraged me to stay with it.*

*Also, this book was written with thoughts of two
coaches close at hand: Jack Saboda and Jim Forjan.
I played for one and still wish I had played for
the other.*

*And finally to my wife, Noreen, who was unlucky
enough to have lived with me as this project ran
almost a year longer than intended.*

Contents

Acknowledgments

ABOVE ALL OTHERS I must first thank Judith Schnell, my editor at Stackpole Books. She doesn't care much about sports, but she cared deeply about this project, and about me. And David Uhler, Judith's assistant, who never once lost patience, even when he should have.

Jim Villaro was the first person I consulted regarding this project. It was 1989, and he was in Fairbanks, Alaska, where I was visiting. Jim was also one of the last persons to read the manuscript. It was 1993, and I was in Brooklyn and he was visiting. His input and support, from start to finish, were invaluable.

I should also thank Geraldine Myers of York, Pennsylvania, who did the lion's share of the transcription for this project, and Mary Kaessinger of New York City, who did the rest. Without their diligence there would have been no book, at least not in this century.

I would have been unable to write *Coach* without the assistance of many people who contacted coaches on my behalf or provided solid leads. Every contact or lead did not result in an interview, but the efforts of the following people are much appreciated:

Gary Abbott, USA Wrestling
Fred Ali, Los Angeles
Mark Bivens, *Murfreesboro Daily News Journal*
Larry Bonham, *Palm Springs Desert Sun*
Tommy Bonk, *Los Angeles Times*

Roger Brigham, *Albany Times-Union*
John S. Bruel
Joe Clark, *The Village Voice*
John Compardo, Allentown College of St. Francis de Sales
Steve Coursin
Jim Gross, Omaha
Jim Guise, *High School Sports*
Margo Ericson, U.S. Synchronized Swimming Association
Janet at the U.S. Diving Association
Johnny Kuykendall, *Lannett* (Alabama) *Valley Times*
Alexis Lipsitz
Kristin Matta, U.S. Figure Skating Association
Jeff Mammenga, *Pierre Capital Journal*
Mo Merhoff, U.S. Rowing Association
John Mitchell, Seton Hall University
John Ogulnik, National Public Radio
Donna Raskin, for being Donna
Kathryn Reith, Women's Sports Foundation
Bert Sahlberg, *Moscow Idahoian*
Robert T. Scott, Executive Director, Hockey Hall of Fame
Rex Spires, *Decatur Herald Review*
Dr. Richard Voy, former Medical Director, U.S. Olympic
    Committee
Abe Winter, *The Bismarck Tribune*
Dr. Richard Yesalis, Penn State University
Dana Yost, *Marshall* (Minnesota) *Independent*

Finally, to the coaches I interviewed. Although they did not all make it past the last cut, they all gave their time, thoughts, hopes, and dreams—little pieces of themselves that, taken together, I hope, have made for a complete *Coach*.

Pregame

The voice comes at you filled with dust and grass burrs, all the way from West Texas and six-man high school football, Texas A&M and the sidelines of the Houston Astrodome. You can hear Bear Bryant in there too; even a little George Allen.

"Coach Bryant has put out a lot of coaches," the voice says. "But when he'd counsel you, talk to you about becoming a coach, he'd tell you not to do it. *Don't go into coaching.* Don't do it—unless you just can't live without it. If you're not happy doing anything else and you got to be in it, then accept the fact that you'll always be working late, you're never going to see your family, you're going to be criticized by everybody, right or wrong. If there's any alternative, take it. If you question yourself at all, find a different line of work."

Jack Pardee, the owner of the voice, played college ball for the Bear at Texas A&M. He was one of the survivors of Bryant's famous trek through the preseason wilderness in 1954. Nearly twenty years later, after thirteen seasons with the Los Angeles Rams in the NFL, he hooked up with George Allen and the Washington Redskins and rode to fame and glory with the Over-the-Hill Gang.

He then ignored the advice he'd heard from The Man Himself. Jack Pardee became a coach. One year as a Skins assistant, followed by head jobs with the Florida Blazers of the WFL (remember them?), the Chicago Bears, the Skins, the Houston Gamblers of the USFL, the University of Houston, and the Houston Oilers.

Jack Pardee isn't the first coach to ignore this particular piece of good advice—expostulated by a man in a houndstooth hat who knew what he was talking about—and he most assuredly won't be the last. "I always knew what I wanted to do with my life," says Bill Whitmore, who for five years was head basketball coach at the University of Vermont. "I'd go to my guidance counselors from the seventh grade on and they'd say, 'What do you want to do?' And I'd say, 'I want to coach.' And every year they'd tell me there were other things to look at. And I'd say, 'No, this is what I want to do with my life.'"

How many coaches are there, from the pee-wees to the pros? How many people do this with their lives? Thousands? *Tens* of thousands? Who are they, these people we call coach? What is it like to stand next to the action and still be completely consumed by it? What does it take? How do they do it, and why? I decided to find out. To listen to coaches talk about themselves. To talk to them about the games we play. To learn the game the way a coach must learn it. To love the game the way a coach must love it.

"I don't know if anyone can understand why we do this" was a familiar refrain, frequently offered. Many times followed by: "I'm not sure I understand it myself."

Why *do* coaches coach? What is it that keeps them coming back to the game? Love? Fame? Fortune? That thunderclap of excitement when the opening bell sounds? Or is it something harder to articulate, something less well defined?

The idea was to explore the territory. Interview an Abe Lemons, who spent thirty-seven years on the sidelines coaching basketball at three colleges, as well as a Walter Lewis, an assistant football man at Kentucky who left the profession after three years. Talk with a Ron Dickerson, now the head football coach at Temple, but at the time the defensive coordinator at Clemson and a past president of the Black Coaches Association. Listen to a man at a major university request that his name not be used—lest he be booted for being gay. Spend a couple of hours with a Don Nelson, the big-time coach of the Golden State Warriors in the big-time NBA, but also spend time with a Pat Ward Seib, a high school volleyball coach, whose career started in the exciting, though hardly glamorous, early days of Title IX.

No grand scheme was devised to select coaches; there was no

formula. If Tony LaRussa of the Oakland A's gets to bring his World Series ring to the table, then Harry Vanderslice of the Ocean City, New Jersey, Little League gets to bring his thirty-two years of experience.

I interviewed 161 coaches in forty-seven states. Of those, 148 appear in these pages. When pursuing the well-known coaches, I aimed a shotgun guaranteed to produce a wide pattern. Since there was no correlation between the difficulty in procuring an interview and its subsequent success, I wasted little energy chasing anybody. The "name" coaches who responded—John Wooden, K. C. Jones, Linda Leaver, P. J. Carlesimo, Chuck Noll, Pat Head Summitt, Joe Torre, George Karl—all offered themselves with few conditions and little fanfare.

I proceeded on the assumption that all coaches, no matter what their game or the level at which they coach it, share a common experience. That there is a vertically inserted connecting rod that joins together the various horizontal levels of the coaching profession into a single identifiable unit. "I ran out on the field for a high school championship, out on the field for a junior college championship game, and then the Rose Bowl and the Super Bowl," says Dick Vermeil, who coached at Hillsdale High and Napa Junior College in California, and at UCLA and with the Philadelphia Eagles. "I don't think any of those experiences were any different to me. In terms of what it felt like as a coach, it was all relative. I always felt a great sense of responsibility to the players. A great *appreciation* for the players who had made the opportunity possible. And I always felt humbled by it all."

This isn't a playbook, a three-ring binder from which can be gleaned next week's game plan. This is a book of voices, collected voices blending into one collective voice, speaking as one coach for all coaches. About what it's like following your team onto the court for the big game. About getting hired, building a team, winning and losing and getting fired. This book is about coaching, but it's also about being coached. It's about paying the price. It's about dreaming, succeeding and failing.

Most of the interviews were conducted by telephone. How else, practically speaking, to talk with Alan Rowan, a hugely successful track coach in Honolulu, or Reggie Joules, a keeper of the traditional Eskimo games in Kotzebue, Alaska, ninety miles north of the Arctic Circle? The average interview ran to over an hour (and forty pages of transcript). I had lists of questions but rarely stuck to a script. No single coach told the complete story. I'd try to find the particular story an individual coach wanted to tell and listen closely. Hand off the ball and get out of the way.

Adhering to the oral-history format proved to be much like what many coaches had observed about their teams: Your greatest strength is often your greatest weakness. Oral history is all in the words, all in the voices. But those same words, those same voices, are the entire game plan.

A few coaches (although not many, I believe) brought their own agenda to the interview. Many coaches fell into a prevent defense when buzzwords like "steroids," "drugs," "recruiting," even "officials" were suggested. To combat that, I collected many voices, amassed many words. As with Nick Hyder's high school football program in Valdosta, Georgia, which deploys 25 coaches for five teams totaling 125 players, there is strength in numbers.

In the writing, I kept in mind an oft-repeated coach's axiom about how best to prepare one's team: Keep it simple. I took all the voices, all the words, and, as coaches do with players, ran them into shape. Then, only the best made the team. Many coaches told me their single hardest job was making the final cut. They were right.

So who are they, these people we call coach? We've elevated these people to an exalted position, heaped upon them many accolades, but the *reason* they coach has got to come from somewhere deep inside. The drive, the dedication, the raw ambition—*that* must be a force within. The external rewards are, by their very nature, too few, too transitory, and too much of a gamble to be relied on with any certainty. What have you won for me lately? The rewards heaped upon them from without seek only to stoke the heat that burns within. But what is the fuel that fires the furnace? What is the spark that sets it aflame?

The high school coach who's the biggest man in town. The head honcho at State with his personal athletic fiefdom. The million-dollar coach who runs onto the field bathed in our wild acclaim and worshipful adulation. We've decided they're important. That they deserve our respect. We've decided they matter.

Well, who do they think they are?

ONE

Game Time

"**B**rian called it 'The Bubble,'" she says. Her name is Linda Leaver and she is the only coach Brian Boitano, the 1988 Olympic Figure Skating Champion, has ever had. The Bubble, Linda Leaver says, was Brian's description of that space where he and his coach would find themselves in those last few minutes before he left her side and skated onto the ice, his game about to begin.

The Game. "That's what it's all about," coaches tell you, reaching comfortably into their bag of clichés. The Game. There's nothing else like it. Game days are not like other days. On game day everything is about the game. It affects the way you sleep, the way you eat, what you do, wear, say. All through the day the game is there, waiting.

The crescendo builds to a grand conflagration, moving at its own infuriating pace. Hour by hour, minute by minute, even second by second. Then, finally, the game. Bands play. Crowds roar. Television lights glare. The locker room provides respite, but it is only temporary, and the coach knows it. Soon everyone must go out there. To the game. The coach looks into his players' eyes, but all he sees are his own eyes looking back.

"I could always feel the energy at the major competitions before Brian skated out onto the ice," Linda Leaver says. "I could feel the energy swirling all around us. It was like being in the eye of a tornado. But where Brian was and where I was was perfectly still and calm and quiet and peaceful.

"All around us was this incredible energy force, but we weren't in it. We were right in the center, completely safe and comfortable and quiet. And we were the only two people who were ever there. No one else could ever get in."

JOHN WOODEN, *basketball, UCLA (retired):* The game you're playing now, that's the big game.

JOHN E. LEE, *football, Walpole High, Massachusetts:* These last ten years I've been able to sleep the night before. The first thirteen years I couldn't. I remember once it was raining and I got out there with a broom, trying to sweep the puddles off the field. Thanksgiving's our big game, and up here there's no way you can control the weather. Usually we get a hard frost or get snow. I've been out there with my wife and my own kids with flashlights scooping it up.

SALLY BAUM, *tennis, Goucher College, Towson, Maryland:* All day I pace the office and go crazy. If I go outside I try to be calm. I try to be the same as I always am. Inside I'm having a cow.

AL BORGES, *offensive coordinator, Boise State, Idaho:* You've got one thought: You're afraid you're going to fail. That's the motivator.

DON NELSON, *Golden State Warriors:* The game is the biggest thing in my day. My life, really, is always around the game. Everything is connected to the game. Even my workouts, it's to tire myself out. I can get so into the game that if I don't do something, I'll explode. I'll walk before the game. Work up a good sweat. My mind focuses on the basketball. By the end of the walk I'm ready.

ANSON DORRANCE, *head coach, U.S. Women 1991 World Cup Soccer Champions:* On game days I meet with each player one-on-one and review not just the game but what's going on for her, maybe even in her life if I'm that close to her. Does one player need more attention? Should I lay off so-and-so? Sensitivity is essential.

JOHN LIPON, *roving instructor, Detroit Tigers (Lipon played ten years in the majors and managed for thirty in the minors):* I liked to sing songs, get them relaxed. We'd be out there stretching; maybe some of the players had a bad day yesterday. I'd try to get them into the right tempo.

From the vine came the grape,
From the grape came the wine,
From the wine came a beautiful feeling . . .

The players, they might think you're crazy, but what the hell, that was part of it anyway.

BOBBY DOUGLAS, *wrestling, 1992 Olympic coach and Iowa State:* Have I prepared these men to meet the challenge? Have I set the example? Have I done everything in my power to prepare them for this moment? My fear is that my wrestlers won't overcome the hoopla and the reputation of who they're stepping out on the mat with. That they fear they're not prepared. I dispel that by saying, "You're prepared." I tell them that before they go out there. "I have faith in you."

DICK VERMEIL, *Philadelphia Eagles (retired):* One of the mistakes I made [before the 1981 Super Bowl] was I kept saying, "This is the Super Bowl! There's no guarantee we'll ever get back. So yes, I am going to do this." I put everything into that game plan. This is the *Super Bowl:* I used that too many times. I think that hurt us. But I didn't want to go home after the game and look at the film and say, "I wish I would have."

BARBARA JEAN JACKET, *track & field, 1992 women's U.S. Olympic coach, and Prairie View A&M (retired):* No one eats peanuts around me. It's been that way forever. Like on the bus on the way to a meet. Peanuts in the shell. Don't get them shells under my feet!

STAN MORRISON, *basketball, San Jose State:* We once had scallops for thirteen straight pregame meals.

TOM BROSNIHAN, *basketball assistant, West Side High, Omaha:* The first six years I coached at Creighton Prep, I had to vomit before every game.

JERRY REYNOLDS, *basketball, coach turned general manager, Sacramento Kings:* It was always a very scary feeling. The fear of losing.

I always felt we were going to win—and there were times I had to be crazy to think that way. Maybe we'd be playing the Lakers in L.A., and before the game I'd say, "We'll do this, make this adjustment." By the time the game started, I'd feel we were going to win. But then, walking onto the court, there'd be this fear of failure. The fear of losing was always stronger than the enjoyment of winning.

MIKE MESSERE, *lacrosse, West Gennesee High, Camillus, New York:* My first championship game, I panicked. Everything went blank. It's like you're not there, not in the flow, feeling what's happening, seeing what's happening.

TONY LaRUSSA, *Oakland A's:* I think you can practice being nervous, handling the pressure. I practice for the World Series all season long. If you get real nervous and feel true pressure during the season, there's a limit as to how much more nervous you can get in the postseason. At a certain point [in the playoffs] you realize: "The losing team goes home tonight." But the way you get through that game, those nine innings, is to treat every game during the season like it's the big game.

STAN MORRISON: Back when I was coaching in high school, I was pacing outside before a big game. We were a decisive underdog against the leading scorer in Sacramento, Gary Foster. I can't believe I can remember his name! I look down and see something crumpled up under this bush. A dollar bill! I run into the locker room yelling, "Look what I found, look what I found!" And then we go out and play our butts off and win. So I always spend game day walking around looking for money. Hell, it's gotten so bad we'll go to an away game and I'll come down and on every other stair there'll be a penny, a nickel. My players are throwing money. It's ridiculous.

OLLIE BUTLER, *basketball assistant, Cal State–San Bernardino (coached thirty-three years in high school):* Joe Shea was my sophomore coach. He used to always draw the old-fashioned six-foot key on the chalkboard, and it always looked like a penis. The players died laughing. He never caught on.

JEAN ROISE, *basketball, University of North Dakota, Williston:* I'm not a fiery, rah-rah coach. Before home games I'll do a devotional and try to relate it to their everyday life. One book I use has a different word for every day. Like maybe the word is "trust," and there'll be some Bible verses about Jesus and how he trusted his disciples. Then I'll relate it to the team, how we need to trust each other. I think they like to hear that God doesn't care whether they win or lose.

TINA SLOAN GREEN, *lacrosse, Temple (retired):* I don't always express my feelings, even with my family. So one of my traditional things before the last game of the year is to give everybody a big hug, to let them know how much I really do care. You assume they know that; they don't always. I tell them that I care for them, that I appreciate what they've done for the program, for the team, for me. "I don't want you to leave here not knowing that." Then I'd give each one a big hug.

ROY CHIPMAN, *basketball, University of Pittsburgh (retired):* One of my assistants filled a wastebasket with crumpled paper and put it in the locker room. We had our pregame talk and then he turned out the lights and told the kids to sit in the dark and think about the game. It's all quiet, and then he lights a match and throws it in the trash can. WOOOSH! Oh, man! Those kids came flyin' out of that locker room.

RON MODESTE, *volunteer football assistant, Santa Clara:* We were playing San Francisco State—a team we had no business trying to beat. [Head coach] Pat [Malley] gave a pregame talk. The punch line was, "Go out there and hit 'em till they puke yellow water!" Two of our best players got so fired up they knocked each other out warming up, and we lost the game.

PAT MANCUSO, *football, Princeton High, Cincinnati:* They did triple-bypass surgery on me on June 30, 1986. You remember that date like you remember your birthday. Two years before I didn't know if I was going to make it. Now here I am running out to play for the championship. Boy. There's no way to measure how you feel.

JIM SATALIN, *basketball, Duquesne University (retired)*: We played the semifinal against Villanova on St. Patrick's Day. The NIT, in Madison Square Garden. I'd just turned thirty. The whole thing was a joyride. I remember before the game walking past the bar—Charlie O's. Everybody from Bonaventure was inside, and I remember saying, "God, I wish I was in there!"

But I remember being absolutely thrilled. We won that game, and then on Sunday afternoon I remember walking out into the Garden for the final. The place was packed. A Garden crowd! I was so thankful to be there that I really wasn't nervous. I looked at it two ways: Number one, I'd proven that I can coach, and number two, I wasn't worried about my future. I remember thinking, "Whatever happens now, I've done this." [Satalin moved to Duquesne in 1982; he was fired in 1989.]

MIKE GEAR, *football, Sidney High, Montana*: We average two thousand people a game—about one-third of the town. I can't imagine what it's like running into a stadium of 105,000, like at Michigan. But I also can't imagine anything more exciting than what we got here.

PAT MANCUSO: I tell our players: "This is the same for you as it is for Michigan playing Southern Cal in the Rose Bowl." You walk out on the field with a smile on your face and you say, "Damn it, we made it!" The preparation, the paperwork, all the practices, the two-a-days, everything—you made it. The coaches are the last to leave the locker room. You breathe a sigh of relief. You really do. When you walk out on the field you have a real sense of completion. We're here. Hurry up, let's play.

ROY CHIPMAN: All you're doing is walking out onto a basketball court, but it's like you're stuck in this fulcrum of light. At that moment that's the most important thing that could possibly be going on. Whether I was coaching in high school, or at Lafayette or at Pittsburgh, there was nothing else happening, nothing else that mattered.

LARRY SMITH, *football, USC (retired)*: I grew up in Ohio. Big 10 territory. From the time I was a little kid I was listening to the Rose Bowl on the radio. I never played in one—that would have been super thrilling—but I coached in two as an assistant at Michigan and that was an exciting experience. But when you're the head coach, you're taking your own team out there.

You'll be standing in the tunnel at the Rose Bowl ready to run out on the field, knowing that this is the most-watched game on New Year's Day; it's the oldest, most traditional bowl. It is the ultimate. You have a hundred thousand-plus people watching you the minute you run out there, and you have a national—worldwide—television audience.

Those things are going through your mind. For me it happened in 1987. And, yeah, there was a flash of "Here I am! Who would've guessed?" Flashbacks of where I started from. Lima Shawnee High School in 1962. In a way you take your whole life out there with you. You run on the field and you get that initial rush. Boom! Then you hit the sidelines. You can't let yourself go wild. Okay now, it's time to coach.

MIKE PRICE, *football, Washington State:* I told the team, "We're going to run onto the field and we're going to be a bunch of wildcats. And when I get to the fifty-yard line I'm going to turn around and I want you guys to *get excited.*" I run onto the field and I'm getting ready to jump up in the air, and I feel this twang in the back of my leg. "You just popped your hamstring!" I turn around and . . . Whoa!!!! They're jumping and stomping all over me and there I am, laying on the ground. They go plowing over to the bench and I can hardly get up and drag myself off the field.

FRANK LAYDEN, *Utah Jazz (retired):* There were lots of times I'd be ready to go, really exhilarated—"Here we go!" Then I'd walk out and see who was refereeing and I'd just go, "Oh, no!"

GENE KREIGER, *women's volleyball, California Baptist College:* In the summers I've taken teams to foreign countries with Athletes in Action. In Indochina, we got off the plane after twenty-three hours of flying and it's 105 degrees and 95 percent humidity. They immediately drive us to this building. Inside there's four thousand people in a thirty-five-hundred-seat arena, everyone's smoking, the doors are closed, and it must be 120 degrees.

We walk in, with the most intense jet lag you can imagine, wearing full sweats because women aren't allowed to wear shorts. Their men's national team is playing. The crowd stops, looks at us, and applauds. An hour later we're playing and they absolutely blow us, off the court.

BARRY LAMB, *defensive coordinator, San Diego State:* Before every game, there's a time when the coaches of the two teams shake hands and wish them well, whether you mean it or not.

WADE PHILLIPS, *defensive coordinator (now head coach), Denver Broncos:* You run out there and say, "Boy! You guys are doing a great job!" And they say, "Boy! You guys are doing a great job!" Coaches have been telling each other that forever.

BARRY LAMB: It comes down to this: If we win, we keep our jobs and you get fired; if we lose, we get fired and you keep yours.

DICK MacPHERSON, *New England Patriots (retired):* I talk about the exactness of the weather: "It looks like it'll be a good day for a game." I say I hope there's no serious injuries. Anything else and you're going, "Now what'd he mean by *that?*"

ABE LEMONS, *basketball, Oklahoma City College (retired):* The other teams always scared me. They always looked so much better than my team. Lord, they're going to kill us! I never saw a bad team warming up, so I said the hell with that, I'm staying in the dressing room.

K. C. JONES, *Seattle Supersonics (retired):* When I'm in the dressing room, waiting to play Houston or L.A. in the championship, I'd say, "We're prepared, we're prepared." And everything's all right. So I come out and I'm on the floor. I'm seeing how they're shooting, what our guys are doing. I'm upbeat. There's the crowd and the players and we're ready. Then you have to wait for the national anthem. All you can do is stand there and think. It's a downer. You say a little prayer. You go from being totally confident to "I hope we can win, I hope we can win."

BOB LUCEY, *football, Curtis High School, Tacoma, Washington:* I love the national anthem. There's just something about it. The whole week of anticipation, it's all there.

HUBIE BROWN, *New York Knicks (retired):* I was standing on the baseline before my first pro game as the head coach with the Kentucky Colonels in the ABA. We were playing the Denver Nuggets. Two friends of mine are sitting on the baseline and there's an empty chair between them. It's right before the National Anthem and I walked over and said, "Don't you guys want to sit together?" They smiled and turned around the placard. It had my father's name on it. He had passed away the year before. He never got to see me coach a pro game.

GAYLE HOOVER, *basketball, Parker High, South Dakota:* I've been coaching for thirty-three years and I still get nervous before every game. There's nothing like game night. We're going to work; we've punched in. The National Anthem plays and I'm just ripping and raring to go. Then the ball game begins and I'm back in it. I can't just sit there and watch; I've got to be part of the game. There's been so many games and so many situations and I've seen the ball go up and down the floor so many times that it's become this long continuation that's been my life all these years.

STAN MORRISON: I sit in the third seat down from the scorers' table. That's a must. I undo the top button of my shirt just as the team has been introduced and they're coming back to the sidelines for the last instructions. Right before the jump ball I loosen my tie. Those things are part of me. I also keep a roll of Lifesavers in my jacket pocket. Wintergreen, always wintergreen.

W. S. DONALD, *football and track & field, Wooddale High, Memphis:* Being on the sidelines, during a game, it's like standing on the ledge of a building ten stories up. Every time you call a play, you're either going to stay on the ledge or fall off. Every time you're successful, you move up a story. You go one story at a time. You've got fourth and one and you decide, Hey, we can make that. But then you don't, and you're standing there thinking, "Hey, man, maybe I should've gone down the stairs." By the end of the game you're either up top, and if the flag waves, you've won. Or you're wishing somebody had a net to catch you.

GEORGE KARL, *Seattle Supersonics:* When old coaches die, the gods give them control of the basketball spirits. And they'll goof with you. It's like they're sitting around a poker table and they have these wild cards they can turn over any time they want. Give this guy an injury. Give this coach a tough referee. There have been games when I've looked up and said things to the gods. "Don't fuck me now. Don't do it now!"

MIKE MARCOULIS, JR., *basketball and baseball, Freemont High, Oakland:* Sometimes during the regular season, when I call a time-out and the team's coming over, I'd be standing there knowing what needs to be said but not knowing how to say it. That's never happened in the championship games. In the championships your senses are more acute, clearer. Bam! I know exactly what I want to say and how I'm going to say it.

PAT HEAD SUMMITT, *basketball, University of Tennessee:* There are games when you feel helpless. We played Iowa at their place in the regional final. They could do no wrong, and we could do absolutely nothing right. I could feel it slipping away. I'll talk to myself—always positive: Stay in the game, keep the players in the game, use your time-outs. I check with my assistants. What should we run on offense? Do we need to press? Do we have the right people in the game? I double-check my own thinking. I went through all the emotions, I tried a lot of approaches. But they didn't work. Not that game. They beat us by sixteen. I'm not sure anything would have worked that game.

JOE RAMSEY, *basketball, Millikin University, Decatur, Illinois:* It's like being a jockey on a horse. The jockey knows whether to give the horse its rein or pull him in or go to the whip. Sometimes a horse will go out too fast, the same way a team is so keyed and you have to rein them in. Take a time-out. At the same time, maybe you get to a point in the ball game where you feel good about the way your team is playing and you want to let the reins out. Or you're in a real close game and it's on the line. You need to go to the whip. Maybe your horse isn't as good as you'd like, but you try to get him to that finish line first.

BRO. MIKE WILMOTT, S.J., *basketball, Creighton Prep (on sabbatical):* This was at the state semifinal. We were playing at Lincoln East and we were playing great and they were playing great. When two teams are playing like that they make each other better, and everything gets really clicking and there comes this thrill just to be a part of all that. I was just watching the game. Both teams were really in the groove, you know? And I turned to my assistant and yelled, "This is a hell of a game, isn't it? This is a hell of a game!"

JERRY REYNOLDS: There'd been some games where I'd felt dizzy. But I was always close to the bench and I'd sit down and get it together. Like most people, I was always thinking it would get better. And of course it didn't.

The night it happened it was pretty much like the other times. It was a close game, against Portland. We had a lead and here was Portland making a comeback. There was a foul at the other end. I thought they'd charged and they called a block. I take off down the sideline yelling and screaming, really upset. I get to half court and I start to feel real dizzy. That's the exact moment when I was really scared. Oh wow! "I need to sit down." That's the last thing I remember until I saw Billy Jones's face, our trainer, getting ready to give me mouth-to-mouth.

When I watched it on the tape afterwards it scared me more. I was real red-faced. I remember telling my wife, "Damn! It looks like I am going to die." I looked terrible. It was scary. The other thing was, the refs gave me a technical when I first went down. I've always been real animated. There's been times when I did a cartwheel on the floor. Another time there was a loose ball and I picked it up and shot a jump shot. So going down like that wasn't totally out of context for me. I guess the refs thought I was playing dead. They rescinded it later. I guess if I'd have died they'd have shot two.

ROY CHIPMAN: They were running by us so fast they were just killing us. I was all over the official—I couldn't blame myself. "You are the worst official I have ever seen." I just had to get it out. The ref turns around—he doesn't scream, he doesn't holler—"Coach, no matter how bad I am, there is no way I'm as bad as your team." I started laughing. And that was the end of that.

STAN MORRISON: A pass was made directly in front of me. Their player reaches out and touches the ball and it goes out of bounds. The official gives them the ball. He makes 100 percent the wrong call. Everyone, including the other two officials, knows it. I walk across the court, right to where the ball went out of bounds. The other two officials can't believe it. "Stan, you can't walk over here! I've got to hit you with a T." I say, "I know, but you've got to wake that ref up." The guy did a nice job the rest of the way.

JACK PARDEE, *Houston Oilers:* A coach spends his entire life fighting off the alligators. A referee is just another alligator.

JOE TORRE, *St. Louis Cardinals:* Sometimes you want to get thrown out. Your team's flat; maybe getting thrown out will get a little energy in there. I remember when I was managing the Mets, I ran out there with the idea of getting thrown out. And the ump says, "I know why you're here, Joe, and I'm not going to do it." I'm screaming and yelling, cursing, and he's just laughing at me.

HARRY VANDERSLICE, *Little League baseball, Ocean City, New Jersey:* You have to be able to laugh at yourself. I'll never forget this—it happened during an exhibition game. A kid rounds third, and the umpire behind the plate weighs about 350 pounds. He's a good umpire, but he can't get out of his own way. I'm working third base [as an umpire] and here comes this kid heading for home and I follow him in. He slides, the ball comes in, everything is simultaneous, there's this big cloud of dust. The umpire watches the play. Then he looks at me, he looks at the sky—real celestial-like—then he looks at third base for what seems like five minutes but is probably about ten seconds. Meanwhile I'm waiting for the call. Everybody is waiting. Out! Safe! Anything. He looks up, blinks his eyes and yells, "Do it over!" I laughed so hard I sat down on third base.

CHUCK TRUBY, *wrestling assistant, Chicago Vocational High:* Go to a wrestling match, and close your eyes and listen. I noticed that at a tournament. My guy had just wrestled, and I was exhausted, so I went up in the stands and laid down on the bench and closed my eyes and just listened. And I started cracking up. Wrestling coaches say the funniest things. They'll repeat the same word thirteen, fourteen times. You know: "Hands, hands, hands . . ." "Get your head up, get your head up . . ." "Single, single, single . . ." I just started laughing.

ED O'BRIEN, *basketball, Bishop Verot, Fort Myers, Florida:* I watch myself on tape and crack up. My assistant says I'm like a guy watching a boxing match. I grunt and groan, throw my elbows at anybody who gets near me. I never realized it until I looked at the tape.

BILL MUSSELMAN, *first coach of the Minnesota Timberwolves (now with a CBA team in Rochester, Minnesota):* The Timberwolves hired me a year in advance. I was on the road watching games that whole season. I studied the coaches. I'd sit at the scorer's table and just watch. Their reaction to game conditions, their adjustments, how they talked to players. Basketball coaches are different. You can get an 8-point run and then the other team gets an 8-point run. You can be up 15 and then down 2 within minutes. One time I remember I started laughing. "My God, I must look like a lunatic along the sideline."

CHARLES TRUBY: At the conference tournament my kid got an escape but the referee didn't give him the points. I run over and grab the referee and do the hold on him. "His hands were like this! His hands were like this!" My jaw almost dropped to the ground. He could have zinged me, but he didn't. But hey, I'll fight for my kids. And why not have fun? I'm only getting paid $1,300 to be a high school wrestling coach. You should be me at a wrestling match. You'd have a ball.

BARRY LAMB: I was at the University of Idaho and we were playing the University of Montana for the Big Sky championship. Right before the half, in about a minute, they scored two touchdowns. They blocked a kick, they scored, got an onsides kick. We stopped them, and the refs are arguing whether there's still one second on the clock, so we get our team off the field. Then refs tell us they're going to let Montana snap the ball without us. So now we're running back on the field and we get lined up and they score and get the 2-point conversion. We'd fallen apart. Everybody figured in the locker room we're going to get our fannies chewed pretty bad.

GEORGE KARL: There's this theory, I think from Jack McMahon or Don Nelson. Every coach carries a six-gun into a season. It's got six bullets, and a coach can only hit his team between the eyes those six times. He has to be real careful about when he does it, or even if he does it.

BARRY LAMB: Keith Gilberston [Idaho's coach], he comes in the locker room and starts laughing. What a football game! Holy smokes! What else can happen? Then he told this joke about a girl from Montana. That cuts the tension and we all laugh. That was it. We kicked the hell out of 'em in the second half.

ABE LEMONS: We were playing Duke in Madison Square Garden, and we were down about 18 by the half. It was a double header and we were the second game. Oklahoma City is a small school and New York scares the hell out of you anyway, so we get out there and we're down and I figure we might as well stay out there. At halftime we did this full-court scrimmage. I thought it might help, but it didn't; we got beat by 18.

MIKE PRICE: I'm not the kind of guy who stands there with his arms folded on the sidelines. I run around slapping kids on the butt and helmet. I broke my glasses when Jason Hanson, our kicker, kicked the longest field goal in history. I piled on and got my glasses broke. That's the third time I've done that. Another time I ruptured a disk in the end zone jumping on a guy. That laid me up in the hospital for about two weeks.

BILL CURRY, *football, University of Kentucky:* I played for Bobby Dodd at Georgia Tech. He wore a business suit and wing-tip shoes on the sidelines. Looked like a million bucks. My first two years as coach at Georgia Tech, I tried to be like him. We went 1-9 and 1-10. I wouldn't wish that on a scorpion. I'd come home and my wife would ask me, "You try to be Coach Dodd today?" She'd hit so close to home. "Be yourself," she'd tell me. I needed to grab people on the sidelines, shake some face masks. I needed to stride up and down the sideline, coach everybody all the time. I had to learn to cut loose.

HUBIE BROWN: You can become so focused and so tunnel-visioned out there that you can shut out nineteen thousand people screaming and yelling, not hear a single sound, and yet you can hear as clear as day every bounce of the ball, every squeal of a sneaker, everything that's said inside that ninety-four-by-fifty-foot rectangle.

JIM ZULLO, *basketball, Shenendehowa High, Clifton Park, New York:* I have this vision of how I want my team to play. I had a team a couple of years ago that was very small. Oh, but could they move the ball! They'd find an opening and one of those little guys would scoot in and make a layup. Just like I pictured it. It's the best feeling in my life, almost. Come down and the ball reverses with three quick passes—bang-bang-bang—and you get the shot you want. Just like I saw it. "All right!" That's why I coach. For that moment.

CHARLIE THOMAS, *basketball, San Francisco State:* I try to get a feel for what's going on. I do the pregame talk and get the strategies down, but once I go on the floor, then it starts to happen. All of a sudden I'll get this feeling. I'll crouch a lot, sit there with my hand on my chin. And then all of a sudden it'll be, "Get somebody in here to guard this guy." It just comes. It's like there's somebody inside me telling me what to do.

I've lost games because I've done things I shouldn't have, but the feeling said, "Go for it," and so I did. We were playing in a championship game, and I left this one kid in. He came down the floor and shot the ball with forty-three seconds to go. It was like a thirty-foot jumper. He shouldn't have been in the game. But that was the feeling I had for who was going to make that shot, so I went with it. I was confident enough to think it was going to go in. It didn't.

BOB ASHE, *soccer, Catlin Gable School, Portland, Oregon (retired):* I made a late substitution once, and the character won the game for us. It was a desperation move; it was no great moment of coaching. But I looked like a genius, and everybody said, "What a great move." I kept my mouth shut.

HUBIE BROWN: We called a time-out to set up the last shot against Denver. This is my first game as a pro head coach, with the Kentucky Colonels, and I have two of the greatest players in the pro game, Dan Issel and Artis Gilmore. But we go into the huddle and Louie Dampier says, "I take the last shot here." So we ran an out-of-bounds for him and Louie hits the shot and we win. That year Louie took the last shot nine times and made them all.

On every basketball team there is only one guy who wants that last shot. Go into a huddle and there are four guys sitting there saying, "Please, God, don't let it be me!" At every level—high school, college, the NBA, and emphasize the NBA. But Louie Dampier tells me: "I take the last shot." My first pro game. I could have said, "Fuck you! I make the decisions around here." Instead, he made me look like a great coach.

BILL MUSSELMAN: Magic Johnson's will to win always stunned me. I remember the first time we played him in the regular season our first year. I've heard this is the first time this has ever happened to the Lakers: They win a game they never led once during regulation. There's six seconds left and they have no time-outs and we're up 2 and they kick it out to Magic. I'm at half court and he comes past, and I looked into his eyes and I saw a vein pop in his neck. And I say to myself, "This guy's going through our entire team." I start screaming, "Pack the lane! Pack the lane!" I'll guarantee you 99 percent of all players would have shot the fifteen-footer. But he knew the clock. Six seconds. Magic got down that damn court and laid it in at the buzzer. They beat us in overtime. My God, what a will to win!

CHUCK JORDAN, *football, Conway High, South Carolina:* You've got to maintain some kind of balance. We finished the season 10-0; we were ranked number one in the state. The first round of the playoffs we had a bye. The next week we had a game against a team with a 6-5 record. We get off the bus at 6:30 for an 8 o'clock game and the stands were already packed, everybody hollering, "DEFENSE! DEFENSE!" Three hours later it's fourth down and we're ahead by 3 when the other team scores and wins the game. In a three-hour time period I experienced as high a point to as low a point in my life. The more you coach, the more you realize how important that balance is. If you're not careful, it can all get out of control.

STAN MORRISON: We're playing at Oregon State. [Morrison coached at USC.] We're up 13 at the half and we score the first 2 in the second half, so we're up 15. They get into a press, the place is packed, we're at their place, you cannot get another sardine in this baby, and all of sudden they go on a run: 16 straight points. I call three time-outs. Their band is right there at the end of our bench. The team could not hear one word I said. It's insane. I had a little point guard, he hits one at the buzzer, off-balance; we win. You've never heard anything like it.

FRANK LAYDEN: We were playing the Lakers in the Forum, and I turned around and Jack Nicholson said good-bye. I said, "Where you going?" "Your team stinks and this game stinks." And I said, "You're right, I'm going with you." The next day I told the team I wished they all could have come with me.

W. S. DONALD: You don't make much money coaching high school. But win a championship, and the kids you worked with and sweated with, they pick you up and tote you across the field over to meet the coach you just whipped. There's hardly words to explain that. It's like getting on an elevator and coming down real fast. You're floating, with joy and light, like you're going to fly.

PAT GRIFFIN, *associate professor, social justice education program, University of Massachusetts, Amherst (former swim coach):* It was at the New England Swimming Championships, the last relay. Our team was seeded third. And they swam out of their heads. We thought we'd lose it on the second leg, but we didn't. We started off with the lead, and our second swimmer went crazy. And the rest of us, we're up in the stands swimming every stroke. There was nothing in our consciousness except our team. When we won everybody erupted. It was such an incredible feeling.

ED O'BRIEN: Three years ago we went 3 and 10, but we won the first round of the districts. We move on to the second game and upset a team that beat us twice during the season. I got to bed around 2:30 in the morning. At 5 o'clock I was on the road to get the paper. I'll bet I read that article fifty times.

SUZIE McCONNELL, *basketball, Oakland Catholic High, Pittsburgh; member of the 1988 U.S. Olympic gold-medal basketball team and 1992 bronze-medal team:* When I was a player, I'd get excited for myself when we won. But now I'm the coach. And after we won the state title, I was excited for my team. Seeing the expressions on their faces. Watching them cut down the net. It was so rewarding, knowing I was instrumental in helping them achieve that.

The bus ride home, that's all we talked about: "I can't believe we won!" On the way up, the girls had mostly stayed toward the back, singing and being silly. Coming home they made their way to the front, just wanting to relive the experience. It was mostly the seniors, the ones who weren't coming back. To listen to them talking about it, reliving what they had just experienced, it was nice to hear that as a coach.

GENE VOLLNOGLE, *football, Carson High, Los Angeles (retired):* We played the number one team in the nation one year for the city championship and we beat them in the L.A. Coliseum. They had to shut the lights off to get us out of there.

HUBIE BROWN: There would be the press conference, and then we'd go eat. Then I'd take the game stats and break them down into my pluses and minuses, and then I liked to see the film of the game to correct the scouting reports. Whether we won or lost, I wanted to know why. Then I could prepare tomorrow's practice. Close the day on the upbeat. Then I could go to sleep. I've ended the day on a positive note, and I was ready for tomorrow.

RANDY JABLONIC, *rowing, University of Wisconsin:* Once they leave the dock, it's their boat race. I've known peers that have had to run behind the quonset hut to vomit. I've known coaches who have threatened to do away with themselves because they feel responsible for the team's loss. I've known guys you can hardly talk to; they can't even think straight after they win.

The toughest race I've ever watched was one my son rowed. I remember Brown or somebody was sneaking through them to win the championship. I could see as the crew came through the finish line area the effort they were making to hang on to the race. I don't think too much about the hurt that goes into rowing. But when my son rowed, I seemed to have this sense for the pain those guys were feeling.

On the other hand, when we won the Cincinnati Regatta, I remember somebody said to me as we were pulling into the lead, "What do you think?" And I said, "We're going to win." That was a very, very satisfying feeling. You've got to realize, there is always an apprehension of the unknown. That undertow of worry. Nothing is going to happen— *this could happen.* It's not going to happen—*but it could.* You can't cheer; you can't run to the finish line. The feeling I had was how much I was going to enjoy the ultimate victory. I knew it was coming. I'd be cast free.

All the labor and work of the year was going to be rewarded. The season would be over and I'd be home free. I would have grabbed the brass ring. I'd be able to sit back and smile for the rest of the summer and enjoy the accolades. "Yes, yes, what a great team. What a great bunch of guys." I knew in advance what all these feelings were going to be.

I wouldn't have to make excuses. There weren't going to be any "ifs" this summer. The great excuse: "if." If the wind had been off the starboard; if we'd taken the stroke higher; if we'd done this; if we'd done that. All those ifs were laid away. I knew that relief was coming. When you don't finish first you have to rationalize, you've got to have a reason. "We weren't good enough" is a reason. "We didn't train enough." "We lacked two good oars." "We did the best we could." You have to have a response when you lose. It's no fun, and it always ends with "wait till next year." But when you do it this year you don't have to wait till next year. This year I wouldn't have to say anything. And I knew all this was coming, walking to the finish line. I knew the rest of the summer was going to be a marvelous, marvelous summer.

TWO

Coach

Even back in 1945 and before all that was to come, Pat Mancuso knew his high school football coach was special. At the time, Chuck Mather was in just his second job as a coach, at Leetonia High in Ohio. His years as the head coach at Kansas, his seasons spent on the sidelines as an assistant to George Halas, these were as yet unscheduled, perhaps only-dreamed-of games.

"When he came to our school, he brought with him a lot of new ideas," Pat Mancuso says. Chuck Mather had coached for one year before the start of World War II, and then had spent his war years at the Great Lakes Naval Air Station, where he got to mix it up with some college coaches also stationed there. In the fall of 1945, the war won, Chuck Mather came to Leetonia, deep in the heart of football country, and to Pat Mancuso, senior.

"He had a poster in his office," Mancuso relates. "This picture of an old man stooping down to help a boy with his pants. A little toddler, like a two-year-old boy, trying to reach for a ball with one hand and pull up his pants with the other, and his bare butt's showing. The title on the poster was 'No Man Stands So Tall as When He Stoops to Help a Boy.' I always remembered that."

Before a person can become a coach, he must first be coached. It's just the way it works. A coach doesn't suddenly materialize on the sideline, clipboard in hand, earphones wrapped around his neck. "Chuck Mather had a big impact on me," explains Mancuso. And now

Pat Mancuso has been the head football coach at Princeton High in Cincinnati for thirty-three years. Ample time to have had a little impact of his own. It's just the way that works, too. Mancuso says, "When I came down here we had a kid playing football for me who was a real good art student. I had him do an oil painting of that poster."

TINA SLOAN GREEN, *lacrosse, Temple (retired):* We had our end-of-the season banquet. My captain got up and spoke. She said that someone had sent her an article about me. I guess it talked about my years on the national lacrosse team, the stuff I'd done to fight racism, whatever. She said she never realized that Tina had done all that. "She was just my coach." I found that very interesting.

WANDA ANITA OATES, *boys' basketball, Ballou High, Washington, D.C.:* When I was in high school, my physical education teacher, who happened to be a white female, told me that I wasn't going to amount to anything. I told her that not only was I going to amount to something, I was going to go to college, I was going to major in physical education and come back and take her job. When I was at Howard University a lot of my instructors tried to get me to change my major. I told them no, that I had this goal. I had to go back and tell that teacher. She had given me that incentive. But I was never able to. I came right out of college and went to Ballou High School in 1965. I couldn't find her. I tried, but I couldn't find her.

BOBBY DOUGLAS, *wrestling, 1992 Olympic coach and Iowa State:* I was raised in a coal-mining community in eastern Ohio. Athletics was a way of getting out. Athletics was a way of achieving prestige and self-esteem. More important, it gave me an opportunity to get an education. I keep coming back to the fact that had I not had the association with George Kovalick, I probably would have never had a chance to be where I am now. Many of the kids I grew up with are either in prison, dead, or close to it. I was one of the fortunate ones.

George Kovalick was my high school football, wrestling, and baseball coach. This guy cared about me as a person, not just as an athlete. Being black and being small in stature, it just gave me a positive feeling about the man—I wasn't used to people treating me as an equal. When I first met George I weighed eighty-eight pounds. When I was in high school I went from 103 pounds to 143; I was a very small person. But that was the nature of this guy. We had John Havlicek and Joe Nekro and Phil Nekro—Hall of Fame people—but they weren't treated any different than the rest of us.

He was a strict disciplinarian and a great "stimulator." I have a different opinion of what motivation is. Motivation lies within the man, and George Kovalick was able to arouse that. It was never how much athletic ability we had; it was the effort we were willing to put forward. This was a man I trusted, a man I believed in. And what he said was true. You don't have to be a superstar, and you can't hit a home run every time you bat.

I remember when I was a sophomore I was wrestling in the finals of the state tournament, and he reminded me of all the work I'd put in and that I'd made the commitment to never lose again. He told me to remember why I had made that commitment, the feeling I had when I made that commitment. Look back to where I'd started and where I was now, and if I was ready to cross the T's and dot the I's, that this was the chance to make all my dreams come true. [Douglas won.]

WILLARD IKOLA, *hockey, Edina High, Minnesota:* Most of the guys I ran around with growing up in Eveleth went into coaching. I think that's because of the coaches we had. Cliff Thompson was our hockey coach. He was a Minneapolis guy, played at the University of Minnesota. After that he went up to Eveleth, up in the Iron Range, about two hundred miles north of the [Minneapolis] metro area. He stayed for thirty-plus years.

Eveleth was a great community in the late '40s. Cliff was a super guy. He didn't have any kids himself. He'd been gassed in World War I and only had one lung. His kids were the kids he coached. Cliff was also the baseball coach at the playground. He had this big Lincoln Club coupe, and he'd take the back end out and fit twenty kids in there and we'd drive all over the Range playing baseball.

Everyone knew Cliff Thompson. There were so many big families up there then. He'd go through three, four, five brothers with each family. He coached a lot of great players. When I was playing for him he had three guys he'd coached playing for the Blackhawks. They used to send up these boxes of old skates. We were all wearing Blackhawk skates. That was a real thrill.

More important, he had so many kids from that small town who couldn't afford a college education—and I was one of them—who hockey gave the opportunity to go to college. I went to Michigan, and later I won a silver medal at the 1956 Olympics. Cliff would come down to the Hippodrome every Saturday morning and watch the little kids. He was probably picking his team four, five years in advance. You always knew when Coach Thompson was at the rink. He used to wear this big hat and coat that came all the way to his ankles, and he'd sit up in the top row. When he'd come in, boy, everybody started working harder and moving quicker. And if you didn't notice him, you sure noticed that all of a sudden everybody was playing. And then you'd look up and there'd he'd be. Coach Thompson sitting up there in his big hat and coat.

WADE PHILLIPS, *defensive coordinator (now head coach), Denver Broncos:* My dad [Bum Phillips, who coached the Houston Oilers and the New Orleans Saints] was a high school coach when I was growing up in Texas. From grade school through high school we made five moves. The longest we lived anywhere was five years in Nederland, Texas, where he won fifty-something straight games. When he went to Jacksonville they were coming off their worst season ever, and he won. Same with Amarillo. He's still a hero there.

Football is king in Texas. The football coach is an important guy, and my dad was that guy. He was all football. I didn't see him a whole lot as a kid. To see him I had to go to the field house and watch practice. He's told me they thought at the time that they had to stay up until 2 o'clock in the morning at the field house to win. They'd argue to all hours of the morning: how the quarterback should take the snap, where the linebacker should be looking. You've got to go through that if you want to learn the game.

Coaching for him at both Houston and New Orleans for ten years, I was around him a whole lot more than I was as a youngster. We talked about a lot of things, and football wise he helped me a lot. We stayed up late and talked football.

DON NELSON, *Golden State Warriors:* I always liked to get down to Boston Garden early. I'd eat a pregame meal downtown about 4 o'clock, and then I'd have time to kill before the game, so I'd talk to [Celtics coach] Red [Auerbach]. He was usually taking his nap about that time; he'd sleep in his chair. I'd pick his brain about basketball. I didn't realize how special it was until it was over. I was trying to figure out how to coach myself, and all those things he'd talked about kept coming back. A lot of the guys, when they had a problem, they had to call Red. All I had to do was remember, and then think like he did.

BILL MUSSELMAN, *first coach of the Minnesota Timberwolves (now with a CBA team in Rochester, Minnesota):* I loved to listen to the coaches talk. I remember one time [as a grad assistant at Kent State], I listened to Frank Smouse and Bob McNey, two of the football coaches. It's August and it must have been eighty-eight degrees, and we're out on the football field and these two guys argued about whether linebackers should use a parallel or staggered stance. One subject, back and forth for hours. I thought, "My God, this is *incredible!*"

KURT ASCHERMANN, *youth league baseball, Sparta, New Jersey; author of* **Coaching Kids to Play Baseball and Softball** *and* **Coaching Kids to Play Soccer:** One of the great things about having a father-coach was being seven years old and going on the team bus to the football games, the basketball games, being the bat boy, and all that jazz. I remember wearing a rubber band on my wrist the entire school year of 1962 as the ball boy for the high school basketball team. All the players wore a rubber band. You did *NOT* want yours to fall off. Nineteen sixty-two was the year of the rubber band, and I still have no idea why.

JERRY POPP, *cross-country and track, Bowman High, North Dakota:* My mom and dad both went through . . . they both went through alcoholic-type treatments. There were twelve kids in our family, and I know they cared about us, but at that time there were other priorities in their lives—they're both straightened out now, thank goodness.

It was Larry Storbeck and Bill Herring, the coach and the assistant coach in basketball, who took me under their wing. They saved me, they really did. I still remember, I wasn't even a starter on the freshman basketball team, and they talked me into the idea that if I played hard and practiced, I could play varsity ball. And that's what happened. Because of them, I became a coach.

BILLY BARNETT, *six-man football, Dell City High, Texas:* My dad's been in the oil fields of Fort Stockton all his life. He provided for us real well, but there's just no way I wanted to lead the life he's had. As a kid I wouldn't see him for six weeks. You don't ever know if you've got a job. It's tough work, real dangerous. He used to have to quit jobs just so we could go on vacation. I never wanted it to get down to that. I worked them in the summers, and when I quit college I worked the fields again. I made gobs of money. Then around 1982 the boom went out and it was getting to where I was getting laid off once a week. I said, I'm going back to school and get my degree.

HANK HAINES, *Blytheville Boxing Club, Arkansas (retired):* One of my early idols was a boxing coach named Joe Craig. He ran the boxing program when I was a little boy. He was a good man, he was a bad man, he was all the things that all of us are. And I loved him. He was born about 1910. A rough boy from Mississippi. He ran a dairy, and he had boxing in his blood. He ran the boxing program when I was little. I would have loved to have worked under Joe Craig. But I wasn't good enough.

Joe Craig, he came up from the mud. He'd been fighting mosquitoes and cows and horseshit out there on his farm. He had a hard life. If you told him you didn't have a hamburger, he'd say that's too bad. Joe knew what real hunger was. I remember once he took a bunch of Mid-South Golden Gloves to Memphis one night and they gave him twenty-five bucks. This was back in about 1940, when hamburgers were a nickel. "Here's your gas money and your meal money for your team." It was the middle of winter, and he had them in the back of his dairy truck. They pulled up in front of a cafe in West Memphis and Joe told his boys to wait in the truck. He went in, sat down and ate and left his boys out in the cold. Then he got back in the truck, and they drove to the fight.

He and I were going to start a boxing club. But hell, he was almost seventy. He'd been working the club about a week when he came home one night, took a shower, put on his robe, came in the front room to read the paper, sat down in a chair, and died. I said to Mrs. Craig, "I'm just so sorry." I'd been looking forward to working with a man I thought was one of the most knowledgeable boxing coaches in America. And Mrs. Craig, she was a terrific woman, she looked at me and said Joe was strong medicine—he made some people well, other people sick. I'm probably that way, too.

CHUCK TRUBY, *wrestling assistant, Chicago Vocational High School:* My junior year in high school my coach was Joe Sowinski. He was an All-American wrestler and football player at Indiana. I loved Mr. Sowinski. He was a sixty-five-year-old man and he took it to everybody, from ninety-eight pounds to the heavyweights. He gave me the idea that the coach has got to get in there and sweat with the kids, get your nose bloody. He was deaf, and he talked real soft. But when he looked at you and took off his glasses, you knew it was your turn to get whupped by Mr. Sowinski.

CARLTON LEWIS, *football, West Point High, Georgia:* Kid Cecil, he taught me everything I know about football. I played baseball and basketball at Georgia Tech. When I finished in '42 they sent me straight into the Navy, traveled all over the world hunting subs. When I got out in '46 I went back to Columbus, my hometown. I had no intentions of coaching, but my high school baseball coach asked me to help out. He got me a job teaching, and then the football coach wanted me to help him. That was Kid Cecil.

Kid Cecil and Dickie Butler were the football coaches in Columbus. They were good buddies, and they were good coaches. Every Sunday afternoon they used to drive down to the banks of the Chattahoochie River in Dickie's car and talk football. They invited me to come with them. They talked football and I listened. Smoke cigarettes and talk football. They were both about fifty; I was twenty-six. They sat in the front; I sat in the back. Never nobody else with us.

After that I came to West Point [Georgia] in '47, so I didn't see them as much. That first year we went 7–3; the next year we won the championship. I was there for twenty-four years, till 1971. We won three state championships and I finished up 185–71–4. There'd be times when I'd be coaching and I'd be in the middle of a game, and I'd realize this was something that Kid Cecil and Dickie Butler had already told me about. Like, say, they'd split a man out on the right and another on the left, and I'd think about what they'd said to do: Change from a six-man line to a five-man line and cover those wide receivers. I went down there on the weekends when I could to ask them questions. Or I'd call from West Point. They always helped me.

GREG CARPENTER, basketball, Whitefield School, New Hampshire: I wouldn't be coaching if it weren't for Bonnie Foley. Bonnie was the women's coach at Plymouth State in New Hampshire. I had her for philosophy of coaching basketball, a three-credit class. I got an A. One of the guys in her class was working as an undergraduate assistant for her, and I started thinking, Jeez, I'd love to do that. When the next year came around, I asked her and she said yes. She was awesome. She let me work the floor, do recruiting, everything. I could pick her brain. She showed me how to organize practice, work a game. I was with her for two years. And the whole time I'm thinking, Why's she letting a punk like me help her out?

RON DICKERSON, defensive coordinator, Clemson (now head coach at Temple): I played college ball at Kansas. Got drafted by the Miami Dolphins—played there for a couple of years, broke my leg. So I went back to Kansas to work on my master's. My plan was to receive a master's in education administration and become a teacher and coach in a high school. Coaching gave me the tool to pay for my graduate work.

Once I got in as a grad assistant, I saw that the players, the black players especially, needed a person they could talk to. It was something that was missing during the time that I was a student athlete. We needed black role models, and we didn't have any. Vince Gibson saw the need, too. He'd seen the need when I was a player, and we'd talked about it even then. A lot of the coaches on Vince's staff were southern coaches. It was tough for them to relate to kids from Pittsburgh, where I was from, or Chicago or L.A. Vince saw the need and felt I was the person to come in. I felt like a pioneer.

RON GREENE, basketball, Calloway County High, Murray, Kentucky: My career paralleled Bobby Knight's—our careers started at the same time—except that he was from Ohio State and he got some very solid advice from Fred Taylor, his coach. I graduated from Murray State in 1962, and after my initial thrust into coaching college basketball, I didn't really follow through with a mentor.

There's the story that goes round that Bob Knight had the Wisconsin job. If the story's true, Coach Taylor told Knight not to leave his job coaching Army for Wisconsin. He told him to wait. He waited for Indiana, and his patience made his whole career. I've always respected Bobby Knight—he's smart enough to seek advice and accept help.

Cal Luther was at DePauw when I was in high school. I elected to go to Bradley the year they won the NIT. Cal left DePauw for Murray State, and I transferred there and stayed on and started out coaching the freshman team. I'd been in ROTC and went to Virginia as a first lieutenant. While I was there I got a call from Cal. He said they were looking for an assistant at Loyola in New Orleans. I was maybe twenty-six, ready for anything. One year later they asked me to be head coach.

I was the bright and shiny penny. We got off to 11 and 1. We beat Michigan State, the University of Washington. I think we beat LSU with Pete Maravich. Then we had some discipline problems. Several players were intoxicated in the cafeteria. I cut four of them. We finished 12 and 10. After my third year I left and started the program at what was then LSU at New Orleans.

I spent nine years there. We were 18 and 5 the first year; had another season at 23 and 1. We played Old Dominion in the Division II finals the year they won it. Then Mississippi State called. Took them from last to second behind Kentucky the year they won the national championship.

Then my alma mater called, Murray State. That's been the most-asked question of my career: "How could you leave Mississippi State?" It's a fair question. What happened was I made an emotional decision, one that I, to be very candid, regretted for most of the time I've spent in coaching. Bob Knight told me one time, "Coaches take more time picking out a pair of shoes than they do surveying a job." Had I stayed at Mississippi, I perhaps would still be there. But we didn't get a bid to the NCAA and we didn't get a bid to the NIT. I was really disappointed. The ironic thing is that the next year the NCAA expanded. Then again, were there a mentor, or someone to have talked to . . . But I've always been independent.

From Murray State I went to Indiana State. They had a better place to play, a larger town, my hometown. My mother and father were getting old. At Indiana State the cupboard was totally bare. They really hadn't won since Larry Bird had left. There were a lot of things that maybe I didn't foresee. For instance, I didn't talk to any of the coaches there who'd been unsuccessful. It would make sense to do that. But I felt I could get it done. I went up there and things didn't work out. I'm ten times the coach I was when I was in New Orleans and ten times better than when I was at Murray State. But in today's market someone has to help you. I wish I would have listened more.

LINDA LEAVER, *Brian Boitano's figure-skating coach:* The way I coached Brian was largely formulated by the fact that for the last half of my skating career I went uncoached. I spent four and a half, five years skating and training myself, waiting for my coach, who was ill, to return. John Johnsen. His recovery was always a couple of months away, and that stretched into years.

There are hundreds of things I learned from that experience. It taught me to understand the principles behind skating, much more so than if I'd had someone standing there saying, "Do this, do that." But it wasn't conducive to great performances. I was the Pacific Northwest champion several times, and I competed in the Nationals. In 1970 I was fourth in the World Professionals. I don't know how much further I would have gone.

But maybe then I wouldn't have wanted to be a coach so much. Teaching myself all those years definitely shaped my coaching. I learned how important emotional support is to a skater. When Brian skates out onto the ice, he goes out there absolutely alone, but he carries with him a backlog of support. When I started coaching I knew I wanted to provide that.

I believe part of Brian's success has been my willingness to let other people who are better than me at a particular aspect of skating have a free reign. I completely released it, rather than saying, "No, I'm the coach."

I've always looked at coaching Brian as a responsibility. A responsibility to his talent and to his commitment. If I couldn't provide him with the very best—whether it's boots, choreography, technical assistance, whatever—then I procured it. I could name thirty coaches who helped me help make Brian better. They were wonderful in sharing with me. I set a goal for myself every year, to have Brian progress more than any other skater, and to be the best skater his age in the world. I felt I could lose him any year if I didn't do a good job. I never took it for granted.

People who hold on to something have exactly that. People who are willing to release it and expand themselves end up with so much more. If you say that you can be the only source from which a person can learn, you limit learning, but when you expand the sources, the sky's the limit.

JOHN YOUNG, *founder and president of Reviving Baseball in Inner cities (RBI) and scout for the Florida Marlins:* When we first started RBI we came in wanting to get great coaching for these kids. Get the coaches from USC, the playbook from the University of Miami. Then one guy said, you know, the main thing here is to get these kids out and let them play some baseball.

That got me thinking about a coach I'd had. Wolfolk—I can't believe I can't remember his first name. This guy loved being around kids, and he was concerned about the community. He didn't know anything about baseball; he just knew that kids should be playing baseball. He was out there every day. We always had enough baseballs. He'd take us for hamburgers after we won. He'd come to practice in a baseball uniform and wing tips. Picture it.

I thought about him and about the players that played back then—Enos Caball, Lenny Randall, Wayne Simpson, who was a first-round draft choice and won fourteen games for the Reds in 1970 before he blew out his arm. And the people that followed, like Eddie Murray, Ozzie Smith, Darryl Strawberry, Leon Smith, Eric Davis. All these good players, and we never had great *coaching.* We had guys who were concerned about kids. Now here I was trying to get a program going and I want to get all these great coaches. I forgot that the man who helped me the most was some guy in wing tips.

BILL WHITMORE, *athletic director, Concord school district, New Hampshire:* I worked summer basketball camps for ten years. I worked for Bobby Knight, Jack Ramsey, Jerry West. I worked at Tennessee, North Carolina, Duke, Kansas. One of my goals was to work for John Wooden at his camp. It was like meeting God. I had this notebook full of questions that I wanted to ask him—only him. Basketball questions, coaching questions, people questions. I'd been working on it for years. Every morning at six I'd be down at the cafeteria. I'd be first in line, and I'd make sure I ate with him, and I'd hit him with the questions and I'd pencil in the answers. It was unbelievable. He never said he didn't have the time.

STEPHANIE VANDERSLICE GAITLEY, *basketball, Saint Joseph's University, Philadelphia:* I was very fortunate to have a lot of success in high school under a very driven high school coach. Pat Daugherty. She was crazy! She'd get in your face and make you want to do it. You're only going to tap into certain players that way, but with me she did. She made me want to play for her.

My senior year was the year we won our hundredth straight league game. It was an away game. We were down 10 in the third quarter and I'm livid. I'm looking over at the sidelines thinking, I am not going to be on the team that doesn't get the hundredth straight win. They got another rebound and got fouled. Right before the official gave the shooter the ball, I stepped into the lane and I looked at everybody on both teams and I said, "That's the last rebound they get." That's what Mrs. Daugherty could bring out in me.

BILL CURRY, *football, University of Kentucky:* [Curry played for Vince Lombardi's Green Bay Packers in the mid-'60s.] Lombardi was a force field. He used to talk about singleness of purpose. When Lombardi walked into a room there was something about him that you could feel. The way he looked at you started you thinking, "Am I doing all I can for this team right now?" A similar personality is Billy Graham. When he looks at you with those eyes you start thinking, "I'd better check my faith *today*."

It's like Paul Horning walking into the training room when I was a rookie. Paul, of course, was an established star. "What are you doing in here, rookie?" And I said, "I've got a pulled muscle." And Paul kind of looked around nervously, and then he said under his breath, "The old man doesn't believe in pulled muscles." I got up and left. And I never went back.

WALTER LEWIS, *football assistant, University of Kentucky (retired):* I remember this vividly about Coach [Paul] Bryant [at Alabama]. We're going to play Penn State; we were number one and number two in the country. The coaches were tight, the players were tight. You couldn't gauge how the players were feeling; I think the coaches thought we weren't as good as our ranking.

On Fridays prior to leaving for the game [in Birmingham], Coach would tell us what kind of dress he wanted. That Friday he didn't tell us anything. So most of the guys went casual. I was one of those guys—a polo shirt and slacks.

We were having our pregame meal when Coach Bryant walked into the room. Coach had this brisk strut about himself. He starts walking rapidly through the tables, and then he raised his voice and started pointing. "I want you, I want you, I want you." He said, "I want everybody in here that don't have a tie on to get out and don't come back until you get one."

I guarantee you, seventy-five guys ran out. Some of the coaches ran out, too. I ran to my room. I started calling people at the hotel. I even called back Tuscaloosa. It was that serious. I had on a burgundy polo shirt, and the guy next door had a green and yellow striped tie. I said, "Give me that!" My roommate had a blue tie, he put that on, and we went back. A lot of guys didn't have anything, so they stayed out. One guy came in, he had on a V-neck sweater without a shirt, and he'd tied a tie around his neck like a regular tie. Another guy had on a leisure suit—remember them? He stopped a waiter out in the hallway and took his little cardboard tie and put that on. We were frantic. I believe to this day he did that to loosen us up. We won 42–21.

You never knew what was going through the man's mind. He always had our attention. What you have to do as a coach is create a curiosity in a player's mind about you—what makes the coach tick, why it is he does the things he does. Coach Bryant had that sense.

A player has to always be wondering what's in the coach's mind. That curiosity helps him probe his own being. Coach Bryant was always planting little things in my mind, and I responded to them, and they made me search myself. I came to believe that a coach has to have a certain type of presence about himself so that players can plug themselves into him. That allows a coach to get the most out of his players.

KATE HORSTMAN, *softball and track & field, Minster High, Ohio:*
I was born in Minster and went to high school here. The only thing we had was a CYO softball team. Then somebody told me about the Fort Wayne Daisies of the All-American Girls Baseball League, a pro baseball team. I started playing for the Daisies when I was fourteen and played for seven years.

My main position was third base, and I pitched. I was versatile; I was the only girl who played every position in the league. We wore this one-piece tunic, like a skirt—real feminine. It was short and we had tights underneath. You could always tell the rookies, they were the ones with the strawberries from sliding.

The league lasted from 1943 until 1954. We went on tour for three years after the league folded. Twelve of us. One year we went out West; we probably traveled five hundred miles a day. We'd play a game, sleep in the cars, drive to the next game, and play again. We'd play men's teams. The pitcher and catcher of the men would pitch and catch the men and the battery of the women would play against the women. It was really grueling, but we enjoyed it. We got to know the world. It was my cup of tea. We had a spirit among us that just doesn't exist today.

Our manager with the Daisies was Jimmy Foxx—"The Double X." Jimmy was a dream. He could really hit the ball. He'd get the crowd started during batting practice by hitting a few over the wall. But the coach who taught me the most was Bill Allington. He was a semipro coach; he never made it to the majors, but he knew the game. A very stern disciplinarian, always learning. At first I hated him. Jimmy, he didn't care too much what we did afterwards. Bill Allington did. There was nothing like being late for the bus. You had to be in bed at a certain time and make sure you ate properly. We were winners all the time when Bill coached us.

Bill's the one who took us on the tour. He was divorced and didn't have anybody except a daughter. Then she got married, so he gave his whole life to taking us around the countryside playing ball. We called him the Silver Fox. He had silver hair and wore glasses. If you work at it, you're going to succeed, no matter what. That was probably his biggest line. All these years later, and I still pattern myself after Bill.

KEN HOUSTON, *defensive backfield, University of Houston (now a counselor at Terrell Alternative Middle School, Houston):* Coach was a great motivator. When I got to the Redskins, I was under the impression that I couldn't play anymore. Then I see guys thirty-eight, thirty-nine years old walking around, and I readjusted immediately. George Allen could change your whole way of thinking. It was the way he handled himself, his knowledge of the game, the hurt if he did not win. His personality, that mystique. He inspired you just by watching him.

We had guys on the team making two hundred, three hundred thousand dollars. He'd give somebody a bicycle if they played well, and he'd have guys playing harder to get themselves a bicycle than they did for their one hundred thousand dollars. On Thursdays he'd bring each player a dish of cake and ice cream. I don't know how he got away with it.

What George Allen did was get himself inside his players' heads. We'd have all those drills in practice, and then you'd go to dinner with him and he'd sit there for three hours and talk. He never took it for granted that we knew. We started over every day. I guess we became brainwashed. A guy would come off the field and say, "Coach, I know exactly what you're thinking. Don't say nothin', I got it." You always knew what he wanted. He poured himself right into you.

JOE NEWTON, *cross-country and track, York High, Oak Brook, Illinois:* I grew up on the southside of Chicago, okay? You were a gangster or you were in sports. The guys I hung with, we went out for sports. We were at the Y, we'd go to the sandlots and play tackle. Then I go to high school. Parker High on the southside. And there at Parker there's this magnificent, tough, rough guy that just became like a second father to me. I've never heard a guy say a bad word about Coach Eddie O'Farrell. He was an Irishman. He was five-foot-eight and 120 pounds. He used to come out at midcourt and shoot two-hand set shots and swish 'em.

I went from '43 to '47. O'Farrell, he never counseled you. It was the way he was and the speeches he made. He'd get mad and throw the ball at you. He'd get mad and throw a chair at you. One time he got mad at me and he said, "Newton, you're going to have to pay to get into the game tomorrow." The next day we go up to the gym. They had the wrestling coach taking tickets. I walked in and he grabs and says, "You gotta pay a quarter." "Who said?" "Coach O'Farrell." My scoring average was 6 points. I was so pissed off I scored 16. It was my all-time high, and we won the game. We come into the locker room and Coach O'Farrell said, "Here's your quarter back."

We loved the guy. We played our hearts out for him. You respected him because he wouldn't take any scrap from anybody. I came back to the school about five years after I graduated and he said, "I used to throw chairs and basketballs at you." I said, "I remember, Coach." And he said, "You'll remember that till the day you die."

BRO. MIKE WILMOTT, S.J., *basketball, Creighton Prep, Omaha (on sabbatical):* It was in high school that I figured out I wanted to enter the Jesuits. And I wanted to coach. After my first two years in the novitiate I took my vows, and then they ask you what you want to do. I said, I want to be a coach. So they sent me to a school for cabinetmaking.

I spent about two and a half years doing the trade-school thing, and then I got sent to Creighton Prep. I told the people there that I'd like to get into coaching, and they found me a spot coaching the 440 runners. I remember the head coach came in and he said to me, "Well, Coach, you ready to go?" This is the first day of practice, you know? And he called me "Coach" and said are you ready to go. That was big time!

This was Dud Allen talking. He was about five-foot-six and kind of stocky. He'd gone to West Point when Lombardi was a coach there. Dud Allen knew football, he knew basketball, he knew track. He wasn't kidding around when he said it; he wasn't trying to pump me up. He was *serious.* I was just starting out and this guy had been doing it for a long time. I'll never forget it. It was like he knew I needed to be called "Coach."

GENE KRIEGER, *women's volleyball, California Baptist College:* I had a couple of coaches who were good influences and a couple who were bad. But one was a Christian coach who showed me qualities that I didn't have but I wanted. I found out he had a relationship with Christ. He was Al Herring. He played at UCLA in the John Wooden era. I liked the way he handled me and the other athletes. He mentioned that there was a meeting of the Fellowship of Christian Athletes. I didn't even know what FCA was, but if he recommended something, I checked it out. They didn't push religion; they talked about Bible verses and the things that Jesus teaches about keeping it all in perspective. By getting sport into perspective, I got better.

Al Herring was the only coach I ever had who didn't swear. That was a biggie. He'd stay stuff like "Gosh darn it" and stomp his foot. It was almost funny. I could play for that type of person so much better than one who ripped me to shreds and ranted and raved and got in your face. Some of those drill sergeants were so negative that my entire motivation for being successful in college was to prove they were wrong about me in high school. There was always the constant pressure on the players, the verbal pounding, never giving them slack, calling them names, the berating, the pushing to make them play harder. You can't see the scars that produces later in kids.

BRUCE WILHELM, *weight lifting and athletics, owner of an exercise-equipment store in Daly City, California:* I'm not real big on coaches. When you're out there [competing], the coach can do nothing for you. That's the moment of truth. You've got to use your own brain, your own guts. When you need a coach to call your plays or always tell you what to do, what have you learned?

Too many coaches want their athletes to be dependent on them. They like to ride their coattails. A lot of coaches live through their athletes. I see it in high schools. These guys running around in those short pants and the shoes. They're always screaming at you, kicking you in the ass, telling you to be a man, suck it up. I look at coaches, and I'm never really impressed.

JOHN YOUNG: It is not a credit to my character, but I had two bad years [out of seven in minor league] baseball, and both years were with managers I didn't like. That was the difference between me and Reggie Jackson—besides a lot of talent. Reggie was able to have great years in situations where he didn't like the manager or the manager didn't like him. I've got to take responsibility for that, of course. But a minor league manager is there to protect the investment of the club. I was an investment. I had big-league talent; I had played in the major leagues [briefly, with the Tigers]. It was his job to set an environment where I could succeed.

TED PETERSEN, *football, Trinity High, Washington, Pennsylvania:* My greatest asset as a coach is not that I played football in high school and college and in the pros; it's that I wasn't a very good player in high school until my senior year and I wasn't a good player in college my first year and when I got to the Steelers I wasn't any good at all.

Because I wasn't, the coaches didn't treat me well. But I never gave up. Rookie camp with the Steelers was the worst experience of my life. I remember looking at guys who were getting cut and thinking how lucky they were. But as long as there were other guys there with me I wasn't going to quit. From not quitting, from persevering, I became a good player.

So I never give up on anybody now that I'm a coach. I don't just pick out the great athletes and praise them. I have this one kid, as a sophomore he tried real hard but he didn't have a chance. This year he came back and contributed. Next year he'll start. He's a winner because he never quit. If I'd coached him the way I was coached, he'd have been gone. Guaranteed. It's not easy for me to compliment; that's not the way I was raised. But I think that's the better way to do it. My father loved me, but he threw compliments around like some people throw manhole covers. The reason for that is because that's how *his* father did it.

I had a tremendous, burning desire to please my coaches. I wanted to work hard and do well and earn their approval. When they yelled at me and ridiculed me to get me motivated, it worked—I mean, they got the result they were after—but it made me hate practice, hate the system, and hate them. It took a lot of the joy out of playing.

And what's the point of that? There's a lot of things that aren't pleasant about accomplishing great things, but you should still be able to have good feelings about it. There are still not a lot of fathers who heap praises on their sons. Some kids overachieve because they never got that approval. The coach often takes the place of the father. When you give them your approval and they find out they're pleasing you, well, I mean, they'll just lay their hearts on the line for you.

STEVE HODGIN, *football, Western Carolina University:* When I left Chapel Hill [University of North Carolina], I got a job at a AAA high school in Waynesville. I worked as an assistant for five years and then took over the head job there. Then I got an opportunity to work with Bob Waters here at Western Carolina. I was offensive line coach from '80 to '86, became the defensive coordinator in '87–'88. That's when Coach Waters died and Dale Strom came in. After Dale left—he was here for nine months—I got the head job.

Coach Waters was one of those individuals you run across maybe once in your lifetime. His great strength was the way he dealt with the players and the coaches. He didn't do it in a forceful way, yet he was forceful. If there was a task to be done, you didn't have to be told by Coach Waters to do it. He made you want to do it for him.

There wasn't any particular day when he called us together and told us he had ALS. His right arm went into a sling at the beginning of the '86 season, but there'd been symptoms before that. It was a long time before they were positively identified. Six months to a year. He went to a lot of specialists until they finally said, "This is it: Lou Gehrig's disease."

He used to come down on Fridays and throw passes to the offensive line. The offensive line really felt special on Fridays. When he got to where he couldn't throw with his right arm, he threw with his left. That's what I remember about Coach Waters. How he kept pushing. There was always hope and there was always the next day. Like being a coach: There's always the next game.

It was probably the '85 season when he had to stop throwing those passes. By the '88 season he went to a wheelchair. Then during that season went on a mechanical breathing-support system. Everybody wanted to do something for Coach Waters. We rigged up a phone in his office where he could lay his head against the receiver. He used to use this bag to help him breathe, like when he was going from house to house. We'd bag him. He'd sit in the back seat, and when he'd blink his eyes we'd mash on the bag. Eventually we got some batteries and rigged something up. It became an obsession to do things before he asked us to. I guess you could say we closed ranks around Coach Waters.

In 1983 we were 11–3–1. We went to the finals of Division I-AA and lost to Southern Illinois. In '85 we were 4–6–1; in '86 we were 6–5. In '87 we were 4–7; in '88 we were 2–9. I guess there'd be people who'd venture that we were distracted by Coach Waters's situation. I don't know. I've got a lot of mixed emotions. But there was no one who was a part of this football team who wanted to see him step down. On the other hand, for him to be able to get into that '89 season, I think we all knew that was going to be questionable. It was a tough decision for everyone involved. They made him an associate athletic director, didn't cut his salary or anything. It was inevitable that it had to happen. They decided not to consider anybody from the inside to become the new head coach. So they got Dale Strom, who'd been fired at Georgia.

Coach Waters died on Memorial Day 1989. In July I had an opportunity to go to Wake Forest. But I decided it was best for me to stay. Coming off Coach Waters, who hardly ever raised his voice, and then to have Dale on the sidelines . . . I guess it was just a bad match. The University of Georgia and Western Carolina are only 165 miles apart, but it might as well be a million. Here's an example: Dale came up to me one time and said, "Who gives the coaches tires?" Well, we got one tire store. It's where all the coaches buy their tires. But Dale, he was used to all the perks.

The first of January, Dale said he was taking a job at Duke. Our AD and then the chancellor asked me if I'd take the job here.

My first game was against N.C. State. We got beat 67–zip. The last time we'd been down there was two years prior to that, and they'd beaten us pretty soundly. That was Coach Waters's last opening game, and now here it was my first opening game, and we're both getting shellacked pretty good.

There isn't a day goes by when I don't think about Coach Waters. There'll be these vivid moments of how he did things. Flashbacks. Like when we're in a meeting of the offensive staff. These guys have got to be tired of hearing me say, "This is the way Coach Waters did it." But it's just a constant thing that stays with me, and always will.

DORIS HARDY, *athletic director, Riverside/Brookfield High, Illinois:* When I was eighteen I was a counselor at Camp Marywood in Michigan. Those were some pretty okay times, canoe trips and all that. And I remember the camp director definitely made an impression on me. It was toward the end of the summer and we were walking back from a campfire before I went to my cabin, and she said she wanted to meet with me. We sat down, as I remember, under a tree. She started talking about how I'd done a really good job and she knew I didn't know what I wanted to do with my life, but she thought I should consider this kind of thing because I worked so well with the kids. "I think you'll enjoy it," she said. I remember going home and announcing to my mother and my father that I was going to become a P.E. teacher. They just looked at me.

I wonder sometimes what would have happened if she hadn't sat me down under that tree. Would I have done something competely different? Maybe taken longer to get where I am now? And I've always wondered what happened to her. I'd like to know. I'd like to tell her, "You were right. I *did* enjoy it."

THREE

Getting Hired

For a couple of years there, he says, he thought about writing his own book. He even had a title: *Not Qualified*. At the time, Ron Dickerson was the defensive coordinator at Clemson and president of the Black Coaches Association. He'd played for Don Shula, coached under Joe Paterno—impressive notes on the résumé. But at forty-four he wasn't what he had set out to be: a head football coach.

Over the years he'd applied for head jobs at a couple of Division I schools. Nothing major; he kept things realistic. The Northern Universities, the Southwest Central States. "I've been in this profession for sixteen, seventeen years," Ron Dickerson says. "With all my background, I figured I had a good shot." But it was as if they kept moving the target. He'd apply for a job; they'd tell him they were looking for a coordinator. So he became a coordinator. He'd apply again, they'd tell him they were looking for head-coaching experience. "They were still finding a way to get you into that 'Not Qualified' category," he says.

Getting hired. Joining the club. Becoming a coach. Ability gets you to the table. Once there it's luck, timing, and contacts, contacts, contacts. The coaching fraternity has ensconced itself within a spiderweb of interdependent strands that holds itself up. To become a coach you must wire into the circuitry as quickly as possible. Get yourself *inside*. A well-placed phone call can light up the entire system.

Some coaches, it appears, have all the luck, all the timing, all the contacts. In truth, it's rarely easy for anybody. "There are three times as many good coaches out there as there are good coaching jobs," says basketball coach Ron Greene, who's made stops at Loyola in New Orleans, Mississippi State, Murray State, and Indiana State. "That's a problem." Yes, it is. And all the more if you're African-American. Or old—which means not many seasons past forty. Or SWANK: Single Woman And No Kids—a deadly euphemism for lesbian.

For his part, Ron Dickerson was reaching that magic age. Soon he would have two strikes against him. If guys like him weren't getting their shots, Ron Dickerson said, the young guys coming up won't bother to take aim. "If it doesn't happen soon," Ron Dickerson said, "I'll have to find another avenue—athletic director, the NFL, something."

Something happened. Ron Dickerson signed on as head man at Temple. His alumni contacts included Bill Cosby. Good for him. A happy ending for Ron Dickerson. The rest are out there, looking, waiting, trying to find their way in.

DOUG BARFIELD, *football, Opelika High, Alabama:* There are only a few great coaches, and there are only a few who are really poor. Most of us are in that middle category: trying our best to get to the top and scratching like mad to keep from falling into the bottom.

LARRY SMITH, *football, USC (retired):* I started to set my goals and ambitions about my second year in college. Time frames. When you get to be twenty-five, where you should be. When you get to be thirty, thirty-five. I became a head high school coach when I was twenty-three; I thought I would be twenty-five, thirty years old. I got into college coaching when I was twenty-six, and I thought I would be at least thirty to thirty-five. So then I said, okay, I want big time, like maybe Big 10 assistant coach by the time I'm thirty-five. I made it by twenty-nine. So I said, I want to be a coordinator by the time I'm thirty-five, and I made it by thirty-three. So I said, okay, I want to be a head coach by the time I'm forty. I made it when I was thirty-six. After that my goal was to make it go.

My family loved Arizona when I was an assistant there, so we always had a goal that someday if the head job opened up we'd go back. Four years later I was able to get it. After about four or five years at Arizona, my goal was to either stay there and be the best head coach they ever had or to nail down one of the top two or three jobs in the country. [Smith moved to USC in 1987; he was forced to resign in 1992.]

ANSON DORRANCE, *1991 U.S. Women's World Cup soccer champions and the University of North Carolina:* When I was sixteen my father was exasperated with me once and he told me something I thought was hilarious. "You're the most confident person without any talent I've ever known." I said, "I'm taking that as a compliment."

CHUCK TRUBY, *wrestling assistant, Chicago Vocational High:* If you don't have confidence you might as well give up. I'm going to be successful at the high school level, and then I'm going to be one of the youngest wrestling coaches at the college level, okay? I'm handicapped, and wrestling has brought me through that. My lungs are scarred and my knees are screwed up from a blood problem. It's hereditary, and you get gamma globulin, and I have to make sure I schedule my treatments so it won't interfere with wrestling. Coaching is about hard work and not giving up and wanting to win, and that's what got me through.

DON NELSON, *Golden State Warriors:* I never thought about coaching. My last year as a player I started thinking about becoming a referee. I went to the L.A. summer league and reffed about ten games. I loved it. Then right about that time I got a call from the Milwaukee Bucks.

Wayne Embry, the GM, asked me to come out for an interview. We'd been roommates. So I flew to Milwaukee to interview with Larry Costello. We were 3 and 14 when Larry resigned. A real tough start. I was in shock, because, being with the Celtics, I'd never lost. I begged Larry not to resign. You have a bad start, you hang in there. And the word was out that I'd be leaving with him. There were ownership changes; it was a real mess.

I was made the head coach, and we're still losing. It was the worst thing I'd ever experienced. I didn't know what I was doing. But even though we lost, it was still fun. The years after that—when I started to realize the complexity of the job and what I'd have to do if I wanted to be any good—I understood what was going to be in store for me. I don't think I really thought I was a very good coach until I had seven, eight years under my belt.

SANDRA CHILDERS, *softball, Marion-Adams High, Sheridan, Indiana:* I'll be honest with you. I would have not done this if I wasn't in a wheelchair. I would have said, I don't need this apple. I'd been down the road with coaching, and I knew how it consumes your time. But since I was in a wheelchair now, it was like I had to do it.

I've been paralyzed from the midchest down for seven years. I have full use of my arms. Before that I coached softball for six or seven years, nine- to twelve-year-olds and twelve- to thirteen-year-olds, and I played amateur softball until I was thirty-seven. I'm forty-six now.

I had a birth defect. An area in my spinal cord that wasn't supposed to be there would bleed, and it was like I was having a stroke. The first time, I was thirty-two. They figured it was an aneurysm. The second time, I must have been thirty-five, and they'd found out what it was but they were afraid to do the surgery because the operation itself might cripple me.

In '85, when it happened again, they said they could go in with microsurgery. Came out like a charm. But there was another defect higher up and that one started to grow. They had to go back in. That's the one that paralyzed me. When that second defect began to grow, I went from October to January slowly losing all sensation, all feeling. It wasn't like I was in an accident and one minute I was whole and the next minute I was half. It was a slow process, and I was able to grieve the loss of the lower part of my body before I even had the last surgery. The only question I asked was whether the surgery would get to my arms, and the doctor said no. So actually when it came time for the surgery it was a total relief. I was going to go ahead and live.

I can't say that there are any real advantages to coaching from a wheelchair, but I also don't think there are any real disadvantages. One difference I've noticed is that I'm much more alert at practice. There are so many things going on. Where's the ball, where are the runners? I break an arm and I'm really out of commission. One other thing: I'm the first-base coach. I'm convinced that with me sitting in the coach's box, the opposing first basemen unconsciously don't want to let a ball get through. Boy, they get them all.

ART COLLINS, *downhill skiing, Reno High, Nevada:* Fourteen seasons ago a group of students came to me and said, "We need a ski coach." I said, "I don't know how to ski." Well, they were real persistent. They asked if I'd help with their preseason conditioning program. I could do that. After I'd gotten out of the service, I'd worked as a trainer at the university here because I went there on a track scholarship for the javelin. Then the principal asked me if I'd apply for the job. And I told him, "I don't know how to ski." But I applied anyway and the principal came by later and said, "Congratulations." I think I was the only one who'd applied.

The first practice I fell getting on the ski lift. I get off the lift and fall over again. I took my skis off and started walking. My skis over one shoulder, the gates to set a race course over the other. I'm hiking around the mountain, following the tracks of my skiers. The soft stuff's about twelve inches deep. The kids are going down the trail to where we were going to practice. All these skiers zooming by as I'm trudging down the hill. "Hi, Coach!" "Hi, Coach!" Thirty-five, forty kids. There was a lift up the bunny hill that would have left me off a half mile from where we were practicing—but nobody told me.

When I took this job, I figured it would be temporary. It was after the first championship, the next year, where I felt like I was enjoying it. I enjoyed the kids and I wanted to stay with it for a while to see what happened. We've won thirteen state titles in a row now. Thing is, after that first group of kids asked me to coach, some girls asked me if I'd be their volleyball coach. I grew up in Southern California. I would have done that for sure. None of this would have happened.

GARY ZARECKY, basketball, Foothill Junior College, California (formerly at United States International University in San Diego): I was coming home from basketball practice at Chico State. I was on a moped. I didn't have a helmet on, and this car came out of nowhere and ran the light. I put my hands up and went through the grill and into the fan. I was thrown back out and landed on a concrete curb and crushed my pelvis. My right hand was severed. They pinned that to my arm in a plastic bag and rushed me to the hospital.

I was in surgery for twelve hours. They asked my parents if they could do experimental surgery—nerve tracing. They put the severed limb on a table and matched up every single strand they could. I was in rehab for almost a year. When you lie in a hospital bed and you've been saved and you know you've been given a second chance . . . you either sit there and cry or you do something. I became a very motivated person. Nothing seemed impossible. When I got into coaching I didn't see too many things that would hold me back. Every time I got down, I'd flash back to that accident and that hospital bed.

ANONYMOUS MAN *at a Division I university:* I used to feel this need to be good so people would never question me. I had to make up for every deficiency so in case someone found out I was gay I'd still be good enough to keep my job. I was on a very hard-driven course. I couldn't allow any setbacks. I always felt like I had to look over my shoulder. There was always this presence, like I was wearing a wet blanket everywhere I went.

It's not like that now. I know so many people in coaching who are gay, so there's a good support system. I know two football coaches here who are very afraid of anyone knowing. And I have that record I was so desperate to establish. I don't have to be the best coach in the world every night.

But something else happened, too. I was confronted by a couple of my athletes, and when I told them, it didn't matter. They thought I was a good coach, and *that* was all that mattered. At the time I was in the pros. A couple of the athletes decided they wanted to discuss it with me. It wasn't a confrontation. It came up in conversation: "Well, what about you?" I've always told myself that if someone has the guts to ask me point-blank, I would have a hard time lying.

I'm still not officially "out." And if someone were to ask me today, I don't know if I would respond the same way. I've learned how administrations work, about what threatens some people. At the same time, when they asked and I told them, that alone gave me more confidence that I was a good coach, that I didn't have to prove myself to everybody in the world. I finally felt like I'd done my job and I don't need to make up for the fact that I'm gay. I felt this great burden being lifted from me.

ANONYMOUS WOMAN *at a Division I university:* The highest rate of suicide among teenagers is among those who have said they have lesbian or gay feelings. Kids need positive role models. They need to know they aren't bad people. I can have an impact on students' lives, even if only in a small way. What I should do is come all the way out. Be a complete role model. But if I come out I lose my job. Then where am I? And where are the kids?

PAT GRIFFIN, *associate professor, social justice education program, University of Massachusetts, Amherst (former women's swim coach):* I would never have come out when I was a coach. Never. You don't know how your team is going to react or how parents will react. And you don't know how the people who hire and fire are going to react. You have to be in a certain place in your life to come out publicly. I wasn't in that place back then.

I was out to two of my swimmers, that was it. It was the right thing for me to come out, privately, to these women. One was struggling with her own identity. The other is a heterosexual woman who I keep in touch with. A couple swimmers found out, and one had a real struggle. We haven't maintained contact, and that makes me sad.

In the early '80s it became important for me to speak out about homophobia in sports. So I intentionally started working toward a time when I could be out and still working in athletics. My coming out was at a conference where I made a presentation. I was on a panel with two men and another women. The other woman and I, we decided it was important to come out as part of the presentation. And I was ready.

I've had very few bad experiences in coming out. That's partly because, coming out publicly, the people who are uncomfortable stay away. Professionally, I think I've been rewarded for the work I've done on homophobia. And, for sure, it's great for the lesbian students. They've told me this: They like having someone who is out and successful. But the real question is whether I'd have come out if I was still a coach. My sense is I would have left coaching to do what I'm doing now anyway. My need to take a stand would have been on a collision course with my need to be secret.

CLEVELAND STROUD, *basketball, Rockdale High, Georgia:* I always wanted to be some type of leader, but I didn't know what I could do. Growing up black in the South in the '50s was not easy, believe me. I graduated high school in 1954; graduated college in 1970. I was thirty-four. I'd married right out of high school and had some kids, so I had to take care of my obligations first.

The hardships I'd had helped me get through. Growing up in a segregated society helped me understand a lot of things. That nobody can keep you from doing what you want to do. Not to get down on yourself. It gives you this hard outer shell that, no matter how you hold me down, I'm gonna make it. It gave me a different outlook than most coaches have.

I started as junior varsity coach for six years. After that I was made the head coach. My first year we went 2–22. The year was a disaster. I had to wonder if I'd chosen the right profession. I started to doubt myself. It becomes like a cancer; it just starts to eat at you, and pretty soon it consumes you.

I'd see the students in the hallways, or the players or my coworkers, and I'd wonder what they thought of me. You hear people say, "I don't care what other people think." Well, I do. I guess it goes all the way back to the time we were growing up in a segregated society, wondering all the time what other people think about you. You grew up thinking there's something lacking, that you're inadequate in the eyes of certain people. You'd be reminded of it by not being able to go into a drugstore; if you went to a restaurant there was a little window at the back; you'd walk down the street and see "colored water" and "white water." I was the first black head coach at my school, the first black head coach in the county. There was a lot of pressure to succeed. When I didn't, right off, all those old fears came back to haunt me.

But that's what I got out of sports. Every game you have to prove yourself. The next year I got a group of young kids and I just started to work. We won seventeen that year, and we've been winning ever since. I think people think of me now as the head basketball coach, just Coach Stroud. Not the black guy they hired over at Rockdale. To me that means a lot.

JOHN NICKS, *Olympic-level figure skating (coached Tai and Randy, and Tiffany Chin):* I fell into coaching. I skated with my sister, and we won the British Pairs Championships between 1947 and 1952. In 1953 we won the European title and turned professional. In 1954 we were in a show in Johannesburg. I fell backstage and fractured a bone in my foot and had it in a cast for months. For something to do, I taught at the local rink.

By the time I returned to England, my sister had married and gone to Vancouver. I went there but found it much tougher than I thought. I finally found work in Trail, British Columbia, a little mining town. They had this wonderful hockey team called the Trail Smoke Eaters. I learned my trade up there. I had to teach at a public rink, sharing ice time with hockey players. I was a so-and-so "fancy skater." But after a period of time we made our peace. I even worked with the hockey players on their power skating.

The turning point in my career came in 1961. The entire American figure-skating team was killed in a plane crash in Belgium. I didn't know them extremely well, but I was still aghast. Two or three weeks later I started getting calls from United States people. One of those people suggested I move to California to replace the coach who had been killed.

WANDA ANITA OATES, *boys' basketball, Ballou High, Washington, D.C.:* I was the football coach for about two weeks. The principal, she didn't see anything wrong with it; the boys didn't see anything wrong with it. It was the other male coaches went downtown and jumped up and down. They didn't tell people they didn't want to beat me. It's that they didn't want to lose to me. I took it to court and lost. We went to the U.S. Court of Appeals, and sitting on it was Robert Bork. All three sustained the lower court's ruling that it wasn't sex discrimination.

CHARLIE THOMAS, *basketball, San Francisco State:* The coaching fraternity has gotten tighter. It's a really close-knit group. Sometimes that can be a problem, because the good-old-boy network weeds out some of the good coaches. If you don't fit the mold, the society doesn't want you. I can think of one guy, he's a great coach. His teams go 24–5, 25–4 every year. But he doesn't fit the mold. So he doesn't get his due, doesn't get invited to the NCAAs. That doesn't make sense.

Go to the Final Four, to the coaches' convention, and you'll see coaches in the lobby. You get a feel for the room and make some contacts. Most coaches hang out for a while, tell war stories, have a few beers, and go their merry way. But some guys stay there all day. What you call an "All-Lobby" team. They come in at 11 o'clock in the morning and stay till midnight. They know how to get to the top. They play the game.

Coaching is a righteous sort of profession. It can go to our heads, sort of change us. I don't want to become one of the good old boys. I just want to show them that I can coach basketball and win and be respected. I want to be able to look at myself in the mirror and say, "Hey, I've done it my way. I don't owe anybody anything."

GEORGE KARL, *Seattle Supersonics:* [After stints with Cleveland and Golden State in the NBA, Karl spent four years in the CBA and Europe before getting back to the NBA.] I made a lot of mistakes [the first time] I was in the NBA. I was young. I was too dogmatic, too aggressive. Keeping your mouth shut and listening is a much better attitude. Back then I was one of the leaders in technical fouls. But I've decided the refs are right and I'm wrong and that's the way the rules are.

I'm not even sure I deserve to be in the NBA now. But what I decided [when out of the league] was that I loved coaching and that I was going to get back to the league by having people say, "Hey, he can coach." I wasn't going to get back in by doing the politically right thing, the politically social thing. I was going to show people I could coach. I think that's what I've done. And I'm proud of that. I didn't show my face; I didn't call a lot of NBA teams [when he was out of the league]. It was: "Here's my record." I was in Albany for two years and Madrid for two years. In Madrid, we were 67–18 the one year. My worst year in Albany was 39–17. The other year we went 50–6. We won all our home games—a record that might be tied but can never be broken. I told myself when I got back in that I was going to stay away from the political end of things and stay with the honest things about the game of basketball.

BARRY LAMB, *defensive coordinator, San Diego State:* There's a couple of different clubs. Once a head coach, you never have to worry about a job. You'll never see a head coach get fired where another head coach won't hire him. It's different with assistants. We sign one-year contracts. You can do a good job, keep your nose clean, make sure your kids graduate, and then the best friend of the head coach becomes available and you're out of a job. There's no recourse.

There's one or two assistants on every staff who keep the others informed: who's getting what jobs, who's getting fired; there's a job opening here, an opening there; this guy might take this job, there'll be an opening at the place he just left. And there's a couple of gurus. You call these guys, they'll know all the scoops. They work the phones hard. A good way in is to work for a brand-new head coach. He doesn't have "his" guys yet; he hires whoever he can find. My first full time job, at UNLV, I was making $18,000 and happier than a pig in slop to get it.

RON DICKERSON, *defensive coordinator, Clemson (now head coach at Temple):* It's not that black coaches were intentionally eliminated— I really believe they weren't. It's just that we were not part of that good-ol'-boy system. About five years ago we said, "We have to break into that network."

If you're at a convention and you see Joe Paterno, go over and say, "Hi, Coach, here's my card." Those are the kinds of things we'd never done before. I must have called forty coaches this year on behalf of other coaches. "I hear you have an opening on your defensive staff. . . "

We don't want a president telling an athletic director, "Hire that black coach because . . . he's black." That's the last thing we want. It's not fair to us, it's not fair to the alumni, and it's definitely not fair to the student-athlete. We want to be hired because we're the most qualified. People get color-blind real fast if the guy can win.

And if we lose, fire us. We know how the game works. People still say they don't want to hire a black coach because they wouldn't want to fire a black coach. I would love to be in the position to get fired! If I just had the opportunity!

TINA SLOAN GREEN, *lacrosse, Temple (retired):* My first experience with racism was at graduation [from Girls' High School in Philadelphia] when they gave out the award for the best athlete. Everybody in the class knew I was going to get it. I love sports; it's sort of an art form with me. Everybody's waiting. And I didn't get it.

I graduated and I couldn't afford to go to college. That's when it started to hit me, the barriers. But I had one teacher, a white teacher, her uncle worked for the employment bureau. I could get a job there to get money to go to school.

At West Chester [University], we were on the lower end of the socioeconomic level—whites and blacks. When it came time to invite people to coach at the field hockey and lacrosse camps, nobody from West Chester would ever get invited. So a group of us decided we were going to start our own camp.

When I started competing on the national lacrosse team, I saw more barriers. I was the first African-American to make the U.S. team. The year I was playing my best it was in the '60s and the team was supposed to go to South Africa. I got cut. My best year. That hit me.

When I [began coaching] at Lincoln [University], they had just begun to integrate with women, and since it was an all-black school the race thing was eliminated. There might have been other factors, but race wasn't one of them. I felt really free. At the time, Vivian Stringer was at Cheney [State, a neighboring school] and so was John Cheney. Vivian's at Iowa now, one of the top women basketball coaches in the country. John's at Temple now; just a great man, a great coach.

Vivian and I didn't know what we were doing then, so John and Floyd Laisure, the men's coach at Lincoln, they took us under their wing. After all he'd already done at Cheney, you'd have thought John would have been invited to all the camps to give clinics. But no. So we had to start our own.

DAVE DOLCH, *football, Morningside College, Sioux City, Iowa:* I didn't go on a personal crusade to become the minority coach—the white coach at a traditional black school—it was just the best opportunity at that time. I was an assistant at Delaware State under a black head coach; I was head coach at Bowie State. There were individuals who were uncomfortable with me coaching. So yes, there was added incentive. I wanted to show young people that people can work together and be successful. Because if you're not, who really cares?

I can't say I experienced being black. But I have a feel for being the minority coach. I learned that the black coaches and administrators were more receptive to me than when it's the reverse situation—the black coach at a "white" school. I learned what it's like with the shoe on the other foot. A strong desire is created within you to prove to yourself and everybody else that you can be successful.

BARBARA JEAN JACKET, *Prairie View A&M (retired) and 1992 U.S. Women's Olympic track & field coach:* I didn't realize how much pressure I had put on myself until August 20 [1992] when I got back to Prairie View from [the Olympic Games in] Barcelona. The tension in my back and everything just released. And I said, "Wait a minute. You mean for four years you've been putting all this pressure on yourself?"

I wanted to be good because I'm a woman and I'm black. They don't think you can be successful, being a woman and the head coach. From 1989, when I was selected, to 1992, that's a long time to have your shoulders tight, I promise you. But I had never been a loser, and I didn't want this to be the first time. Because basically coaching is supposed to be a man's world. I knew there hadn't been but two black head [women's] coaches in the whole Olympics. The first was Dr. Nell Jackson, my coach at Tuskegee, and the second was me. Me. Head Olympic coach. I mean, I had six assistants, three men and three women, and all six were white.

I had never been part of those five circles before. What everybody says is when they start talking about those five circles, everybody goes crazy. I didn't want to get crazy. I just wanted to be successful. Not doing well, that's what I feared. Not doing well as a coach, as a person, as a friend to the athletes. I wanted to be excellent. That's all.

JOHN LIPON, *roving instructor, Detroit Tigers [Lipon, seventy-four, played in the majors for ten years, then managed for thirty years in the minors, with stops in sixteen cities, starting in 1959. He also coached with the Cleveland Indians for four years, and for two months in 1971 was the interim manager]:* Sparky Anderson [Detroit Tiger manager] will tell you I've had the best job in baseball. And others say I had the most important job. What I did have was an awful lot of patience with young people. Players have to know you're behind them 100 percent—I've bailed a few of them out of jail, too. I always tried to build up their confidence. Baseball has a tendency to beat you down. There's going to be games, streaks, whole years when you can't do anything. It's very easy to get disappointed. We play a game every day. If you can't sleep after a game, you're in trouble.

I won 2,176 games against something like 1,900-and-some losses. That's fifth on the all-time-win parade. But it's when you see a player come on, that's what's exciting. I had Jim Bunning in Pueblo. He won one hundred games in the American League and then in the National League. Now he's in politics up in Kentucky. [Bunning is a co.igressman.] Lou Pinella, I had him. He always had temper problems; I tried to calm him down. When a player comes on and develops, you like to think you were a part of that. Then you have other guys who don't make it. There was one guy, Tony, he was my favorite player, a great hustler. But we had another prospect coming on and I had to move Tony out. That's the toughest part of managing, and Tony was the toughest. I patted him on the back and let him go. At the club-house meeting, I tell you, I had tears in my eyes.

Not getting the permanent [managing] job in Cleveland, that has to be my biggest disappointment. Gabe Paul became general manager and he told me I didn't have a big enough name. He said he'd let me know. It ended up I called him and told him I was going with Detroit. I had enough years in to know how the game's played. But that's all right. I look at the managers in the majors, they get old quick. If I'd been in the majors, I wouldn't have lasted this long, no sir.

K. C. JONES, *Seattle Supersonics (retired):* [Jones was fired as head coach by the Washington Bullets in 1976.] There was a tough period of maybe two, three years. Then I picked myself up. I decided it wasn't all that dark out there. I got a job as an assistant. I was putting food on the table and taking care of my family. I told myself I wasn't going to get another head job. I was ready to go with that when things turned around, just like that.

I was up in Chicago where all the coaches and general managers watched the players in the predraft camp. Red Auerbach met me down-stairs one morning and said, "Let's go to my room." He asked me if I was interested in the head job with the Celtics. I said yes. I had this urge to tell him I wasn't worried whether I got it, because by then I was at peace with myself, but I just said yes and that was the end of the conversation. He said he'd get back to me.

Red left on Friday. Sunday morning I got on the plane and the flight attendant says, "Congratulations, Mr. Jones." I said "Thank you." Then another attendant came up and said, "Congratulations, Mr. Jones." I said thanks again, but what for? She said, "You're the new head coach of the Celtics." I said, "Sure." So she got a newspaper and there it was. She brought some champagne and paper cups, and there were just a couple of people in first class, so I said, "Well, whether it's true or not, let's celebrate."

AL BORGES, *offensive coordinator, Boise State, Idaho:* It was Steve Weaver's idea. He was the radio guy [when Borges was the offensive coordinator at Portland State]. The idea was to have the fans call some plays. They could hold up a card with a red Run or a green Pass.

Pokey [Allen, the head coach] brought it up when I was interviewing. I said, "Sure, Coach, I love it." I got the job, and I was hoping he'd forget about it. But my second year he brought it up. "What do you think?" I said I wasn't too fired up about it. And he said you were. "That was before I had the job." When you're in a game, you're thinking about a lot of things, but I guarantee one of them is not turning around to get the call from the fans.

So when's the perfect time to have the fans call your plays? There isn't any. I decided on the second series of the second half. We run it once a year, the first home game of the season. The first time we got the ball on about the forty-eight-yard line. The fans called for a pass, so we threw a play-action thing. Then they said run and we ran a sweep to our halfback and he put it in the end zone.

BOBBY CREMINS, *basketball, Georgia Tech:* I wanted to play in the NBA. When I didn't I went to Ecuador; I was running away, but it was super. Then I tried out for the 1972 Olympic team. I figured if I made it I'd make the NBA. But I didn't.

I had worked at the basketball camp at Davidson, and one of the assistant coaches told me there was an assistant job open at Point Park College in Pittsburgh. Point Park is two buildings connected by a bridge. I lived in one of the buildings. Their gym was the YMCA. Then my college coach, Frank McGuire, brought me back to South Carolina as an assistant. Then I got a break. I became a head coach when I was twenty-seven; I went to Appalachia State in 1975.

I loved the old days. I loved it back when I was young and single and wild. Not having any money, always having to hustle. The people you meet, the early steps of your career, nobody knowing who you are, nobody *caring* who you are, never getting asked for your autograph. When I think of those days, I miss them. I always wanted to be where I am now, but they were fun days.

You've got to be ambitious. But there is a fine line, a danger zone. I once heard a person describe the fine line as being a jockey riding a horse. You've got to know when to hit the horse and when not to hit the horse. Sometimes the best way to let things happen is to let things happen. When I was at Appalachia, I used to try to get interviewed for Duke and N.C. State. I couldn't get the time of day. I tried everything. I'd call this person, I'd call that person. I'd run around doing everything. Finally I said, "This ain't working. Keep winning and let them come to you."

I go to the Final Four and I see myself in a lot of the young guys looking for the next job up the ladder. And I envy them a little bit. I remember how excited I was and full of enthusiasm. I'd like to walk over to them and say, "Hey, slow down, let it happen. Don't be so anxious to get to the big time. Enjoy this while you can."

JIM VAN HORN, *formerly a volunteer basketball assistant at Allentown and Lafayette Colleges, both in Pennsylvania; he owns a sports-marketing company:* I had the security of my own business. I never put it on the line. And that is meant to be respectful of the guys who do. The guys you'd see working the lobby at the conventions, looking for their next job. They had their own vision. I respected what those guys were going through. Because to make it, you have to be willing to put it all on the line.

I always feel sorry for these guys when the hammer comes down. And it always does. Say a guy is the first assistant. The program has a bad year and they come down on the head coach and the staff goes with him. He's been traveling the country scouting and recruiting, being away from his family. Now he has to go home to that family and tell them: "We have to start over someplace else. We've got to do it again." I was willing to put in the time, and I was reasonably successful. But I was never going to put myself on the line like these guys did. I was never courageous enough, I guess, to put myself in that vulnerable a position.

BUTCH VAN BREDA KOLFF, *basketball, Hofstra University, Long Island:* These young guys, they gotta learn to relax. Thirty years ago you'd go to the Final Four and guys would have whatever little money they had in their budget, and you'd see them at the hotel having a big steak. Next night they're down at Ted's Steak House, where you get a steak for a dollar thirty-nine and a schooner of beer for forty cents. Final night they're looking for the hospitality room, looking to eat and drink for free.

Last Final Four I went to, I went to the hospitality room and everything's quiet. In the old days we didn't have money but we had a lot of fun. These guys make the money but don't have fun. I said it loud enough for some of the guys to hear. One of them looked up and said, "You're right."

PERRY CLARK, *basketball, Tulane University:* When I got to Penn State, assistants could be on the road all the time. I'll bet you my first three years I was on the road three hundred days a year. I was married and it was tough, but I loved it. It gave me time to sit with coaches from all over the country. I'd just sit there and suck up as much knowledge as I could.

JIM VAN HORN: That's where assistants find their glory—in how hard they're willing to work. And I never heard anyone complain. I think they took real pride in telling each other how busy their schedules were. I spent a couple years as an assistant at Allentown College [of St. Francis de Sales, in eastern Pennsylvania]. It was a brand-new school with a program that wasn't off the ground. I got temporarily transferred to Connecticut by my company, and so I spent a year commuting back and forth, all over the place. I never thought about how nuts it was. I didn't mind doing it. It was my red badge of courage.

AL BORGES: They did an article on me in the paper. They called me "the football junkie." I'm thirty-six years old and I've never been married, in large part because of my commitment. I'm not saying that's good; I'm just saying that's my style. I may make it and I may not, but I'll be damned if I'm not going to make it because I didn't give it the right effort.

A girl I'd been with for four and a half years decided this wasn't what she wanted to deal with anymore. I'll never put her down for that. I regret losing a great girl. But I know too that it had to happen. Ambition is like anything else. You wake up one morning and you realize this is what you want to do—*I really want to do this.* It's like you have no choice.

NICHOLAS MARIOLIS, *basketball, St. Nicholas Church G.O.Y.A:*
St. Nicholas had an A team and a B team. The guy who coached the A
team didn't want to coach the B team anymore, so they asked for volunteers to coach the B team. You had to be over twenty-one and be a
Greek Orthodox Catholic and belong to St. Nicholas. I'm a true Greek,
take my word for it. So I stepped forward. The game was St. Nicholas
against St. Constantine. We got beat 45 to 3. All I could do was put my
hands on the back of my head and say, "Is this what I really want to be
doing?" I asked myself the question and I said, "Yes, this *is* something
I'd like to do." That was fourteen years ago.

AL BORGES: People say athletics is not all that important. But you
know what? It is. Because so many people care about the game. The
competition. The sense that they have something they can cling to.
Some people live their whole week just so they can watch a football
game. It's important to them—maybe it's too important. But as long as
people care as much as they care, I'm going to keep doing what I'm
doing.

KEITH KEPHART *was a strength and conditioning football coach at
Iowa State, Kansas, South Carolina, and Texas A&M:* I don't have any
desire to be the guy that sits behind the big desk. I don't have big
enough nuts for that, to be quite frank.

BILL GUTHRIDGE, *basketball assistant, University of North
Carolina:* I've been here since 1967. In 1979 I told the people at Penn
State that I would take their head job. But I called them up the day
before the press conference and told them I was going to stay here as
an assistant. I have not interviewed for a head job since.

It's been a great run. Dean Smith is the greatest coach ever. We've
won at least twenty-one games a season for twenty-three, twenty-four
years in a row. We've won twenty-five games more times than any other
coach. I've been to the Final Four eight or nine times. We won an NCAA
Championship [a second in 1993], the N.I.T., ACC championships.
We won a gold medal in the Olympics—I was Dean's assistant with
John Thompson in 1976. I was with him when he was inducted into
the Hall of Fame. I'm happy to be riding the train.

There is money to be made being a head coach. Maybe I'd be making more had I become one. But I'm making more money now than I ever thought I'd make in my life. How much do you need? I enjoy my life, and that's more important. To be honest, I'm not real sure I have a contract. As long as Dean Smith's here, I have a job.

This is the only place where I could have done this. Any other place I would have moved on to become a head coach. And I think I would have been a good one. But at this point I can't imagine walking onto the floor without being next to Dean Smith. I have the best job in college basketball.

JOHN WOODEN, basketball, UCLA (retired): If there hadn't been the war, I probably would have stayed at South Bend High School until I retired. I enjoyed my work there very much. I liked the people, I liked the town. I was happy. I see no reason to make a change when you're happy. I was contented without losing ambition.

But during the war we lost our home when I couldn't keep up the payments. When I came back they offered to sell it back to me for three times what I'd paid for it. I got my same teaching job back, but not the coaching. I decided not to stay. Two very fine high school jobs opened up, two of the finest in Indiana. Then the Indiana State job opened. I thought, "Okay, since I'm going to leave anyway, why not try college?"

HUBIE BROWN, New York Knicks (retired): I was never looking to the next level. Being a high school coach, I was just trying to be the best I could be. I was thirty-four years old, with three children, and I was making $18,750. I was coaching year-round; everything overlapped. I was very happy. Then William & Mary called and offered an assistant's job for $7,000. I still remember sitting on the steps on the William & Mary campus with a friend of mine at 2:30 in the morning. I'm looking down that little street in Williamsburg and I'm saying, "How can I do this?" And the answer was that if I didn't do it now I never would.

JOE NEWTON, cross-country & track, York High, Oak Brook, Illinois: When I was about forty years old, I had this burning desire to become a college coach. We'd won three state high school championships; I'd done well. I had three or four chances. I went for an interview at Northwestern, my alma mater. But I would have had to have taken a twelve-thousand-dollar pay cut and work eleven and a half months. I said I have a wife and three kids, I'm not going to do that. So I never left.

HARRY VANDERSLICE, *Little League baseball, Ocean City, New Jersey:* There's always somebody telling you to take a chance, break away. But I never did. My family grew so fast! Income-wise, I couldn't handle it. But I'd have loved to try.

HUBIE BROWN: There are going to be times in your life where you are going to be asked to go backwards in order to go forward. This will be the critical time in your life. Can you make the decision? It doesn't mean you have to go. You just have to be happy with the decision.

JOE NEWTON: Everything worked out. My goal my whole life was to be an Olympic coach. That was my dream. George Bernard Shaw said, "If you dream the impossible dream long enough, it becomes possible." I dreamed for thirty-four years. In 1988 I became the first high school coach on the Olympic staff. It was my destiny that I stay here.

WALTER WILSON, *basketball, Haskell Junior College (formerly Haskell Indian School), Lawrence, Kansas:* When I came here, I wanted to do a good job and then go on. But I also came in wanting to help Haskell. Being a Native American—I'm Choctaw—I wanted to give something back. But I also had ambitions for moving on. Now that I've been here a while, I feel this is probably where I'll retire.

It was tougher than I thought when I came here. There were a lot of obstacles, and there still are. Native Americans aren't known for their height—that may be the biggest one. We've probably played every junior college in Kansas, Texas, and Oklahoma. The competition level is extremely tough. Everybody has somebody six-foot-eight except Haskell. You have to have tribal membership or be one-quarter Native American to go here, so that limits us.

There wasn't a lot of stability. That's gotten better within the last two years because of a change in the administration. But for a while it was back and forth, and during those times I was thinking I made the wrong step careerwise. But if it was a lot tougher to win at Haskell, there were good things about being here. There's a lot of Native American culture, and the school is built around it. Native Americans are as athletic as anyone. But there's always been a problem with them continuing to play or continuing with their education. That's Haskell's role—it can be the next step for those kids.

It's just been within the last two years that I really made the decision to stay. Last year we were 17 and 13. It was a big turning point. This year we were 21 and 5—the first twenty-game season in seventeen years. Last year I was offered the high school coaching job where I had planned on going when I first got here. I turned it down. I wasn't ready to go. I'm feeling more and more like I made the right decision. I didn't see how I could be helping here by leaving.

It's not that someone else couldn't do a better job. I just felt I could be a good role model here. That it might be worth it to stick around. I've had students call me: "You were a big influence on me. You're the reason I stayed with my education, the reason I'm working with the tribe." There was a time when the coaching here was the only thing. Now it's the opposite. I've changed. It's the teaching, the being here when they need someone. The coaching, that's just a plus for me now.

LINDA WELLS, *softball, Arizona State:* I grew up in Pacific, Missouri, about twenty miles west of St. Louis. I had an older brother and five male cousins next door. I grew up playing in the backyard, doing hoops, elbowing my way through. Because of that I was a very successful female athlete. By fourteen I was playing in a women's softball league in St. Louis.

I went to college thinking maybe I'd do music, maybe chemistry. I played field hockey and volleyball in the fall, basketball in the winter, and tennis and softball in the spring. Doing all that, my interest turned to physical education. I graduated in 1972 and went to the University of Minnesota to pursue exercise physiology. I had no thoughts about coaching. It wasn't an option.

At an early staff meeting they wanted to know who would like to pick up an extra six hundred dollars to coach a sport. Well, not only does my hand go up immediately, but I looked around and could see that I was one of the few women who really knew sports. By 1974 I was the head coach of volleyball, basketball, and softball. I was making nine thousand dollars. The men's baseball coach that same year was making twenty-eight thousand dollars. I was twenty-one, twenty-two. I'd never had a job for nine thousand dollars—wow, that's a lot of money! And nobody had ever told me that there was a great job like coaching.

But you put in three, four years and you start looking around. Wouldn't it be fun to have a car? But you can't because the money's not there. But then here comes Title IX. It starts pushing the issue of equality, the equality of opportunity. All of a sudden, female coaches aren't making nine thousand dollars anymore. They're starting at twenty and getting twenty-five.

But here's what happened. My first year there were no men coaches. By 1981, the year I gave up volleyball, probably 70 percent of the coaches [for women's sports] were male at Division I. The men who wouldn't coach three sports for nine thousand dollars would coach one for twenty-five thousand. A lot of women, for a number of reasons, made the decision to leave coaching. Some of that was squeeze: You're out, he's in.

Remember the pool that we were dealing with back then—a pool of women who didn't get to play. Compare them to the boy who grew up dribbling the ball. We were asking women—who maybe didn't have the self-esteem, the belief in their knowledge of the sport—to compete for jobs with men who were coming right out of the old male model. They knew everything about sport, they were better, they were bigger, taller, and stronger. Boom—they're in.

So now there's a whole generation of girls who have grown up to become young women who have had the opportunity to play sports. But they haven't been taught that they can coach.

MARGE RICKER, *fast-pitch softball, Orlando Rebels (retired):* I was always what they called a "tomboy." That's an obsolete term now. Orlando was a small town then. We didn't have Title IX; we didn't have TV. People played sports. I got into softball and played in a city rec league. They were all men coaches. Somebody's father or boyfriend. I always thought I could do better.

Pearl Harbor was bombed when I was a senior in high school. The boys in my class went right in the service. Women couldn't go until they were twenty, so I did the Rosie the Riveter stuff until I turned twenty, when I enlisted in the Army Air Corps. We had teams on the base and since we were in the air force we could fly to other bases. I was the only pitcher. We had these noncom guys coach us. I always thought I could have done it just as well.

I got out in '46 and played in the city league in Orlando. We had a coach and he did a good job, but he had his family, and I decided that I was going to organize my own team and be the coach.

If I have to choose between a good guy coach and a bad woman coach, I'll take the good guy. But I don't know if men really know how to relate to women. They take it to one extreme or the other. Either treat you like little girls instead of athletes or treat you like you're a guy. Guys coach through intimidation, screaming and hollering. Very few women buy that. Men are more inclined to think, Okay, we're treating everybody the same. Women are more inclined to realize the individual differences. What works for one player won't necessarily work for another. And for most men it was just a sideline anyway. He's coaching because his sister's on the team, or his girlfriend. Then you'd get the boy-girl thing.

I organized my first team in 1951. I was twenty-six, twenty-seven. We were known as White Turkey then, after a restaurant. They sponsored us for three years, until in 1954 when I organized the Rebels. That team I coached through 1985. We qualified for the national tournament every year but one. We were a perennial threat.

PAT WARD SEIB, *track, Gibson Southern High, Indiana:* I was here the first year Indiana started the girls' program in volleyball. I wanted everything the guys had. I wanted to be just as good as the guys were at coaching; I wanted the girls to be just as good as the boys. You had to do everything yourself. Find your own officials, make your own programs, set up your own concessions, find someone to sing the national anthem. The things the male coaches didn't have to worry about. The women coaches helped each other. It was a struggle, but it was an exciting time.

The male coaches didn't want us to get started. You know: "Girls? Yuk! Get them off the court." We had to put our own lines down for the volleyball court. But we couldn't use tape. We put our lines down with white shoe polish, and after every game we had to clean them off because we couldn't mess up the look of their basketball court. One time the basketball manager came in and cleaned the lines off and we had a game that night. I had to put the lines back down again.

It's a lot easier these days. Everything's organized now; it's more competitive. There's so much more skill now than there was back then. But a lot of times kids nowadays don't care. They don't realize how much time and effort you put into it. Everything is done for them. And the coaches—if they only realized what we had to go through! It would be worth their while to put down some lines. You have a different perspective when you've been out there on the court on your hands and knees with a bottle of white shoe polish.

SR. LYNN WINSOR, B.V.M., CAA, *golf, Xavier College Prep, Phoenix, Arizona:* I always had the idea in high school that I wanted to be a sister, but I was reticent. I wanted to "live life." So I went to Arizona State, then I worked for the Phoenix Parks Department. I entered the convent in '67, the Sisters of Charity of the Blessed Virgin Mary out of Dubuque. Most of the girls were right out of high school. I was the grandmother. We organized leagues. We used to have some rousing games— tennis, volleyball, basketball. Since I already had gone to college, while the rest of the novices were taking classes, I went over to St. Raphael's and coached and taught P.E. I felt I needed to get out and work with the kids.

After two years in Dubuque I went to Iowa City, where I got my master's and taught P.E. at Iowa City Catholic. Then I went to St. Louis for three years, where I coached softball and worked with basketball and volleyball. Then I came to Xavier here in Phoenix, where I went to high school. My first year was 1974–75. I taught P.E. all day and coached basketball, softball, and golf. I coached basketball for ten years and softball for four. Golf is where I ended up. We've won twelve state championships in a row, a national girls' record.

Everything worked out. God has been good to me—I will never dispute that. I'm probably the most fortunate person in the world. The goal of staying in religious life and being a sister was always more important than being a coach. If I'd been told to put the athletics behind me, I would not have liked it, but I would have done it. However, the good Lord took care of me.

BILLY WILLIAMS, *coach assistant, Cleveland Indians:* When I played the game, it was my whole life. There wasn't very much money, there wasn't much fame. But by playing in the minor leagues for seventeen years, I did two things: I found myself a pearl of a wife, and my family got a good raising. And I met a lot of great people.

When I was playing baseball it was tough on blacks. You had to put in your time in the minors. I felt that if I stayed long enough and kept having decent years, I was going to get a shot to play. Well, I did, even if it was for only ten days with the Seattle Pilots. I played in three games, against the Orioles; I didn't get a hit. But my kids can say their dad is an ex–major leaguer.

I got out of baseball in '69 and opened a clothing store. The first eight years it was great; the rest damn near killed me. This is my third year back [in baseball]. I spent one year as a coach, then one year managing the rookie team—their big-money babies. We finished first. The third year I was in the big leagues.

I don't regret not getting into coaching when I stopped playing. I feel the same way when someone asks if I feel color was a problem when I came through as a player. That was yesterday and today is today. What happened, happened. I think I could have got ten or twelve years in, but it never got done. I don't have that hurt inside me. I was always too busy playing baseball.

I had plans then; they didn't work out. I have plans now. If I get two, three years in, great; if I get five years in, great. I'm happy I'm in this uniform. That's enough for me. Everyone wants to progress up the ladder. I can't worry about that. If I do my job here, then those things will happen. If they don't, fine. Hey, take the bitter with the sweet.

BILL MUSSELMAN, *first coach of the Minnesota Timberwolves (now with a CBA team in Rochester, Minnesota):* I coached in the CBA for five years [prior to the Timberwolves]. I coached the Tampa Bay Thrillers for three years. We won three championships. The third year the owner moved the team to Rapid City [South Dakota] right before the play-offs and we still won. I didn't want to live in Rapid City, so I moved to Albany. I figured that was my best chance to win a fourth. We did. It's a tough league, but I enjoyed it. I don't think any coach on this planet could go win the CBA championship four years in a row like I did.

I wanted to get back to the NBA, no question. But it wasn't like it was gnawing away at me. [In 1972 Musselman's University of Minnesota team was involved in an on-court melee with Ohio State, still considered one of basketball's most infamous brawls.] It was a bad incident; the game got out of control. It's just something that happened. But it hasn't been brought up as much as you'd think. My last year in Albany people were saying this guy's got an unbelievable record. We were trying to go 54–0. Why isn't he in the NBA? And they'd say, well, it must be *that.*

The reason, probably more than anything, was Cleveland. [Musselman coached the Cleveland Cavaliers to a 27–67 record from 1980 to 1982.] Not winning in Cleveland—under ownership that had brought in four coaches in four years [and traded away four years of first-round draft picks]—being in an unstable franchise probably had more of an effect than anything.

I had to pay my dues to get back to the NBA. I had to work hard constantly. But I would have worked hard anyway, even if I never got there. There are only twenty-seven NBA head jobs, and they're not easy to get. People would say to me, "Jesus, it must be like purgatory coaching in the CBA." You've got to be kidding me! I was not embarrassed to be coaching in the CBA. They were the happiest years of my life. Better than small college, major college, any job. I had successful teams that played hard. I was satisfied. What's the difference between that and the NBA? Fame? Money? I've never taken a job for money.

There are guys who, once they've been in the NBA, are too proud to coach in the CBA. *I like to coach.* I'd like my next job to be an NBA job. But if it's not in the NBA, that won't be the end of the world. Some guys, they've got to have the cream job. Me, if I'm coaching, I'm happy.

KURT ASCHERMANN, *youth league baseball, Sparta, New Jersey;* *author of* **How to Coach Kids in Baseball and Softball** *and* **How to Coach Kids in Soccer:** All minor league managers are named Sparky. If they're not, they should be. They're all named Sparky and they all managed in Duluth. And like the players, they're looking to get to the big time. Up where it's good, because it's sure not good where you are.

Actually, I only knew one minor league manager named Sparky. Nearly killed me one time when we were playing golf and he drove the cart off the side of a bridge. Nice man, horrible manager. We were in a sixty-game league, and I think we were like thirty-four games out of first place by the all-star break. Sparky was a different kind of duck. He played ten years in low minor league ball and was kept in the organization because he'd been so loyal. His only talent was he could put a nickel on the web between his thumb and forefinger and flip it over. He'd make a move and the coin would go "blup." Probably won a lot of bets in bars with that.

I got let go after my second year. I'd had a great spring training, I thought, and I'd just finished playing the best game of my life. Picked the tying run off third base in the ninth inning. Storybook stuff. I was walking through the hotel lobby in Duluth—yeah, I think it *was* Duluth—and the manager called me over. "Come here, kid," like in a Jackie Cooper movie. I strut over. "We're making a change." I remember thinking to myself, "Here we go, babe!" And he said, "We're sending you to Caldwell." Caldwell was down, not up.

When I look back on it now, my minor league career was dramatically impacted by the Vietnam War. My draft number was thirty-four. I'd been very active in the antiwar movement on campus, which was blasphemy at Springfield College. My brain was elsewhere, and when I went away to play baseball in the minors, this thing I'd played my whole life for, I really didn't give it a full shot. By the time I got released I was ready to go home. I knew I wasn't going to make it. If I had it to do over again, I would have begged the Cubs to hold on to me. Send me down to Caldwell and I'll pitch batting practice. I'll work through the system. Me and Sparky. I would have become a Sparky, no question, just to stay in baseball.

One-on-One: John McLendon, Jr.

He was the first coach in the nation to win three consecutive national college basketball championships. His five college teams won 76 percent of their games and fourteen conference championships. One team was voted the number one team in the nation by a wire service final season poll, and four other times his teams were named national champions. He was named national coach of the year. Twice he was a member of the U.S. Olympic coaching staff, and two other times he was an assistant on World University Games teams. He won two amateur-league national championships and two international titles. He coached in the old ABA and the even older ABL. In thirty-four years he won 740 games. He learned the game at the knee of Dr. James Naismith, the inventor himself. He is the author of three books and is generally acknowledged as one of the true pioneers of the game of basketball. His name is John B. McLendon, Jr., and chances are you never heard of him.

I was born in Hiawatha, Kansas, on April 5, 1915. My youngest sister was born in the middle of the influenza epidemic and my mother died. That was 1918. My two sisters and my brother, we were given out to relatives. My dad was a railway mail carrier. My brother and me, we were sent to southeast Colorado to live with our grandparents, who had just left Hiawatha to homestead a plot about twenty-two miles northeast of Trinidad, down in the corner, on the plains.

We stayed out there about three years. In the meantime my dad remarried. My second mother—that's the way I refer to her, because she was nowhere near the stereotypical stepmother—she wanted us all to reassemble. So we were all taken back to Kansas City, except my older sister. The family that had her disappeared, and we were not reunited for another forty years.

Back in Kansas City my mother enrolled us in school. I went to Dunbar Elementary. Dunbar was segregated. Then I went to Northeast Junior High. This is where my interest in basketball came in. I was ten years old and going into sixth grade. And for the first time in my life, I saw an indoor basketball court. A combination gym-auditorium, with the basketball court up on the stage. There was a man there named P. L. Jacobs. He was there to welcome all the visiting schoolchildren. Then I saw him shoot a basketball. The old two-handed set shot. I couldn't believe you could shoot the ball and make it go through that ring from such a distance so many times. That was the beginning of my life with basketball.

I went out for the team when I got to Sumner High School, but I never made it. But I had a deal with the coach, A. T. Edwards. Anytime I didn't make the team I could be the student manager and sit beside him. I got to listen to a lot of basketball.

I was getting ready to go to Springfield College, where basketball was invented. That was my goal. I put aside a little money and Dad said he'd help. But when the time came to go, we didn't have the money. This was in the midst of the Depression, 1932. But in the meantime my Dad found out that Dr. Naismith, the inventor of basketball, was at the University of Kansas, not more than forty miles from our front door. But before going there, my psychology teacher in high school, Beltron Orme, told me I didn't need to go anywhere if I wanted to make a basketball team. He was the coach at a segregated branch of Kansas City Junior College. I made the team and learned the life of a substitute. Every coach ought to do that.

Then I went on to Kansas. I went to Dr. Naismith's office and told him I was his new advisee. He wanted to know who had told me that, and I said, "My father." And Dr. Naismith said, "Well, come on in; fathers are always right." He had piercing blue eyes. He looked directly at you when he talked. He was Scotch-Canadian, and when he got excited his Rs would roll a little

bit. I had never met anyone at that age who was absolutely oblivious of who you were in terms of how he treated you. Let me put it like this: The first time I ever had a white instructor was at the University of Kansas. I don't know what I was expecting, but in Dr. Naismith I found only an exaggeration, really, of the good side of people.

Dr. Naismith was ahead of his time. His main thing was conditioning, how to motivate a person to get into the best physical condition. "There's no way you can motivate somebody who's not in shape to perform," he'd always say. He gave me the idea of the kind of game I would like to coach.

I remember one day we were walking through the gym, and there were little kids playing. Somebody gave them a ball, and Dr. Naismith said, "Let's watch." I'm watching them chase the ball, and I say, "What am I supposed to see?" And he said, "This is the way basketball ought to be played." "Tell me," I said, "what am I looking for?" And he said, "Whenever one player has the ball, that's where the defensive attack begins, and whenever the other player gets the ball that's where the offense begins." Right there— watching a bunch of kids, listening to Dr. Naismith—that's where I got my beginnings, how I wanted to develop players to play all over the court.

I went to the University of Iowa

for a year to get my master's. Then I started off at Kansas Vocational School in Topeka, but that was just for a month. My roommate at Iowa—Dr. William F. Burghardt, that's who he became—we made a deal that whoever got a job would hire the other one. I couldn't do that at the vocational school, but he could at North Carolina College. Three years later I became head coach and was for twelve years. I left there and went to Hampton Institute '. Virginia, which is now Hampton University, for two years. Then I went to Tennessee State from '54 to '59. We were the first team in basketball at any level to win three consecutive national championships, the NAIA, from '56 to '58.

I left Tennessee State when Harold Enarson became president at Cleveland State. Not a single white institution in the U.S. had ever hired a black coach, and he said he'd like to put an end to that. Then Ed Sweeney hired me to coach the Cleveland Pipers in the Industrial League—the first time a black man had ever coached beyond the college level. That league became the American Basketball League—I coached in that under George Steinbrenner, which is a story in itself. I got fired by George and went with the State Department, and when I came back from three years in Southeast Asia I went to Kentucky State for three

years. Then I went back to Cleveland State from '66 to '69, and then went to the Denver Rockets in the ABA, '69 to '70—they became the Nuggets. For the next twenty years I was with Converse doing national and international promotions.

The reason I left Hampton Institute was I was a charter member of the National Athletic Steering Committee, which was trying to integrate basketball on a national level. The president at Tennessee State wanted to see if I could get it going. He had an understanding with the governor, Hubert Ellington. As long as we didn't play any schools in the state, we could play all the integrated teams we wanted. We had the first integrated tournament in the South. And there were times we'd have one or two of the teams from in the state come around for a private tournament, and not even the governor knew about it.

We were the first team from a historically black school to win an integrated national tournament, the NAIA in Kansas City. I had refused to play there until they integrated the hotels and the eating places. We won three times in a row—the first time any school anywhere had done that at any level.

I coached in North Carolina, Virginia, Tennessee, and Kentucky. The one thing I had to do in that setting was avoid confrontation. If you're traveling by bus, you had to figure out in advance what you can do to keep from being confronted by someone in front of your players—to be put in an undignified position in front of your players. Otherwise, their belief in you can weaken. So you tried to avoid those situations. Players don't have to agree with you; they don't even have to like you. But you have to maintain that respect.

I made a rule: "Let me do the talking." There were certain things that could cost you your life. I remember once our bus driver got caught speeding. They made us go up through these woods to the justice of the peace. We didn't know what was going to happen. Then they found out we'd just won a tournament and they kind of lightened up.

The coaches in the South, we had our own underground railroad. We knew every gas station where we could be serviced without a problem. I never got on a city bus, because you had to keep moving on a bus, farther and farther back. I never had my team eat in a restaurant. Our dining service fixed us box lunches. We arranged to sleep on the campuses of other historically black colleges. I coached fifteen years at North Carolina College, and I don't think I stayed in but maybe three hotels the whole time I was there.

Take for instance the time we were getting ready to go to Kansas [for the NAIA tournament] the first time. I had six guys who had never played against a white kid. I wanted to cover all the bases. Fort Benning had a team. The official would call our players all kinds of names when they handed in the ball. We won the game, and afterwards the colonel in charge asked how we were treated. I said everything was fine, except the officials were quite insulting. The colonel says, "I'll call them in right now." And I said, "Well, I appreciate that, but can give you me a one hundred-mile head start to Atlanta?"

When we got to Kansas City, the first team we were going to play, their band started playing "'Bye, 'Bye, Blackbird." I said, "Let's get out of here and talk this over." I wanted them to come in and think about where we were. "The only way to get respect is to put a whipping on this team," I said. We beat that team 134–66 and won the tournament. We never had another incident.

I coached players who could have played anywhere, for anybody. When they did a twenty-five-year history of basketball at North Carolina College, to mark its twenty-five years in the Central Intercollegiate Athletic Association, from '27 to '52, Sam Jones was the last person picked on the all-twenty-five-year team. I think Sam understood—as good as he was, as famous as he was with the Celtics. The best player in the history of North

Carolina College is a fellow named Reginald Ennis. But who knows Reginald Ennis? Before the white schools integrated, we got all the great black ballplayers that these days go to the schools everybody's always heard about. We're a whole history of basketball that nobody knows about.

There was a time, especially in the '30s and '40s, when most black athletes at historically black colleges didn't believe they could play basketball as well as the people they read about in the newspapers and heard about on the radio. All I ever wanted was for my team to be able to play against anybody. It was a stimulus to try to get an opportunity someday when my team could play against anybody, and to have that team ready when the door opened. I tried my whole five years at Tennessee State to get a game at Madison Square Garden. Never did.

The Basketball Hall of Fame wrote a hundred-year history of basketball. Year by year, and it doesn't even mention the NAIA. They picked the top twenty-five teams from the last one hundred years; not one NAIA team. The University of Kansas had a guy write *One Hundred Years of Basketball at the University of Kansas.* Right

here in Kansas City where I won three national NAIA championships. I went to school there. I'm not in the book. I bought one and then sent it back.

I'm the last surviving member of Dr. Naismith's class. Fog Allen and Adolph Rupp and John Bunn and Frosty Cox, all those guys are gone. I'm telling this story from him to you. I'm the only person who can do that. This isn't a beef, it's just the way things are. Maybe I should write my own book and call it *The Invisible Man of Basketball.*

McLendon won three NAIA titles in 1957, '58, and '59 with Tennessee State; he coached at North Carolina Central, Hampton, Tennessee State, Kentucky State, and Cleveland State; his teams won the Central Intercollegiate Athletic Association eight times between 1941 and 1952 and the Mid-West Conference six times from 1955 to 1966. The Associated Negro Press voted him national champion in 1941, and from 1956 to 1959 he won the National Negro Championship. He won National Industrial League and AAU titles in 1961. In 1965 he won the World Championships for players under six feet tall and the World Cup Championship.

FOUR

X's & O's

His first job as a head coach was at a high school in Massachusetts. He'd put in eight years as an assistant at two high schools in Tennessee, paid his dues. His parents were getting old and his dad was sick; Massachusetts was home. Besides, it was time to be his own man.

So John E. Lee came back to Massachusetts, to Walpole High School, the head coach. "I was coming to a program that quite honestly had been a disaster," John Lee says. "It couldn't have been a better situation—there was no place to go but up."

Rookie head coach. First-time guy. All of a sudden you're no longer off in the corner of the field with your seven defensive backs. All of a sudden yours is the last voice the team hears before it leaves the locker room. All of a sudden this is *your* team. All of a sudden you're The Man. What do you do? Where do you start? What do you say? These questions possess a particular terror for the first-time coach. But you needn't be a rookie to lose sleep searching for answers. A coach is only as good as the next win, the next season. Every year starts with a clean slate. So you built a team last year; *can you do it again?*

John Lee has been at Walpole High for twenty-three years now. There have been many wins, more than a few championships. And yet, he says, he can remember like it was yesterday running onto the field for his very first game as a head coach.

Coming from the South, he was used to football being a bit more than just a game. Worse, he was now the head man of a team that had never won before, didn't know how to win, and had no idea what price was to be paid if they ever decided they wanted to win. The team wore these embarrassingly hippielike powder-blue uniforms with black shoes. And now here he came, the new head coach, running after them. "All I could think," John Lee admits, "was, Boy, what a mistake you made!"

John Lee's team lost that game. It lost the next game. It lost the one after that. But the team finished 4-4-1. By the end of that season, John Lee says, he had the best team in the league.

GREG CARPENTER, *basketball, The Whitefield School, New Hampshire:* When you start, you have this picture of what coaching ought to be. Then you do it and you realize it's not at all like you envisioned it. You end up eating a lot of crow.

JIM SHORT, *wrestling, Simley High School, Inver Grove Heights, Minnesota:* When you're a kid you think sometimes coaches pick people they like rather than the people who are the best. So I went out for wrestling. I knew that if I was the best in my weight class I'd get to wrestle.

I was kind of short when I was going through school. I gave up baseball by the time I got to high school. If I'd stayed with it, I'd have seen that it was me, my inability to deal with being little. I had a kid's perspective. I felt coaches played favorites. I've changed my mind on that. I've been involved with team sports now as an athletic director for five years. The coaches here are as driven as I am. They play the best. They are out there to win.

KERRI HEFFERNAN, *Boston Beantown Women's Rugby Club:* Former players who become coaches need support groups, because coaching isn't anything like playing the game. I played rugby for ten years. I began my fifth year at Florida State. I fell in love with it. When I graduated I took a job in Houston, and they had a team and I played there for a year. The Houston Heathen Hearts. By then I was obsessed. I decided Boston would be the best place to learn the game. I was a graphic designer; I quit my job and moved to Boston.

I loved it up here. I was on the best rugby team in the country. It was rugby heaven. And I had wonderful coaching. Kevin O'Brien—

he's won five national titles. One of the few men who understands innately how to coach women. You can't yell at us and you can't exhort us out of fear. Women don't respond to that.

My best years were '88 through '91. I was the queen. I made all the national teams. I truly believed I was the best. It's very rare in your life that you shoot for a goal and you achieve it. Trotting out onto that field in your U.S. jersey and the crowd is going wild . . . I still get choked up about that. Then in May of '91 Beantown lost the Nationals. I thought we should have won and I was pretty despondent. I wondered if it wasn't time to move on. Then that summer I tore my anterior cruciate. A bunch of us had always wanted to play rugby in dresses. The joke was we would wear bridesmaids' dresses—you know, those dresses with the billowy sleeves that you never wear again after the wedding. Most excellent dresses.

Anyway, I tripped on the hem of my dress. A very noble way to go out, lying there in my pink dress. The next year I helped coach. But it drove me crazy. You have to switch gears and be identified in a different context. I remember the first game we huddled up, and then the team ran out onto the field. I hated it. It was worse when they came back—everybody all dirty and sweaty, and you know you're not part of it no matter how much you kid yourself.

That next summer I tried a comeback, and I blew out my back. In a way it was a blessing. "Okay, that's it." The injury was really scary, a I-hope-I-can-walk-again thing. I realized to be thankful for what I can do and not have my ego so based in what I once did.

The team approached me to take over as the head coach. Eventually I said yes. It was like going back to square one. Athletes know what we can do physically; we often can't translate that. I was having to break all this stuff down and think about the game in a whole different way. Players would say, "What do you mean?" And I'd say, "Do it. Just do it." I finally realized that wasn't a good enough answer. It's still difficult. I had to look at the way I learned myself. I wasn't translating information; that's why people weren't getting it. It wasn't because they were dumb or they weren't paying attention or they weren't trying. It was because I couldn't tell them.

SUZIE McCONNELL, *basketball, Oakland Catholic High, Pitts-burgh; member of the 1988 U.S. Olympic gold-medal team and 1992* *bronze-medal team:* I was twenty-three my first year [as head coach at Oakland]. I had worked a lot of camps and I had taught players. But now here I had twenty-five girls and I was responsible for all of them. The basketball season was in my hands. What to teach them? Where to start? When I first got started I assumed way too much. I had played at the college level and the Olympic level. It's what I was used to. It only took me a couple of days to realize I had to go all the way back to the beginning.

WADE PHILLIPS, *defensive coordinator (now head coach), Denver Broncos:* As long as you can teach players what you want, they'll respect you. I've seen coaches fall by the wayside because the players had no respect for them. That's tough. It's embarrassing. And it worries the other coaches because all coaches are in this together. There was a coach once when I was in Houston, the players ran over him. They'd walk off the field and leave him there saying, "Come on guys, you need to stay out here." It was awful. They didn't feel he knew any more about the game than they did.

SANDRA CHILDERS, *softball, Adams-Marion High, Sheridan, Indiana:* There's not much you can't teach from a wheelchair. You just have to learn how to talk, how to explain. To do orally what you used to just *do.* I remember once trying to teach a drag bunt. No matter how many times I told them, "Drop back on your back foot," when they'd go to do it, it didn't come out that way. Finally there was this one girl. I dropped down under her when the ball was coming and moved her feet. She was terrified. She didn't even try to hit the ball. But it was the only way to do it. Since then they've gotten used to me coming up and moving their legs. I'm telling them something and they'll say, "Show me."

RANDY JABLONIC, *rowing, University of Wisconsin:* The average spectator who looks at a crew out on a lake marvels at the symmetry and the perfection, how well they all mirror each other. The fact is, they're not rowing very much alike at all. There's a bit of magic in there, a little Houdini in putting a team together.

Every position in the boat is different. The coxswain steers. He has to sense the speed, the psychology of the crew. The stroke is the quarterback; he's got to have a great sense of rhythm and timing. Up in the bow, the boat's light; it's sliding back and forth. You need a loosey-goosey guy who can handle that. In the middle of the boat are the engine-room people—the big, powerful sweeps. They give the boat a pulse. Every position is different. The average person doesn't understand that.

The catch of the stroke—when the oar hits the water—is no different than when two football linemen square off. But on the release of that stroke, suddenly it's a bird, an eagle soaring. You have to turn all that violence of pulsating power, all that energy, into maintaining the speed of the boat, preserving the delicate balance and smooth rhythm, actually sneaking into the next stroke without wiggling the boat around. Sometimes I think I'm lucky. Maybe I have this innate skill. But I can see what it is that makes a boat go. When I'm searching for the right combination, moving guys around the boat, I'll just know when the boat looks alive. I feel a bit like I do when I go to an optometrist. He'll say, "Is this better or is the former better?" And he'll switch the lenses in front of my eyes. "Yes, number three is better than number two." The selection process is based on knowing what lenses you've got. I have a list of people who have established themselves in a pecking order. Now I have to experiment. I've got to balance my left eye and my right eye. "I can read the bottom line now!" That's what it's like: I can see clearly now.

SID JAMIESON, *lacrosse, Bucknell University, Lewisburg, Pennsylvania; founder and president, Iroquois Nationals (retired):* I'm fifty-two years old and I'm a Native American—Mohawk Indian. In our culture, at birth, lacrosse becomes a part of you. We believe the game of lacrosse is part of all Native Americans. The Creator has given us this game as a means of demonstrating to Him what our personal worth is, what our personal values are, what kind of personal character we have. To many Native Americans, lacrosse is a "religion."

We always begin play with a prayer. It is not us against an opponent. It is us demonstrating who we are to the person who gave us this game, the Creator. Lacrosse is a way for the people in the community to come together. When we play a game against a team with a different-color jersey, it is not just the game that is important. It's how you play the game. It's the conduct of the game. It's the toughness, the hardness. You have all that space and all the free-flowing movement. Plays just kind of happen; they just kind of exist out there. It's more of an event than a contest.

There were a couple of people who had the idea to start the Iroquois Nationals: Chief Oren Lyons, the Faith Keeper for the Iroquois Nation, and Wes Patterson, who had played lacrosse for years and years. It was in the mid-seventies. We saw the Nationals as a way for us to redevelop that sense of community. We saw it as a great program to bring back our people. The young people needed something positive, something spiritual; there was a hole in their lives.

It took two years to get a team on the field. The first event was in 1983. We played Syracuse, the number one program in the country. We got thumped pretty good, but that's okay. Just getting the team out there, a lot of people didn't think that was possible. I remember I said to [the team before the game], "This is the beginning, this is the first, this has never happened before." We were going out there as a nation. My heart started to pound and my chest was this big and the hair was standing up on the back of my neck. "Here we go. This is for real!"

We're trying to pass our lacrosse down from one generation to the next. Our program is for the thirty-year-olds, but more importantly it's for the ten-year-olds. We need to be able to demonstrate to the youth of our nation that this is something they can do to help them grow spiritually, it will help them grow physically, it will help them grow in a moral sense, in an ethical sense. It's a way out, so to speak, for a lot of the young kids. We need to provide these kids with a positive program. In that sense it's exceptionally valuable to us.

Our first international trip with the Nationals was to England. I don't travel with a U.S. passport; I use my Iroquois passport given to me by my nation. Going overseas as a nation, that established our legitimacy. The little baby has grown from concept to idea to a team representing your whole nation. There's no way lacrosse will ever be just a game to me, to any of us. No way. It won't. Because it's not.

ROY CHIPMAN, *basketball, University of Pittsburgh (retired):* I still remember the first team meeting I ever had. I was living in Freeport [Maine] in the summer, and I wanted to set up a summer program. I got a speeding ticket getting there. Once school started and the football season was over, we weren't allowed to start basketball for a week. I remember going into the gym, just waiting. And then that first day practice was at three o'clock. I remember being there early, making sure the balls were there, going over what I was going to say. I had a speech all set. I had a book I'd made up with everything that we were going to do. I'd worked on it all summer. That was probably the biggest day of my coaching career, bigger even than my first college job.

STEPHANIE VANDERSLICE GAITLEY, *basketball, St. Joseph's University, Philadelphia:* I coached a freshman team at Archbishop Carroll while I was student teaching. That age was too young for me. I was too nice. Remember when Luke and Laura got married on *General Hospital?* I can't believe I did this! I let that team watch the wedding. They were pleading and whining, and I gave in.

JEAN ROISE, *basketball, University of North Dakota, Williston:* I took over a losing program [at her first high school job], the kind of team the rest of the schools stomped on. I was twenty-four. My assistant was new, and I remember after that first practice we went back in the office and sat down and I said, "Did I sound like I knew what I was talking about?"

LaDONNA WILSON, *basketball, Austin Peay State, Clarksville, Tennessee:* I graduated from Missouri Southern and came to Peay as a grad assistant. I did that for a year. The next year I was the assistant coach, and then I got the head position at twenty-five. I had to learn a lot in a short time to learn it. I talked to anybody I could get hold of, all the clinics I could get to. There were all these things I needed to know.

That first year was rough. There were moments when I wondered if I wasn't in over my head. A lot of people would have hung it up. We ended that first season winning five games. It seems like thirty years ago now. I reached the down point in the middle of our conference season. We had won one game, and we had just lost to Eastern Kentucky by about 30. It was an away game, and I remember standing outside the locker room in the hallway after the game. Going in to talk to the team was going to be about the hardest thing I'd ever done. And I'm asking myself if this is really what I want to be doing with my life.

Larry Inman, the head coach at Eastern Kentucky, walked past. As a coach, you try to conceal your emotions. But I was way beyond the point of concealing how discouraged I was. He came up and encouraged me to stay with it, to keep it up, that things would work out. That had a big effect on me. Maybe I can get through this. Things gotta get better. They can't get worse.

STEPHANIE VANDERSLICE GAITLEY: My first couple of years when I was head coach at [the University of] Richmond, I would have died to have been an assistant again. I missed the fact that I couldn't be as close to the players as I wanted. I wanted to make sure everybody was comfortable and their social life was good and they were happy. And it seemed like nobody was ever happy. We finished up 7–21. The next year, when we finished 13–15, was my toughest. We signed five kids and had everybody back. We ended up with six more wins, but it wasn't any fun. I was pregnant and I felt horrible. And nobody was happy because not everybody was playing.

I came to grips with things the next year, the 21–8 year. It was December and we were 1–3 and I'm saying to myself, "Maybe I'm not as good as I think I am." Frank [her husband and assistant] talked me through. "You're not stupid, you're not a quitter, it's one of the reasons I married you, blah–blah–blah." Then he finally said, "Grow up!" I couldn't even get mad. He was right. I stopped sulking. We ran off seven straight and all of a sudden we're over the hump.

JAMES REYNOLDS, JR., *football, Martin Luther King, Jr., Senior High, Detroit:* It took eight years to turn the corner to where I felt it was my program. The coach before me was a very good coach—he's been in the pros for ten, twelve years—but he was so tough that he couldn't keep kids. We were fighting discipline problems, tradition, everything. I was a twenty-six-year-old head coach going by trial and error. Everything I did, I did out of instinct.

Then I lucked out. I got three people on the staff that had graduated from here. They knew the people in the community. That started the turnaround. All my coaches now are from the East Side. They're all from the community, and they realize the importance of pulling together.

We've been working at it now for nineteen years. The educational problems took a back burner in the beginning—we spent a lot of energy on domestic problems. But we've turned the corner. When I first came here, the teachers sent their own kids to other schools. Now all the teachers have their kids here.

The teams we had to beat were Detroit Northern and Detroit Cass Tech. We played Northern in a driving rainstorm and beat them 3–0, with the first field goal we ever kicked. I think the next year we shut out Cass, 15–0. Perseverance worked out. But it took eight years. At one point the choice high school job in the city came open and I had a chance to switch with the coach there. We were going to flip jobs. He was literally coming into the building and I was going out. I turned around and went to the office and told them no. The kids had stuck with it, and I wasn't going to quit on them. I'd stay and try to make it go.

CHUCK JORDAN, *football, Conway High, South Carolina:* My first practice as a head coach, a kid went down with heat exhaustion. "Coach! He's passed out!" I go running over and then I look up, and I instinctively wanted to holler, "Coach Gault!" He'd been my head coach at college. And then all of a sudden I realized, "Hey, wait a minute. It's me! I'm in charge!" Just like that it hit me.

WADE PHILLIPS: Every coach gets tested. I got it early on. I was coaching Elvin Bethea [with the Houston Oilers]. He was an all–pro and had been through a lot of coaches. We were working on a slant drill. I wanted him to step laterally down the line. He did it wrong, and I made him do it again. It's the first drill we're doing, and here I am this twenty-eight-year-old son of the head coach [Bum Phillips]. "Elvin, do it again." So he does it again and he does it again and when he gets it right I say, "Good job, Elvin!" And Elvin turns around and yells out, "HEY BUUUUM!" Bum was up in the tower, at least a half a field away. Everybody turns around and looks at him. And then Elvin yells, "Wade's over here coaching his ass off!"

JEAN ROISE: I remember my first game [as a high school coach], because my three best players couldn't play. They'd gone to a national softball tournament and had missed the first couple of practices, and you had to have so many preseason practices in to play. I told the other coach to take it easy on me.

I lost my confidence that first year. I remember feeling I had to prove myself to the kids all the time. I'd talk about what I'd done, the teams I'd played on. My senior year at Kansas State we made it to the final eight; when I was in junior college we finished third in the nation. I sure liked to talk about it, because it gave me confidence. I was scared to death they were going to think I was no longer a winner. And I prayed a lot. I'm a Christian, so I prayed a lot because I really doubted myself.

I see now that it was my ego getting in the way. I coached fundamentals and tried to keep things simple. I got my confidence back. I quit worrying about the winning and losing. I know now that when my team wins or loses it's not me winning or losing, it's them. It took me maybe four or five years to realize that.

JENNINGS BOYD, *basketball, Northfork High, West Virginia (Boyd coached Northfork High to nine state titles, including a national-record eight in a row):* It's unbelievable how excited a young coach can get. I was a screamer and yeller and chair kicker for probably two years. Even at time-outs I'd rant and rave.

I remember I wanted them to look like they were well coached. I wanted people to say, "Gee, those kids got a good coach." I wanted everyone to think that it was me. I don't remember how things evolved, but I can remember all of a sudden saying, "Hey, the kids aren't responding to all this yelling." They played worse after time-outs. When I screamed at an official, it affected the kids. So I quit it. At time-outs now I have the starters sit on the bench and I kneel in front of them, and I actually talk in a lower voice than usual, to make sure I got their ear.

Maybe what got me to change was I bought a new pair of Florsheim shoes and wore them to a game and kicked a chair and split the toe. Split the toe wide open. Fifty bucks. Maybe that's it.

DARLENE KLUKA, Ph.D., *assistant professor in health, counseling, and kinesiology, University of Alabama at Birmingham (retired volleyball coach):* It was my first year coaching college after nine years in high school. I had never gotten beat 15–0. And in one of our early matches we got beat 15–0 three straight. I came unglued. Took them into the locker room and ranted and raved for at least twenty minutes. It did me wonders of good, but it did the kids zero good. I ended up benching the seniors. It was so straining and draining. If I'd managed that situation in a different way, I could have left them with their self-esteem.

I realized I'd done it wrong right away. I went home and didn't sleep. I've taken inventory of that incident many times since. I would come back to it time and again. To figure out not only what I'd done but what I *should* have done. It was a great learning experience for me. But it was really devastating to some of the kids, and I didn't mean to do that.

BOB WOOD, *tennis, University Liggett School, Grosse Pointe Woods, Michigan:* I'm a much better coach now than I was fifteen, twenty years ago—and yet we're winning less often now. When I took over the program here I wanted it to be the best high school program in the nation. Winning consumed me. It was the only thing. I wouldn't be able to sleep a week before the state meet. The drive to win, it clouds your judgment. It does with all young coaches. Who installed this need to win?

I know there were times when I looked the other way. Because if I did something—suspend somebody, kick somebody off—I was significantly hurting the team's chances of being successful—of my chances of being the winning coach. A smashed racquet on the court? I'd look the other way. Somebody yelling out, "Goddamn it"? I'd turn to somebody and say, "What'd he say?"

I'm a much better coach now. Other things became more important to me, in terms of the individuals, of making them better men and women. There wasn't any specific point in my life where things changed. There wasn't a tragedy, a divorce, anything. But you know when I think it was? This will sound snobbish, but here goes: We were so successful that it didn't matter whether we won the state championship anymore. "There has to be more to it than just winning this thing."

HARRY VANDERSLICE, *Little League baseball, Ocean City, New Jersey:* The first year is for the ego; after that, the hell with it. I watched the other coaches, the way they'd yell if a kid made a bad play.

And I said, "Gee, I must really be a pain in the ass!" Who'd I think I was, Casey Stengel?

I remember once, early on, I was giving the kids a big speech: "What's the name of the game?" "HUSTLE!" I'd yell it out and they'd yell back. But the whole time I'm not speaking to the kids. I'm showboating, because the parents are up by first base. I'm getting carried away, really getting the votes. And I finish up real big. "What's the name of the game?" "HUSTLE!" "Now go home and help your parents with the dishes!"

After I'm done one of the kids walks over to me and says, "Big Bear"—they called me Big Bear—"you talk pretty good, but your fly's open." Put me right down on my kneepads, right on the ground.

JOHN KEMMERER, *basketball, Riverdale High, Fort Myers, Florida (no longer coaching):* It took me two, three years to figure out that you don't have to get three technical fouls a game. It was an ego trip and it took years for me to get over it. I watch other coaches now and get embarrassed. "Look at me!" "I'm the coach!"

I remember my first game. I was scared to death. We were playing some class AAA team, over at their place, and this is the first game I ever coached, and we win in overtime. We should never have beaten them. But I'm screaming and yelling and we beat them. They come to our place later and kicked our butts. It took me a couple of years to figure that out, too. Hey, you've got to *coach.*

NAN AIROLLA, *volleyball, Providence Catholic High, New Lenox, Illinois:* I've seen coaches throw tantrums, throw towels, kick chairs. I sit there thinking, "Can't you pull it together?" I have never, ever seen anything good come out of a tantrum. There's this one team we play, the coach screams all the time. Once the tantrum starts, all learning stops. You're wasting everybody's time. You've embarrassed a teenage girl—the worst thing you can possibly do and still expect them to listen to you. All learning is officially done.

Besides, I've seen coaches make a big deal out of traipsing across the court to the referee and in the process of stalking over there, fall down. It's not worth it.

JOHN KEMMERER: It took me a long time to figure out that these kids basically know what the hell they're doing. We played this team with two high school all-Americans on it, plus this six-foot-nine football-playing center. Boom! Going into the fourth quarter they are kicking our ass. They're singing "Amen!" My little guard, little Moochie, he makes a suggestion during a time-out and gets 15 points all by himself. Boom! Boom! Boom! We tie it up and win in overtime. And I'm standing there thinking, "Boy, I'm a great coach!" Hell, no. I listened to a kid. That's all.

JERRY POPP, *track and cross-country, Bowman High, North Dakota:* There was one time here that was devastating for me. We had 106 kids suspended from fall sports for drinking, out of a school of probably 220. Our football team canceled the rest of its season; girls' basketball canceled the year. I lost every girl on my team over the ninth grade. I lost all but three boys. We were right in the middle of this consecutive-national-record thing; I think we had five or six straight state titles in a row.

I can remember going into that meeting, and all these kids stood up and said they'd been drinking. I remember that I was just furious. How could they do this to *me*? This is a small community. A lot of the coaches party, and I was right there with them. These kids made me think about being a role model. I realized these kids look up to their coaches, that some of them end up really loving their coaches. I'd never stopped to think about that before. I realized how important the team was to these kids. Instead of it just being important to me.

DAVE LAFFERTY, *girls' basketball, Vinsin High School, Huntington, West Virginia; boys basketball, Ceredo-Kenova, Kenova High School, West Virginia:* Coaching two teams, coaching against my son, it's made me look at sports differently. How important should sports be in your life? Is it a live-or-die situation? No, it's not. You prepare as best you can, and you have as much fun as you can. But it's not winner take all. There better be more to it than that.

I've seen injuries. Coach for twenty years and you're going to. I watched my oldest son get his arm snapped in a game. A player bent him over his shoulder and popped his arm. I had to cope with that.

Why are we playing? When I used to coach just one sport, I worked it real hard; it meant so much to me to win that it'd kill me to lose. At the end of the season when you get beat in your final game, I'd think about that for months. I once had a 9-point lead with ninety seconds to go, and I lost on a last-second shot. I thought about that forever. It was like a death in the family. I'd be at school and have a class, and I'm thinking about it as I'm trying to teach. Just always trying to figure out how I could have gotten control of those last ninety seconds.

It sounds like a contradiction, but by taking on another team, intensifying my life, team, I was actually able to take a lot of the tenseness out. I lost a state championship with the girls. It hurt, but I didn't have any time to think about it. That game was on a Saturday, and on Monday I had practice with the boys. You pick up and go on.

There's more to it than winning, although I can still lose sight of that. I remember once we were playing the number one team in the state, and my best player was sick. She had the flu, and she shouldn't have played. She scored 23, 24 points. At one point I yell at her for not running the floor. She looked at me: "It's not like I'm not sick." I'm ripping my best player. She shouldn't be in the building, and I'm asking for more?

BILL WHITMORE, *basketball, University of Vermont (retired, now athletic director, Concord school district, New Hampshire):* I went one year to Alabama, and then I transferred to St. Bonaventure. But my last two years at Bonnie's there were some very good guards. My playing time was going to be minimal, so when I was offered the opportunity to coach at the local high school, I figured I'd learn more about coaching by coaching than sitting on the bench. By the time I got out of college I was turning down head high school coaching jobs.

I ended up taking a head job in upstate New York. Rushford. They'd had six losing seasons. The community had five thousand people, mostly dairy kids. Basketball was a rallying post. They wanted the basketball team to win. I said, "Fine, let me coach." I told them I was going to make mistakes, but I wanted everybody to know that I was the "expert." Which, of course, I wasn't.

I ran the program first-class. I wanted practice uniforms, I wanted a completely revamped locker room. I ordered the best uniforms. I wanted a bulletin board. After every game they got a six-page statistical report. I wanted the kids to travel first-class. We raised money to buy blazers and matching pants. I wanted them to know that you had to do things the right way.

Commitment to a *team*. We did everything together. We were always having birthday parties. Academically we had kids who did a 180-degree turn once they got on the basketball team. I took one kid, he had no parents. He was just hanging out. He needed basketball; basketball didn't need him. Teams don't keep kids like that anymore. Basketball gave him something the English teacher never could. Another kid, everybody told me he was a thief. The first day, I handed him the keys to the equipment cage. "I want you to get two balls. And understand one thing: I'll trust you for the rest of my life as long as you don't screw me once." I never had one thing taken. Things like that are more important than winning.

The first practice we went for three and a half hours. I had twenty kids try out; lost half of them. "This guy is nuts!" But the ones who showed up the next day were the ones I wanted. That first month we didn't take a day off. We prided ourselves in practicing all the time. There was one game, against a bigger school, where I told the kids during a time-out that if we lost we were going to be in the gym at 7 o'clock the next morning. The kids went ashen. We ended up losing in overtime. But it was the best thing that ever happened to me. After the game I'm saying we're going to be in the gym at 7, and one of the kids puts his hand up and says, "Coach, you're killing us." I thought about that, and then I said, "You know what? You're right. We're taking the day off." We didn't lose another. If I'd have said, "Baloney, you're coming in," I'd have lost them.

The night we won the state championship there was a parade of hundreds of cars back to Rushford, and we had a bonfire at the high school. I could have been elected mayor. Even now, sixteen years later, I still see it as the best coaching experience of my life. Going up the ladder you get to see the cesspools in this business, no question. But Rushford—coaching at that level, with those fans, the whole community rallying around the team—that was pure coaching.

FRANK LAYDEN, *Utah Jazz (retired):* A coach who doesn't have authority can't coach. You have to control your own destiny. When I was coach and G.M., when I'd pay my players, I'd hand them the check myself. *I am the guy who's paying you.*

MIKE MARCOULIS, JR., *basketball and baseball, Freemont High, Oakland:* One of my first jobs, I worked with a man named Harris Flowers at a junior high in Oakland. He was real hard on the kids. But he had a way of getting to them. He used to tell me: "They're scared to death of me." But he would always say you can't coach by fear alone, because once the fear's gone, what's left?

What he did was give those kids something they really wanted. All kids want discipline. They don't necessarily have it, but they like it. Because with discipline comes organization; it brings a seriousness to things. "This is what we have to do to accomplish our goals." Deep down, no matter how bad a kid is, he wants to have positive things happen to him.

Harris Flowers let the kids know he loved them. He was a father figure. He could play all the roles, and he did it real well. You run a fine line with a lot of kids between being the disciplinarian and being a care figure. As the coach, you have to make them understand that.

ABE LEMONS, *basketball, Oklahoma City University (retired):* Teams are very fragile. People don't realize that. Everybody you got makes a difference. The key is to survive. That's all I ever tried to do, survive.

In 1980–81 [at Texas], we started out winning fourteen in a row, and then our best player got hurt. Mike Wacker. Would have been all-pro, no doubt in my mind. We were fragile. Teams we were beating by 15, we were now getting beat by 1. Ended up 16–11.

I wasn't at the game when Wack got hurt. My brother was getting bypass surgery in Oklahoma City, and I was up there. If I'd have been at the game, I might have had Wack in a different play. Maybe I call a time-out, and that time and period would not have happened. It's like you just miss being in a car wreck or something, and you say, "You know, if I hadn't stopped to get that Coke. . . ." With Wack, it was one of those deals where a quirk of fate changed a lot of people's lives.

Mike was a special person. He was a happy-go-lucky guy and a pleasure to be around. He had a charisma about him that made your day go short. We got blown out of a couple of games after that, but most of them were heartbreakers, last shots, down the drain. We couldn't find his points in the lineup. It's the only time when I really started to hate the press. I didn't have any answers. I didn't know what to do. Then you go out again and lose another heartbreaker. I was in trouble. We had a freshman guard and a sophomore forward and a sophomore in the pivot, and we was just *fragile*.

JERRY REYNOLDS, *basketball, coach turned general manager, Sacramento Kings:* Ricky [Berry] had a chance to be a real star. Late in his rookie year we started him. He was a great 3-point shooter. We had a team very much on the rise, I thought, and Ricky was going to be a big part of that. He had some special skills. Everything looked real good.

His death was a huge blow. It happened in August. I'd seen him the week before. He looked terrific. He'd been working hard. So it came as a total surprise. I guess these things always do. Gosh, he looked so good.

He shot himself in the head. I don't think anybody really knows what happened. The best guess is that he had marital problems and it was on his mind. He was a very sensitive person. I don't think it had anything to do with basketball. The basketball part was the best of times and the other stuff was the worst of times. Maybe he didn't know where to turn. I don't have a clue.

It was maybe two, three days later when I first thought about it in terms of being the coach. Our slim chance that we were on our way up had just become the reality that we were on the way back down again. Ricky was a major piece who couldn't be replaced. The team is still set back. It'll probably take ten years to recover. Players are such a valuable asset in this league. They are *the* asset. Lose one like that, with no warning, and it's not like you can just go out and replace him. You may get players like him with similar skills, but all that means is that if you still had that one player with all these other players you'd be that much better off.

I don't know if there is any grand lesson to be learned from all this. It affected my career negatively—I might still be coaching, I don't know. I do know that you don't want to leave any stone unturned. Hell, if there is a philosophy in the NBA, it's that when the good times are there you'd better enjoy them. Even a weak team has some good times. Looking back on my time as a coach, when we did have some good times I didn't enjoy them. I was worried about the future. Better to live life as it comes.

FRANK LAYDEN: What happens a lot of times is a head coach is afraid to hire good assistants. He's afraid he'll be upstaged. I never worried about that. Two of my assistants at Utah were ex–head coaches. Hire the best and they'll make you look good. When I interviewed assistants, I'd ask them what their goals were. "To be a head coach." Good. I'll help you become a head coach. I just don't want you to be the head coach of *this* team.

JOHN WINKIN, *baseball, University of Maine:* The first thing I look for is loyalty. There are a lot of things that affect loyalty. Pressures from parents, the press, alumni. I don't want an assistant coach around unless he's completely loyal to me. If he's not, I'll advise him to go.

BILL MUSSELMAN, *first coach of the Minnesota Timberwolves (now with a CBA team in Rochester, Minnesota):* Money breaks down loyalty. Assistants want the high salary job; it can get very cutthroat. Things don't go well, there's some injuries, the team's losing, it gets real easy for somebody to say to the owner, "We should have done this"—and put a quick doubt in his head about the guy doing the head job.

DON NELSON, *Golden State Warriors:* I had an assistant; I think he thought that if he could discourage me enough he'd get my job. This was early in my career [with the Milwaukee Bucks], and it's the worst experience I've ever gone through. He would discourage me in any number of ways. After a tough loss, he'd beat my head in on how dumb I was. Or when I'd be coming up with ideas I wanted to try, right away he'd say they wouldn't work. He was undermining in a hundred different ways. And he was succeeding. I didn't think I was a very good coach. I didn't even take credit for being the head man. I called us co-coaches, saying we were in it together. The more credit I gave him, the harder he was on me.

It was Wayne Embry, the G.M., who stepped in and made me fire the guy. And to fire him myself. Wayne knew we had to get rid of the guy—that I couldn't always be relying on this strong assistant. I was scared to death. He was my security blanket. He really had me. Then all of a sudden there was no strong assistant. My career took off after that. Boom.

JACK WHITE, *Pop Warner Football, Canton, Massachusetts [White was diagnosed with diabetic retinopathy in 1981; he coached totally blind for five years]:* I see the game through the eyes of my assistants. I run the defense and another coach runs the offense. They tell me down and distance, what play they're running. There's a constant flow of information back and forth. It all happens pretty quick. I've got a good memory and I log it all in my head and we make a decision and go with it. With their help I create a picture in my mind of what's going on.

BOBBY DOUGLAS, *wrestling, 1992 Olympic coach and Iowa State [on being the Olympic coach]:* The coach and his assistant are not the keys to being successful at the Olympics. It's the people you bring in who help you get the job done. There were a lot of people behind the scenes [of the 1992 team] who never get mentioned. Jim Sheer. All of USA Wrestling. John Dupont was a lifesaver. Art Martori. The single most important thing is to make sure the right people are in the right place at the right time.

You take on the weight of the world [when named Olympic coach]. You take on the weight of each athlete in each weight class. You get inside of him. One of the first steps I took was to find the people who were closest to each athlete and try to help them help him help me help us win the gold medal. I don't know if I explained that properly. You look at it from a very personal point of view. For example, you have to find out how important it is for a Bruce Baumgartner, who won the gold, to have his wife and his son and all his people from Edinboro State behind him. You go to Bill Ferrel and Asics and say, "I want Bruce to feel like a million dollars when he gets to Barcelona. And, Bill, I'm going to rely on you to do that." Bill said, "We're going to send a telegram to Bruce the night before and we're going to let him know there are one hundred people in Edinboro that are going to see him wrestle." I told him the most important things for Bruce will be to have his high school coach call the night before and say, "Bruce, we believe in you."

Do that for ten athletes, and you know what? You get strung out. We had to have certain people in John Smith's corner. What do we have to do for Chris Campbell? Chris was thirty-eight years old. We had to get his firm behind him. Make sure Chris and his wife think Bob Douglas is 150 percent him and her. Those are the things you have to do.

When you start doing all that as the coach, you realize you would never want to do it again. Because the athletes have no idea what it is you're doing. You're talking to an athlete and he's saying, Where's the video that you were supposed to set up for me? And you're saying, I was doing something else that I thought was more important, and he's raising hell and on the verge of collapse. Athletes, when they get to that point, where they're going for the gold, they all have needs. I'll always help out, but once is enough. I've had my moment.

LARRY SMITH, *football, USC (retired):* It took me two years to realize I couldn't do everything myself. That was the single hardest thing for me to master. I don't think it was my ego getting in the way; it was this feeling of *responsibility.* Hey—I'm the head coach! I'd coached every position as an assistant, so to stand there and let my assistants do their job, that was frustrating. The guy who taught me how to handle it was Charlie McClendon, my archrival.

Charlie had been at LSU for umpteen years. He was going into the last year of his contract and it hadn't been renewed, and he knew he was going to retire. I was going into the last year of my contract at Tulane, my first head job. I hadn't won much, and I was trying to figure out how.

One night Charlie and I were at a charity function and we're having dinner, and we're talking and all of a sudden he said, "You and I are kind of in the same situation. I'm in my last year. You're in the last year of your contract and you've got to win." Then he said, "I don't know about you, but here's what I'm gonna do. I'm going to have fun coaching the game of football. I'm going to let my coaches coach and I'm going to have fun." Charlie hit it right on the nose. It's helped me more than anything else I've ever heard.

BARRY LAMB, *defensive coordinator, San Diego State:* Once you reach a certain age in this business, if you haven't been a head coach, you're not going to be a head coach. Schools hire guys under a certain age. Because the only head job an assistant coach gets is a rebuilding job, and the mentality is that you need a young guy with an infinite amount of energy.

I've been involved in four rebuilding programs. There are so many hours involved in going over every little thing. From academics to team morale to training rules to coaching quality. The way you travel, what they eat. In one, we had to retrain the players in how they acted on the field, how they practiced. In another, we had to put in an alcohol abuse program. A completely different player-accountability program. You're changing attitudes. It's a huge undertaking.

GLEN MASON, *football, University of Kansas:* You have to realize that if it was a winning program, A: they wouldn't be firing the coach, or B: they'd be hiring a guy with a big name. You go in knowing it's going to take time. You figure everything that's already been done is broke. You develop a plan and a strategy that will help you keep your sanity when things get tough. Because things are going to get tough.

FRANK LAYDEN: I never gave a team a goal they couldn't reach. I set very modest goals for the early Jazz teams. I told them I thought they could win twenty-five games, so let's try to win thirty. When they were good enough to win thirty, I said let's try for forty. You have to get closer to winning before you can win. See what it looks like, what it feels like. Losing by 2 was better than losing by 3; losing by 1 was better than losing by 2. You have to learn how to almost win before you can really win.

DICK VERMEIL, *Philadelphia Eagles (retired):* I remember one thing vividly about my first meeting [Vermeil took over a 4–10 Eagles team]. I said, "This is not the start of a new program, it's the start of a crusade." I interviewed every player. They'd all been losers the year before, but individually none of them had ever lost: "It wasn't my fault." I got rid of the bad people—the drug users, the pushers, the lazy people, the smart asses—and stayed with a better character of person each time we made a cut. I remember guys retiring on the field, walking off. We made it very tough.

It takes a long time to establish credibility as a football coach, to get to where the players trust you and will listen. I always felt that if we had a strength as a coaching staff it was that we brought people together. *Extremely* close. It's one of the reasons we ended up succeeding. You can't sit down with a player often enough if you're talking about the right things. When I came to Philadelphia there were seven players living in town in the off-season. I think we had thirty-seven living in town my last season. I'd have full-team dinners out at my house—the players, the coaching staff, the whole organization.

We were able to eliminate the selfish thinking. Motivation is a reflection of an attitude. Defined in the dictionary, it's an inner urge that creates change. It's a collective attitude. That 1980 Super Bowl team had the finest collective attitude I've ever been around—high school, junior college, college, or pros.

That first year [1976] we won four games. They'd won four the year before, so where were we? But we didn't have many good football players. If they'd had good players, the coach before us would have won. But we were improving in a lot of things that were showing up in the won-lost column. I felt us turning the corner in 1977. We still hadn't had a first-round draft choice, but the guys were getting better as individuals. And I hired outstanding assistant coaches. We kept getting better as coaches, better as players. I could see it coming. We were playing better through all four quarters. We were tough to beat. Take pride in your improvement.

The turning point was beating Pittsburgh in 1979. They came in undefeated, as I remember it, the world champs. And we beat them. All of a sudden people realized that, Hey, this is a team that is going to have to be confronted. Running off the field, you could feel the confidence level of the team and the coaching staff shoot up.

JENNINGS BOYD: We won the first title in 1971. In '74 we started that fabulous streak [a national-record eight straight state championships]. In '75 we were voted the best team in West Virginia. So now we won a couple in a row, we win a third and what's the topic of conversation? The state record is four in a row. Hey, maybe we can tie the record. And we worked and we worked and we won. The next year was all geared toward setting a new state record, and we did. We won six in a row, and it was like there wasn't anything significant about that until someone found out the national record was seven. That really created excitement.

No one in his right mind could ever have dreamed of winning the way we won. I'm not so immodest as to say I didn't have a bit to do with it. But the players had a *whole lot* to do with it. We had the type of kid who, by the time he reached the sixth grade, he was talking about being a Blue Demon when he got to high school. And we were lucky. The flu that every team gets in February? We didn't get it. We had some minor injuries, but we were lucky. Extremely lucky. My wife's saying, "No you weren't. You were blessed."

I was in the right place at the right time. The first year I coached happened to be the year of consolidation with a black high school. That was a time when blacks at the professional level and college levels were striving for recognition, and that filtered down into the high schools. Our young black kids were striving for recognition. It was amazing. This was back in the days of the big Afros. Most of the kids on our teams were black, but all the kids kept their hair trimmed neat. We wore blazers to every game; we wore white shirts and ties. They didn't like it at first; they grew to love it. They were the Northfork Blue Demons.

ANSON DORRANCE, *U.S. women's 1991 World Cup soccer champions and the University of North Carolina:* You need chemistry. Chemistry is rapport between the players, rapport between the players and the coach. Chemistry in a women's team is more important than chemistry on a men's. A men's professional basketball team is not really a team, it's sixteen franchises melded together with, more or less, the common goal that each individual will benefit individually. Players come together so that each one can be successful. And chemistry isn't necessary so long as you are successful. You can be successful even if your chemistry is horrible. That's harder to accomplish on a women's team, because their interconnectedness is more important for their harmony and playing.

Chemistry is ongoing and constantly changing. It can destroy a team. It's not like, "We've got chemistry now, we've taken care of that."

Players are always upset with someone or something or everything. There were times during the World Cup and the year leading to it when our chemistry was unbelievable. There were times when it wasn't. There were days when our chemistry held us together through the worst of times. There were days when I thought it would blow us apart. Things players say to each other, things players do. Insensitive gestures, insignificant statements. All the little things that make up human behavior.

I remember sitting down with the team before the year started and telling them the plan was to go into the World Cup as the favorite. I knew we had enough girls with that kind of drive and ambition. We were actually at our peak six months before the Cup, in Bulgaria and Haiti. We were unbeatable. It was a feeling of incredible power.

Then the injuries started. Michelle Akers-Stahl was hurt for a stretch; April Heinrichs was hurt and not 100 percent in China [site of the World Cup]. Joy Biefeld had a pulled hamstring, Christine Lilly developed a hip pointer in our first game. Mary Harvey had a shoulder injury. We played Norway twice in August without Michelle and April, and we lost both games. The World Cup was only three months away and we were playing poorly. We were burned out and fed up. We'd played a lot of soccer. I was worried we'd peaked early.

It was a hell of a ride, an amazing experience. Everything had an effect on how the team was doing. Everything. Even little things like moving our luggage. At the end of a baggage-moving ceremony we'd have four or five people upset with the four or five who sat there and did nothing. These little things add up. A player says something to another player about a third player. Invariably, it'll get back to the third player. That's not to say all things are negative. We had one girl on the team who was an outstanding player but nowhere near the top. But her effect on team chemistry was so powerful there was no way I was going to cut her. You've always got some girls who are doing things for other people and are always concerned. That can build the chemistry back. It's this constant tapestry-weaving experience that you've got to always be plugged into.

FIVE

Tricks of the Trade

What you have to do, she says, is "pull out the spirit." Finally, in the end, that's what a coach does. Because there comes a point where the coach can no longer coach the body. She can only run an athlete through so many hoops, push her through so many drills, work her through so many practices. "You impart the knowledge of technique, but the athletes, they're the ones who have to go out there and run," says Dr. Dorothy L. Richey, professor of physical education at Chicago State, a former track coach, and one of the first women to be named a college athletic director for both men and women. "You cannot run down the track for them. But you can make them believe that they can do it. Because if they don't believe it, they are not going to achieve it. I found that to be the real challenge of coaching. To get them to depend upon themselves, to go out there and find themselves."

Motivation. Inspiration. Exhortation. Finding these intangible, elusive qualities within an athlete is the real secret of coaching. Every coach will tell you that. You don't win if you don't have talent, but all talent does is get you in the game. Can you make it play, perform, *produce?* "There's something else, a higher level, that an athlete can achieve," says Dorothy Richey, who learned at the knee of the legendary Dr. Nell Jackson, the first African-American woman to be named an Olympic track and field coach, and Richey's coach at Tuskegee Institute in the mid-'60s. "It's another whole dimension that you have to get to." But to arrive there a coach must climb inside an athlete's mind, a team's psyche. It is rarely an easy journey. You have to push and pull, massage and manipulate. Withhold approval, shower with love. Do you press ahead or back off? No two kids are the same, and every team is different.

Many coaches are reduced to mumblings of explanation when pressed to illuminate what it is they actually do and how they do it. Either you can or you can't. If you have to ask the question, maybe you won't understand the answer.

Can you pull the spirit out?

JANET ELY-LaGOURGUE, *diving, Mission Viejo Nadadores:* Athletes are not real good at expressing themselves, at being vulnerable. That's why I think I bring something extra to coaching, because of what I went through as a diver. It has to do with what was going on in my family, the death of my mother when I was in Munich at the '72 Games, the breakup of my family, my brothers and me.

I left home at fifteen to train. I wouldn't recommend it, though I think I benefited. My mother was very sick with cancer. The first time I made the Olympics, I thought, "Luck." It happened to me; I didn't make it happen. The second time, I felt I had a major part to do with it.

When my mother died the family sort of . . . dispersed. I think we all felt very fragmented. I think that's very natural. It was just very sad. I didn't quit after '72 because I knew I hadn't reached my potential. I don't know how much of it was that I felt lost and that diving had become my whole world. When I won the Worlds in 1975, psychologically I wasn't on top of my game. I was on the verge of a breakdown, but I couldn't get out of the thick of things to take care of it. I'd made diving everything, and I didn't know how to work away from it. And it was only one year until the Olympic Trials again.

Then at the [1976] Olympics, during my second compulsory dive, I brushed my feet on the platform on a back dive. The added momentum flew me right onto my stomach. From thirty-three feet up. I got all 2s on that dive, and I placed ninth, one place out of making the finals, when you start over with a clean slate. I continued diving after the '76 games, but I was devastated.

I had a great coach who nursed me along. Brian Robbins. The year he started coaching, in '76, a handful of the top divers went to him. He had an interesting perspective. A kind of Eastern philosophy, meditation and focusing on the quiet aspects and the strength of being calm and quiet, which was really important for me at that time. He helped me deal with myself, confront myself and say, Whoa, look at yourself here.

If I hadn't come upon this coach, I don't know, I might have quit. But I learned to enjoy diving again, to have that passion that I used to have for diving, which I believe is what makes anybody great. It was Brian who made me see my fears had nothing to do with diving and everything to do with all the other things. So I went for another Olympics. But I ended up having back surgery, and that Olympics was the one that Carter pulled us out of, in '80 in Moscow.

Tipping my feet on that platform was no accident. People said it was just one of those things. I don't believe that anymore. If an athlete's in tune, she knows about those things. I knew there was potential for me to hit my feet. I was coasting on my training. I didn't do it on purpose, but if I'd been more into it, I believe that it's something that would not have happened.

You really do have more control than you realize. Some athletes, I think, are blind to thinking that some accidents are preventable. They don't want to know that they have that much control—as an excuse, in case of a poor performance. Self-discipline, self-control: that's what it's all about. If you're being honest and truthful, you realize you control those things.

CHUCK NOLL, *Pittsburgh Steelers (retired):* It's not a natural thing to want contact. You have to prepare yourself for it. It's a choice a player has to make. It's overcoming self more than anything else. Exterior motivation—the fans in the stands, his parents or relatives, whatever—that's not going to make it. He has to do it because he wants to do it as a player. He's not going to do it for the coach. He's playing a game where he is physically threatened—he isn't exactly in the safest spot in the world. He has to do it so he can survive. I don't think a coach can force somebody to do that.

TED PETERSEN, *football, Trinity High, Washington, Pennsylvania:* There's another motivation: pure athletics. There's something inside a man, I guess, that likes the challenge. There's something inside a man that likes to be a team player. Jim Otto [long-time Oakland Raider center], he has to get plastic knees. And yet he says he'd do it all again. It's all about approval. Just like it was when you were a kid.

BILL MUSSELMAN, *first coach of the Minnesota Timberwolves (now with a CBA team in Rochester, Minnesota):* I was a back when I entered Wittenburg University. The back coach was young, and he used to run us hard. I used to watch the linemen; they'd be down on one knee while the head coach, Bill Edwards, was telling jokes. It's eighty-five degrees and I can't even move, and I'm watching the linemen laughing and joking. One day Bill says, "Hey, Scrap"—they called me Scrap Iron—"how would you like to become a lineman?" I said, "Oh, yeah." What I learned from Bill Edwards was not to run your kids into the ground. We only did three hits a day. But we'd do it with the whole team watching. You couldn't hide. The players loved him. They would *play* for him, throw all caution to the wind. If they don't want to play for you, forget everything else.

JOE NEWTON, *cross-country and track, York High, Oak Brook, Illinois:* You've got to know your athletes, who you gotta pat on the butt, who you gotta hug, who you gotta yell at. Everybody's different. Learning how to motivate, that's the secret. I make it a point—at every practice, every day—to say out loud the name of every kid on the team and at some point to shake every kid's hand. "Isn't that right, Joe Smith?" "What do you think, John Jones?" It's that personal contact, letting them know that they exist. I believe in the eternal verities, that's the secret. Society can change and people can change, but truth is truth and honor is honor and courage is courage. I'm wacky and out of date, but as long as they know you're sincere, maybe they'll put up with it.

BARBARA JEAN JACKET, *1992 women's Olympic track & field coach; Prairie View A&M (retired):* Sometimes I have to walk up to someone and say, "You get on my nerves. All that talent and you don't use it." Say that and they be whispering behind your back: "I'll show her!" Then when she comes off the track and she's done it, I'd say: "It took me to say you weren't going to be anything before you did something." There are times you have to do that.

Every year there are different buttons you have to push. Some you have to psych, some you don't. You have to hold some hands, some you don't. Then there are times when you just have to say, "Little girl, why are you talking so much? Show me." It's a whole lot of different things. I used to have this one shot putter. Her name was Woody. I'd grab her and jump all over her. It wasn't physical; I was just talking noise. But my mouth scared everybody. If I could jump on Woody, I could jump on anybody.

SR. LYNN WINSOR, B.V.M., CAA, *golf, Xavier College Prep, Phoenix, Arizona:* How do you motivate kids? What do you do? What can you say? I remember once when [future professional] Heather Farr was a freshman here. She was a great golfer, even then. It was the state championship, and Heather had played horribly through the first nine. I could see her coming and I had to figure out what I could say. When she told me her score, I pretended that I'd fainted. Her mother was talking to me and BOOM! I went right down on the ground. Heather drops her clubs and comes running over. "Sister Lynn, what's wrong?" The other coaches thought I'd really fainted. I woke up and said, "Your score just knocked me out." The focus went off her and onto me, and the next day she went out and won her first championship by two strokes.

TOM HOUSE, *assistant to the general manager, Texas Rangers (and former pitching coach):* If there's something that separates me from the coaching mainstream, it's that my burning desire as an instructor is to be able to *answer* questions. Coaching is information, instruction, and inspiration. It's as simple as that.

Clyde King was one of my role models. He's an academic baseball guy. He looked at the game a bit differently. He had answers above and beyond the spit-on-it-and-go-get-'em stuff. He got me to the big leagues. I had four and a half years in Triple A ball when Clyde took over as manager of the Richmond Braves. "Let's find out if you can be a pitcher." I was a marginal major league player, but I was a lefty who could throw a curveball for a strike—and I got nine years in the bigs.

I teach the basics. It's just that instead of answering the what, I give you the why—at least I hope I can. I have my Ph.D. in psychology and have done research in biomechanics. Most coaches come at things with a seat-of-the-pants approach. That's okay, but you can't cookie-cut. My education has provided me with a way to look at psycho-emotional makeup and understand why things occur. A kid might be having performance anxieties that have nothing to do with baseball. Problem identification is half the solution. We have our pitchers throw footballs. To make a football spiral you have to be mechanically sound. It's like having a coach on every throw.

Anything I've ever done has been proven and reproven, re-searched and objectively sold to me before I bring it up. I've never had any trouble with the pitchers that I've worked with. Nolan Ryan has been the best thing that's ever happened to me. When he joined the Rangers, he came to me before spring training. "Let me look and learn," he said, "and if I see something I like I'll ask questions." He came to me about two weeks into the season. But let's face it: I didn't *teach* Nolan Ryan anything. What I do is remind him of things.

Baseball is a money game and a medical game. The two M's. I believe the type of instructor I'm trying to be is the kind of instructor who will survive into the next century. Athletes are not dumb. The longer a guy can play, the better he's going to be financially. He does not want to do anything that might be career threatening. To put an athlete on the field you have to make sure the physical therapists, the trainers, the support staff, and two or three other opinions have en-tered into what's wrong with this guy. You have to put everyone's mind at ease, from the insurance company that insures the arm, to the front-office that is paying for that arm, to the athlete himself who knows that if the arm doesn't work it's not going to make the kind of money it should be making.

Today a coach had better be able to tell a youngster, "Look, this isn't career threatening." Or, "You can throw X number of pitches." Or, "You can give me what you got." If you can tell him that, look him in the eye and tell him, he'll do it. If you can't give him all the in-formation he needs, then you've got your hands full.

BUTCH PASTORINI, *volunteer football assistant, Santa Clara Uni-versity:* I played for Pat Malley when I went here. Pat could make us believe. He pushed all the right buttons. I remember once he took me out of a game. I sneaked back in. He sent the other guy back in and called me over. Now, I'm so mad I'd like to hit him. He's got this dead-serious look on his face, and he reaches into his pocket and pulls out a quarter and says, "Go to the snack bar and get me a cup of coffee."

Pat could turn any game into a crusade. I remember playing Chico State. We had one player, Craig Smith, who had transferred to Chico. A couple of days before the game Pat starts getting letters from Craig talking about what the coach from Chico was saying about Santa Clara. He'd read us these letters and, I mean, "We're going to kill those sons-a-bitches!" How can they say that about us Catholics? We kicked their ass big. After the game I went up to their coach and yelled, "So what do you think of us mackerel-snappers now?" That's what he'd called us in the letters. It wasn't until years later that I realized those letters were a figment of Pat's imagination.

I hurt my knee my senior year. Before the San Francisco State game we went to Mass and then Pat said, "Go down to the stadium and see what they did." We go down, and the stadium's been painted all over. One sign said: "Too bad about your Little All-American." I wanted to kill them. Of course, Pat had done the whole thing. A kid who'd played a couple of years ahead of me had asked what he could do to get the team up for San Francisco State. Pat told him to paint the stadium.

BILL CURRY, *football, University of Kentucky:* The two giant role models in my life were very combative, very aggressive coach figures. One was my dad. He was in the infantry during World War II. He was a hand-to-hand-combat instructor and a national weightlifting champion.

In high school it was Bill Badgett. One day he decided to have "Bill Curry Day." I was not a good football player. Obviously Coach had observed this. He decided to have a tackling drill in which I would not be allowed to go to the back of the line until I'd tackled big Roy Betsill.

Well, we proceeded to have this drill over and over. There was blood and snot and tears, and it dawned on me that I was going to stay out there, for an eternity if necessary, until I tackled him. I couldn't quit—my dad was at home. So I closed my eyes and knocked the day-lights out of him. Everybody cheered and hugged, and Coach Badgett, he almost smiled. A breakthrough! It was a rite of passage. It was the beginning of my football career. My guess is Coach Badgett set me up. He may have even spoken to Roy and said, "Let Curry tackle you. We've got to turn him into a player."

ED CHEFF, *baseball, Lewis-Clark State College, Lewiston, Idaho:* I boxed when I was a kid. Boxing isn't a fight, it's a sport, and there are skills that carry over to other sports. We put our guys through a boxing program, and everybody has one match at the end. It may be the only time in their lives where they'll be able to say, "Yeah, I was in the ring." One of the most pressured, exciting things they'll ever do in their lives is get in the ring against another guy. There's a lot of apprehension, fear of the unknown. For some of the guys it builds up over the five weeks. We got guys looking like they're going to pee down their legs. Once you fight through it, you find out it wasn't near as bad as you thought it was going to be.

RANDY JABLONIC, *rowing, University of Wisconsin:* Anyone who's ever rowed in a championship race has crossed the pain threshold. Going to that edge, where you ask your body to respond and it doesn't, *that's* a frightening thing. There's a fear of failure that rises even greater than the pain. A fear of falling short, of failing your teammates, of not being able to serve the primary cause. That's what a rowing coach is up against.

You reach for things to bring this feeling on so they know what it is and won't be afraid of it. We have rope runs. We start out with everyone hanging onto a rope, and we run until there's only one guy left. It stirs the perseverance and discipline of a man to reach out, to see what he is worth. What can you contribute to the whole before you have to let go of the rope? There's a real symbolism to holding on.

FRANK LAYDEN, *Utah Jazz (retired):* Some coaches, their downfall is they have to prove that they're right. Sometimes being right is even more important than the winning. Phil Jackson of the Bulls is a good example of how to avoid that trap. I was broadcasting for the NBA network and we had a lot of Bulls games with Michael Jordan. Phil, he was a bit of a rabble-rouser in his early days, and he still has a bit of the hippie in him, and he brought that to the table. He had a real run-in with Stacey King. Stacey made the statement that he wasn't going to practice if he didn't play. Phil didn't allow it to become a shouting match, a contest of who was right and who was wrong and who was going to give in first. Phil has the ability to step back and look things over. He didn't panic. He didn't allow himself to become the issue. He made sure Stacey King remained the guilty party. Phil could have destroyed the team just to prove he was right. A lot of coaches, that's exactly what they would have done.

JOE TORRE, *St. Louis Cardinals:* You try to give the players a calm about things. A sense that you're not panicking, even if you are. Let them know that you believe in them, no matter how badly somebody's doing. Make them believe that you believe in them. That takes a lot of work. It's tougher to play this game than it's ever been. Nobody pats them on the back anymore. If they do well, they're supposed to because they're making lots of money. If they don't, they're bums—because they're making lots of money and they're supposed to. But they're still the same people who were making the minimum wage of six, eight thousand dollars when I started playing. It's one hundred thousand dollars now, but that's not their fault. They're still the same kids.

When I first started managing I thought it was a power thing. I'm the manager; do what I say. Well, that used to work. You could be a little mysterious and make your job look like more than it was. But you can't threaten players anymore—the guarantees are in their court. I used to have a lot of rules: You can't lay out in the sun, can't swim, can't play golf. Now my only rule is get to the park on time.

What you have to do is be available and don't give them any excuse not to do what they're supposed to do. You've got to make sense, give them a feel for what you're trying to accomplish. I'm doing it to win this game. I'm not doing it because it will get you three hits and improve your batting average. I want them to respect the fact that it's my job to make those decisions, and if I don't make the right decision, then I'm the one who'll get fired.

K. C. JONES, *Seattle Supersonics (retired):* The one thing [Boston Celtic coach] Red [Auerbach] had, and he used it very well, was this sense of fear about him. He used that to get your attention. That's a valuable weapon for a coach to have. And with that, he'd blow us away once a month, just to let us know he was still around.

Red knew how to walk the line. Because if you go beyond that little taste of fear, you go beyond it into hatred. If the players hate you, you're in trouble. Red liked to keep you on the defensive. His style was to keep you off kilter. He knows fans, he knows players, he knows officials. He's one of those geniuses. He'd pick on the players who could take it. If he didn't want to chew out [Bill] Russell, he'd pick on Satch [Sanders]; if he didn't want to chew me out, he'd pick on [Tommy] Heinsohn. Those guys could deal with it. But he got his message across to everybody.

JOHN WOODEN, *basketball, UCLA (retired):* I don't know if I could say I feared becoming complacent as the championships started to mount. But I was always aware that it could happen. When Bill Walton and his group came the first year, we had an undefeated year. I told them at the end of that season that next year was going to be even better. Then I said, "But by the time you're seniors you'll be intolerable." There is always the possibility of a team's becoming complacent. The coach's job is to prevent that. I do feel the Walton teams came closer to fulfilling their potential when they were juniors than they did when they were seniors.If you're not hungry you won't function. You have to keep them hungry and thin and avoid becoming satisfied with themselves and feeling that what they've done in the past is going to affect what's coming up. You've got to get that across to them, and it's not easy. The better they do, the more pats on the back they get from outsiders. That leads to their feeling they're a little better than they really are.

W. S. DONALD, *football and track & field, Wooddale High, Memphis:* They say black kids are better sprinters, but I don't believe it. They're just hungrier. Most of my track people are black now. But back in 1973 we were about the only school in Tennessee that wasn't integrated, so I had all white kids. At States, some black kids came up to my kids and asked what events they were running. They said the sprints. These black kids go, "What?" Yeah, well, we run 'em and we won 'em.

They can say this and that about the higher hamstrings or Achilles tendon, but I don't believe it. I had a white kid years ago, nobody could touch him. Ran a 9.2 one-hundred-yard dash. Yes, sir, that's movin'. Fastest kid I ever had. Take the kids from different neighborhoods and put 'em all on the same program and you'd get the same results out of all of them. The missing ingredient is that some kids are willing to work harder.

I call it paying the price. Getting up early to lift weights, work on the fundamentals. Too many white kids today, they don't want to pay that price. Track ain't fun! Run eight, ten repetitions of two hundred yards and your head gets to swimming, your legs get rubbery, you want to throw up. It's a beating, and it's every day.

I've approached white kids who I know, just by looking at them, they've got the ability. They let you know they'd rather do what they're doing because it's no sweat and it's not work. They've got their car and a job to pay the insurance. If they could show up on Friday and run, they'd do it. But that's getting paid for not working.

MIKE PRICE, *football, Washington State:* When I was at Weber State we were in a losing streak; we'd lost three and we were playing Idaho State next, and they were number one in the country. We were sitting in the locker room before practice, and I said, "I do *not* want to go out there."

Bob Bratkowski—he's with the Seahawks now—he started talking about how he'd just seen these guys on the street with their hair all spiked and painted blue. Well, it was Halloween, and Idaho's colors are black and orange. Bratkowski says, "Why don't we spray our hair orange and go out to practice?" The coaches thought we were nuts. But we had a great practice and we knocked them off.

RANDY JABLONIC: We have the "Grand Row." I don't know if I'd call it the "Naked Row," though it has on occasion become that. The last practice before we head to Nationals, we gather in Willows Bay with all the boats from all the events going to Nationals, and then we promenade back to the dock. One year somebody brought some fireworks, and then we started with "Stars and Stripes" and "Pomp and Circumstance." One year we concluded with a bagpiper. And it's been said that a freshman coach stood up on the bow one time with nothing on and led the parade in. I don't know if it's true or not, but let's just say a couple of boats maybe follow suit from year to year.

MIKE PRICE: Some seasons you do something crazy; other seasons you don't. It depends. I remember once at Weber before a Portland State game, it was pouring down rain. I didn't want my receivers to start thinking they were going to drop the ball. So I told my assistants to lead the team out and dive on the fifty-yard line and slide across the field. They forgot about dropping the ball.

Usually it's all of a sudden: "We gotta do something!" I dressed up like a Sun Devil one time. I came out like a duck hunter before an Oregon game; I looked like Elmer Fudd. At Weber I dressed up like Robo-Cop. I had the police and the fire department put on their lights and sirens and escort me out to the middle of the field. I stepped out and told the team that I would be with them on Saturday. I liked that one.

Sometimes I'll do it just for fun, but usually there's a method to the madness. There was a USC game that was real important. One of our first national-TV games, and we were undefeated. A couple of students suggested this one, actually. They had a horse and one of them dressed up like Tommy Trojan, the USC mascot. I'm out on the field talking to the team about how sick and tired I was about all this USC stuff. And then all of sudden here he comes riding out onto the field, Tommy Trojan. I go nuts. "That's it! We don't get any damn respect. I've had it!" I pulled out a starter's pistol and shot him. He fell off the horse and they drug him off the field. I think half the kids thought I'd really killed him.

ED CHEFF: One of the worst things athletics teaches people is to be so structured. So we play "golden rules" basketball. A gym full of guys, fifteen, twenty on a team, throw the ball up in the middle of the court and say, "Go." There are no rules. They have to develop their own ethics, their own code of conduct. There's a lot of creativity. These games develop a structure from within. It's amazing. There's a tremendous amount of competitiveness and discipline—way more than when someone has defined the rules for you. You get insight into a kid's character playing these games. We're trying to throw their egos out and start talking about other things that are important to being athletes. There's a difference between being confident and highly motivated and being an egotistical guy who thinks he's something special. You might be a future first-round draft choice, but you're still playing golden rules basketball.

BOB WOOD, *tennis, University Liggett School, Grosse Pointe Woods, Michigan:* Every year I match everybody up and we practice shaking hands. The seniors laugh. I don't care. I feel shaking hands is very important. I do this with my girls, too. They'll pass me later and say, "I shook hands with one of my father's friends and he complimented me on my handshake." You can't ever take anything for granted when dealing with kids. Kids will make you as proud as you can possibly be; they'll leave you with your chest bursting with pride. And then thirty seconds later they can destroy you.

CHARLIE THOMAS, *basketball, San Francisco State:* Kids are looking for discipline. I think that they don't get it, they don't have it, but they want it because they know that's the only way they're going to make it. Sometimes we think they don't know that. They *know.* They say things and they do things when they're hanging with the fellows, but deep down they want somebody to show them the way.

MIKE MARCOULIS, JR., *basketball and baseball, Freemont High School, Oakland:* You are *the* person in these kids' lives. And I'm not saying that boastfully. It's just that you are. There are a lot of other things you have to do with these kids besides try to win games. If you're not responding to them, if you're not out there saying, "You okay?" "What's the problem?" "We need to talk"—if all it is for you is get to practice, play hard or you don't play, if we win we're great, if we lose you're fucked up—then you're not doing your job. You're abusing your power.

Because you are the man. You're the man during lunch when they all come up to talk to you, walk around with you, this or that, blah, blah, blah. They think you control everything. They think you're in control of everything. You are the man. And it's coming at you from fifteen different directions. Sometimes I feel the lives of all my players is my life too.

STAN MORRISON, *basketball, San Jose State:* Athletes get spoiled. They anticipate a different set of rules: "If I get a speeding ticket, the coach will take care of it because, after all, I am a basketball player." I want them to deal with life. My expectations are greater for them than for nonathletes. Because they walk around campus with a neon sign on their forehead that says, BASKETBALL PLAYER. People know them who they don't know. Their behavior, how they conduct themselves, how they think, how they react—all that takes special planning.

We serve tables at a homeless shelter every Thanksgiving. I want my guys in sweatpants and sweatshirts with "San Jose State" on them, and I want them to smile at a guy, give him some food, pat him on the back, and say, "Hang in there, buddy." I want my players to know what can happen to people for any one of a hundred reasons. That there's another world out there where not everybody gets three squares a day.

FRANK LAYDEN: The little things. Like a ten-thousand-dollar bonus to a player if he goes back and gets his degree. We started book clubs. I bought eighteen books and gave one to each player and told them to get interested. I'd encourage them to go to the theater on the road. I'd plan sideline trips: Tonight we're having a team meeting—at Candlestick Park. It is amazing how many players have never been to a major league baseball game. None of these things, by the way, have anything to do with surviving in the business. But there was more to it than that. These NBA players have a lot of potential. There's a lot of bright kids playing pro basketball who have been shortchanged by the sport they play.

ANONYMOUS MAN, *coach at a Division I university:* I was fortunate to come out of the closet after the AIDS issue had really struck. I'm very conservative in activities and *very* safe. But I've also had to confront AIDS head-on. About three years ago my roommate developed pneumonia. Then we found out it was AIDS. I'd met him playing baseball. He's my best friend—never a lover situation. He has suffered greatly. It's been *the* difficult experience of my life.

It's a horrible trade-off, but the good thing that has come out of all this is that I see myself as being more insightful as a coach. I'm more sensitive to the kids' needs. I'm more able to show them that I care about them. I'm closer to my athletes than I've ever been. And I've allowed them to see that I have weaknesses too.

STAN MORRISON: This year we had two AIDS workshops. Based on the stories I'm hearing, the casual talk, there is a lot of activity going on. And we have a superstar on our campus who does a date-rape workshop. A young man needs to understands that no means no. She also does a thing with my team to empower them to say no. Empower young men to say no to young women who are making themselves available to these guys. The pendulum has swung.

GLEN MASON, *football, University of Kansas:* My first year here we were 1–10. We played Nebraska and got beat 63–7. I thought we did a hell of a job, and that's the truth. We got waxed by Oklahoma State and Oklahoma. The game days weren't tough at all; that was the easy part. You're in the game, you've got that competitive spirit, you're letting it all go. The tough thing was facing the players every Monday. It's easy when you're successful. But we were getting waxed week in and week out, and every Monday you have to walk in and have sixty kids looking at you.

[QUESTION: So what did you say?] You lie! You've got to find something good to tell them. You've got to find something good to tell yourself. I wouldn't use the films. Who wants to see 63–7? I'd cut out the good stuff and show them that. Absolutely. Everybody knows the doom and gloom; you've got to give them some hope.

BILLY WILLIAMS, *coach assistant, Cleveland Indians:* Find something positive to get them to tomorrow. Maybe the best today didn't materialize into a win; you still try to take something from today to get them into tomorrow. When he makes a great catch, when he makes an excellent pitch, you come over and sit down next to him, and you put your arm around him and say, "I'm going to tell you something: That's pitching," or, "Let me tell you: That was a catch."

TINA SLOAN GREEN, *lacrosse, Temple (retired):* A person has to learn how to be an athlete. I had one group, it took them four years, until they were seniors, to win themselves a championship. Some kids don't realize what you have to put into it.

SALLY BAUM, *tennis, Goucher College, Towson, Maryland:* It takes a lot of hours. You have to break down their heads. You start with little goals. The object today is to hit it ten feet. Next week we'll aim for twenty, then thirty, then we'll go for the corners, right side, left side, alleys. It can be frustrating for athletes to have their game broken down like that. They're going to get worse before they get better. And it's tough on the coach, because you're the one who's making them worse before they get better.

TINA SLOAN GREEN: I was so disgusted after the Maryland game. We were down 2–1 at the half, then Maryland scored the first goal in the second half and we just gave up. It was an away trip, and they all wanted to ride home with their parents and friends. I said, "Everybody gets on the bus." And I really lambasted them. Not for losing, for giving up. The next day they came back and they worked. "Just keep working," I told them. "Keep working, keep working. Don't give up, don't give up." They had to learn what it takes to be an athlete.

It was after the Lafayette game their senior year when I could tell they'd finally learned. That was one of the most rewarding experiences for me as a coach, to see them feeling like athletes, understanding what it was. They had to win the game in order to stay in the race for the post-season. And they didn't give up a point. I could tell by looking at them, their body language. They were following the game plan—and they were enjoying it. When they came off the field, you could see they were physically and mentally drained. I said, "What's it feel like?" And they said, "Can we bring it back with us?" They had the feeling, what it takes to be a winner.

SIX

Players

He coached high school wrestling coach for twenty-nine years. That's a lot of young men in singlets and ear protection, a lot of young men sweating and groping and lying exhausted on the mat in his wrestling room. A lot of young men with arms raised in triumph at the state finals. And, yes, a lot of young men with arms left unraised in defeat.

But ask Bob Siddens, the now-retired wrestling coach at West High School in Waterloo, Iowa, if he will name a favorite wrestler, that one special kid from all those years, and he'll hesitate. Perhaps because the obvious answer is too easy. Bob Siddens coached the teenaged Dan Gable, who went on from his Waterloo wrestling room to become the greatest wrestler in U.S. history, a ferocious competitor who won a gold medal at the 1972 Olympics *without relinquishing a single point to any opponent.* Siddens witnessed that Munich triumph, and he has surely watched with quiet pride as Gable became the country's premier college wrestling coach, at the University of Iowa, as well as the 1984 Olympic coach.

But to come right out and say Dan's the one? Bob Siddens won't do that. Because what about the rest, the five, six hundred others? All those other guys who gave him all their sweat and blood, who made him laugh and cry and scream and yell? What about them? They're doctors now, and dentists and businessmen and teachers and wrestling coaches. Heck, he says with pride, one of his wrestlers is an artist. And he's proud of them all, every single one.

So when you ask Bob Siddens for a favorite story about a favorite kid, it's not about Dan Gable. It's about this kid named Rich. He was another of Siddens's state champions; he turned the trick twice, first as a sophomore, and then as a junior. "He was an interesting individual," he remembers. "People didn't understand him." But maybe Bob Siddens did.

During the summer before his senior year, Rich went to the Junior Olympics. He beat the Russian and won a gold medal. He came back home, Bob Siddens remembers, and, well, he was just a kid, you know? He celebrated, drank some beer, got caught. "I had to make him ineligible. He lost football and wrestling for his senior year."

And that would have been that, except that Bob Siddens told Rich he could still come out for wrestling; he just couldn't wrestle in any of the matches. "I had coaches say to me, 'Why are you doing that, after what he did to you?'" They didn't understand. "Richard didn't do anything to me," Bob Siddens says. "When he got back from the Junior Olympics, he didn't think, 'This is going to hurt Coach Siddens if I get caught drinking.'" Rich didn't miss a practice that entire year, and he got a full scholarship to college, where he won a national championship.

"I'm not trying to take the credit," Bob Siddens says, but he will allow this: "He needed somebody right at that time." And Coach Siddens was it. "What would have happened if I hadn't done that? I don't know. Maybe it would have worked out all right." Then again . . . "Maybe he would have gone helter skelter," Bob Siddens reflects. "Maybe if he hadn't had the opportunity to stay with the program, he'd have gotten sidetracked. You just never know."

KEN HOUSTON, *defensive back coach (retired), University of Houston (now a counselor at Terrell Alternative Middle School in Houston):* I played in the NFL until I was thirty-seven. By then you've seen a lot of coaches. You start looking for the coach who's sensitive, the guy who's treating you like a human being, who understands that it's only a game. Because people make the game. Take this into coaching and it'll help you, because you'll always keep your hand on the pulse of the team.

Sometimes your players are going to get beat. And when they come off the field they know they got beat. Right then they want me to tell them something they don't know. They want to know why. "Tell us something we don't know, Coach." At that moment it is *real* easy to put your kids away for good if you're not careful. I don't care how good a coach you are, whether you get fired, retire, *whatever,* someday the game's going to be over. Coaches forget that. Someday we're going to have to walk off the field, and all we'll have is the people we coached.

ROY CHIPMAN, *basketball, University of Pittsburgh (retired):* Leave your problems where they are. Don't bring them onto the court. Maybe the AD's on your ass because you're not winning or the fans aren't coming. The easy thing is to take it out on your players. You have to always be aware of that. I remember the losing streaks. Everybody would be down—me, the players, the coaches. I'd sit in meetings and say, "We are going to be positive. Find me a reason to be positive."

TINA SLOAN GREEN, *lacrosse, Temple (retired):* The things you take for granted, your players take seriously. They remember everything you say.

NAN AIROLA, *volleyball, Providence Catholic High, New Lenox, Illinois:* I run a grade-school camp. I had this one girl who played in the fifth grade who then played for me in high school. She came up to me when she was a senior and said, "Do you remember the time when I was in the fifth grade and I was at your camp? You put me over on this court and you put Susie over on the other court. And I know it was because I was so little and skinny." Seven years later and she's telling me this. "I always said I'd come back and show you."

There was this other girl. She was my first challenge. A real hot dog. We went round and round. You couldn't win without her; you couldn't win with her. We struggled for four years. I learned more from her than I did from all the other kids. To this day I'll get a call from her every six months or so. "Remember when we were in your office screaming at each other?" Of course I do.

That's why I stay with it. Because every once in a while you'll get a kid to come back ten years later and she'll tell you: "Because of you, because of this *one* conversation we had, I went on and did this." They've even told me it's helped them deliver their babies. "When I had my baby, the doctor said do this-this-this, and when I did it he said how coachable I was." And I say, "I told you that stuff was going to pay off."

HANK HAINES, *Blytheville Boxing Club, Arkansas (retired):* I had a black middleweight that I was just so fond of. His name was Lee McNichols and he won the Novice AAU Middleweight Championship over in west Arkansas. I had three or four boys in the tournament, and after Lee won we were going around, getting gas and something to eat. We're getting in and out of the car, and every time, Lee got front seat. One of the white boys in the back gets to wondering why Lee always got to ride in the front seat. Just kind of razzing him. Lee sat there looking straight out the windshield and, without looking back, says that's because he's the champ now. The guys in the back, they liked that. When I took Lee home, to the projects, we pulled in and Lee has this big beautiful trophy, and he gets out and all these little black kids run yelling that Lee's home, Lee's home. And I thought, "Good. Lee McNichols is a hero down here. He ought to be."

ANN LEBEDEFF, *tennis, Cal-Poly Pamona:* Her name was Xenia Anastasiado. She was from Athens. She was a senior and a great girl, a great player. Funnier than hell on the court—temperamental, a real actress. She could be a complete bitch or she could be funnier than anything. When I came to Cal-Poly I saw her and all I could think was, "Jesus! What a player!" She was driving home from practice one Saturday and this guy ran a red light and hit her. Came down a hill at about forty-five miles an hour. BOOM! She never regained consciousness.

I got the first phone call because Shelley, a girl on the team, and her mom were driving to Kmart, and they saw the accident and followed Xenia to the hospital. I hadn't been at practice that day because I had to go to the hospital for some minor surgery. I'd come home that same day, and I was still kind of out of it from the anesthetic. Shelley made the call, but she was so shaken up she put the nurse on. "Do you know a Xenia Anastasiado?" I said yes. They said, She's in the hospital," and I said, "Is she hurt?" I thought it was a joke. I never thought it was critical. But the nurse said, "Yes, she is." To think that someone could be snuffed out that fast.

That next Monday, about five minutes before I was going to get in my car and drive to school, I found out I had to go back in the hospital for a hysterectomy and six weeks of radiation. I didn't tell the kids until after the memorial service for Xenia. That Monday was really weird.

Xenia's gone, I find out I have cancer, I talk to the team for the first time, and then we have a match. Then I come home and there's a letter from Xenia. She had mailed me a get-well card.

Someone told me the girls on the team aged about twenty years just by having this one friend die. I mean that in a good way. Coaches are always telling their kids: "You're going to remember when you're fifty that I told you this." My girls don't have to remember. They lived it.

I never had a team play through so much adversity. It was like getting picked up in a spaceship and you all go through the same things together and then you get dumped back down on earth. We came out seventh in the nation. They lose Xenia and then I'm not around for a month. They would hit and then they'd talk. Nobody on the outside wanted to talk to them, but they needed to, and that's what got us through the season.

At Nationals, it was really strange. We're getting ready for our first match, and I happened to look up at the sky. There's this huge X, this jetstream that a plane had left. It was something you'd see on *The Twilight Zone*.

I know this will sound corny, but when all this happened to Xenia and then to me, I took it that I had a second chance as a coach. I'd tell the team that. I got a second chance and she didn't. Here we are bitching and moaning—but we have another moment, and Xenia doesn't. We dedicated the season to her. We had taken our team picture right before Xenia's accident, and when they came back we had laminated pins made from Xenia's individual.

We have Xenia's picture up in our office; I like her smile. I think about her every time I pass a Greek restaurant. I think about her every time I see someone on the court who's temperamental or really funny. She made me laugh. One of the girls this year—she's a senior now and this is my fourth year—she's the only player I have who knew Xenia. There's a real bond between us. The girl who was our all-America for three years graduated last year. She was a national champion and was one of Xenia's closest friends. Sometimes when we talk we'll say, "God, Xenia would have loved this." I've kept her letters—the get-well card and a Christmas letter saying she was looking forward to the season, that she was so glad she had a new coach that she really liked.

DERRIL KIPP, *girls' basketball, Maine West High, Des Plaines, Illinois:* The year we won States we had nine seniors. That's tough. I always try to play a lot of kids, keep them involved. We do a lot of things other than the basketball—dinners, assemblies, all that. Make them all feel as important as the starters. You have to take extra steps to keep those kids feeling like they're important and that you want them there and that they're not just scrimmage bait. There's lots of things that go on through the season, but that's the hardest of them all— keeping everybody happy.

OLLIE BUTLER, *basketball assistant, Cal State–San Bernardino (coached high school for thirty-three years):* I don't have a lot of faith in a lot of the high school coaches coming up these days. They're in high school to make a name and move on. Up to the glamour. And I don't like that. I don't think they have much interest in the kids who aren't going to be their stars.

I've always admired the kid who comes out every day, who busts his butt in practice knowing he's not going to get a lot of playing time. I'm worried these kids will get caught in the shuffle. That nobody's going to put their arm around their shoulder and say, "You tripped over the lines painted on the floor, but I appreciate your hard work and I'll see you at practice tomorrow."

JOHN WOODEN, *basketball, UCLA (retired):* I used to tell my players that I liked them all the same, that I was going to treat them all the same. Then I changed it. "I won't like you all the same any more than you like each other all the same or like me all the same. And don't expect me to treat you all the same, because I won't. I'm going to try to give each individual the treatment you earn and deserve, and I know that won't all be the same. And I'm not infallible, so watch out."

JIM SATALIN, *basketball, Duquesne University (retired):* I coached for twenty-some years. You can't do something that long and not ever miss it. But I don't miss the recruiting, and I don't miss the alumni. And, to a certain extent, I don't miss the players, either. There are some kids you do not miss, that's the honest truth. Ask any coach why he's coaching, and he'll tell you: "I'm in it for the players." But that's because they can't tell you the truth: There are some kids you just never enjoy coaching.

ABE LEMONS, basketball, Oklahoma City College (retired): Players are like heart transplants. Put them on one defense and they'll reject it. Find something to fit the team, don't make the team fit you.

BOBBY DOUGLAS, wrestling, 1992 U.S. Olympic coach and Iowa State: More coaches have been ruined by trying to have an iron fist and treat everybody the same. That's a fact. There are certain athletes that you've got to treat different. Some wrestlers can't run; it tears them down. But maybe they can do forty miles on a mountain bike — I'll trade for that. You can use a talented wrestler as a stimulant for the rest of your athletes. But it's difficult. He may be so far ahead that you have to slow him down. Or you can get a gifted athlete who's capable of beating 90 percent of the guys without being in shape. All of a sudden you've got 80 percent of the rest of them saying, "If he doesn't have to do it, I don't have to do it." Or they see a wrestler who can't run sitting on the sidelines, and all of a sudden everybody thinks the best way to get in shape is to sit on the sidelines. It's a balancing act. You have to make sure everyone understands that you understand what's going on. It can be a dangerous thing.

SR. LYNN WINSOR, B.V.M., CAA, golf, Xavier College Prep, Phoenix, Arizona: Heather Farr put this golf program on the map. There is no other way to say it. When Heather came here, it was like the sun rising in the morning. First it shines on the trees, then it bounces off the trees and touches something else. Heather changed me. We're steadfast friends. We call each other once a week. With her cancer, we've become very close. [Farr died in November 1993 of complications from breast cancer.] With someone like Heather there comes a real responsibility to the talent. For sure. It's like when you're a kid and you get one of those little chicks at Easter time. Remember? You have to treasure something like that. Make sure it grows. This little feathery thing, and it's your responsibility. That's how I felt about Heather.

CHARLOTTE DAVIS, national head coach for U.S. syncronized

swimming since 1985; founded the Seattle Aqua Club in 1971: I started with Tracy [Ruiz] when she was nine [in Seattle]. By the time she was ten I knew I had something special. The first time I saw Candy [Costie], she was swimming for another club. I thought to myself, "WOW!" When they were twelve I sat them down and told them they were going to be national champions—at the time there was no Olympics, and the rest of the world wasn't at the U.S. level.

They laughed and giggled. It happened to be a day when they were goofing off. I pulled them aside after practice, and I told them. "You guys want this?" I had no idea how long it was going to take. I wasn't concerned with that. I was concerned with the fact that they understood that I thought they were special. It's exciting, it's exhilarating when you're a coach and you realize you're responsible for the kind of talent they had. I felt I had the ability to take them to the top. I never doubted myself. But they had to understand what possibilities the future held for them. [Ruiz won the solo gold at the 1984 Olympics; Ruiz and Costie won the duet gold. Ruiz won the solo silver in 1988.]

MIKE MARCOULIS, JR., *basketball and baseball, Freemont High, Oakland:* I had this one kid, he came from the projects. I don't know who his father is; I never met his mother. We went round and round. I had to kick him off the baseball team his senior year after he bad-mouthed the opposing coach. But I got him into a junior college in Wyoming. A black kid in Wyoming. He survived, got his A.A., came back to college and played a couple of years and graduated. He's doing real well.

I had another kid, his junior year he wanted to give it up. He'd had a couple of bad games, said he was going to become an electrician. I told him he couldn't quit. Don't give up on baseball. He goes to Fresno, plays three years, gets picked by the Giants in the first round, signs a bonus for $175,000. Someday he'll be a millionaire.

But you don't get through to every kid. There can be sixteen years of bad influence, a lot of poor self-esteem to fight through. And so you have kids who just don't make it. I had this one kid a couple of years ago, a tenth-grader, never would go to class. His brother was in the drug life. But I kept at him: "Why don't you get it together? Give it a shot." Finally, his junior year he comes out, plays, does well. Then comes a day and he doesn't want to run. You don't run, you don't play. Two weeks later he says he wants to play. So he starts playing. Plays well. Plays *great*. Doing fine in school, a real bright kid. Then he misses another day. "I had to get my brother out of jail." That was it. He stopped going to school. He got shot.

I had another kid, played for me as a junior. His senior year he played well again, but then I notice that he's out on the street selling drugs. "What are you doin'?" He got shot. Paralyzed from the waist down. If that doesn't cure you, nothing will. He's selling drugs from his wheelchair.

ALAN ROWAN, *track & field, Punahou School, Hawaii (retired):* I was born and raised in Hawaii. My folks migrated from Winnipeg, Canada, back in 1924. I coached for forty-one years; thirty-eight years at Punahou. My brother was the original impetus when we were kids back in the '30s. He got involved in the community sports programs. Being the younger brother, I tagged along.

We had some good programs on the islands. I won my first medal in the fifth grade for running the fifty-yard dash. In those days we were detached from the rest of the world, so to speak. It was all by ship. The island we were on, Maui, the population was about thirty-eight thousand and most of them were either employed in sugar or pineapple. The plantations pretty much controlled the islands. They provided housing, food, hospitals, they provided for just about all our needs. That was another time altogether.

The plantations provided the sports programs and created recreation for the employees. And everyone got caught up in it. I started out in a seventy-five-pound basketball league. I remember our fifth- through eighth-grade track meets would have five hundred youngsters in the all-island meets. In the fall we were into barefoot football. Plantation against plantation. The people enjoyed what they were doing. That's my background: You were supposed to enjoy it. As a coach that's something I've tried to convey to my teams.

That's why when a youngster turned out for the [Punahou track] team, there had to be a place for him. We carry youngsters who we know aren't going to make it, but because they take the time to come out, we're going to give them the opportunity.

When I was at USC, I ran the hurdles behind the two guys who finished second and third at the Helsinki Olympics in 1952. I could have said, "Forget it." The only way I had a chance was when they hit a hurdle. But I had a beautiful experience at USC because of the interest that the coaches took in me.

I'll never forget when I was a freshman. Dean Cromwell was the head coach. Probably the greatest track coach of all time. We were taking starts, and Dean had just finished working with Mel Patton, who at the time held the world record for the one-hundred-yard dash. And he walked by, and as I got into the blocks he came up behind me and hit me on the butt and said, "Good going, champ!" That's all I needed.

STAN MORRISON, *basketball, San Jose State [formerly at USC]:*
My assistant coach at USC, David Spencer, was the one who told me about these two young men at Dobbins Technical School in Philadelphia. "One is really polished, Bo Kimball. The other is a rugged kid who plays so hard it's unbelievable, Hank Gathers."

Bo was in the starting lineup early. Hank was a diamond in the rough. He wasn't ready to play yet. But he kept working at it. I'd never seen a more alive guy. He had a vitality, an energy. He wanted to learn. He was the worst free-throw shooter in history. I'd stay for an hour, and hour and a half after practice working on it. I talked to him about the dart theory of shooting. When you throw a dart you use the wrist. Why? Because your wrist never gets tired. Hank bought that. I said, "It's just like I said: You're the strongest man in the world." We got him up to 72 percent. I even let him shoot a technical foul once. He looked over and winked and shot the thing. He made it, too—it'd be a lousy story if he didn't, right?

When I got fired at USC, Tommy Lewis transferred to Pepperdine and Hank and Bo transferred to Loyola Marymount. I wrote them every year on October 15, the first day of practice. The first time Hank collapsed was in December. It was in a game against UC–Santa Barbara, where I was then the athletic director. I called the next day, and I said, "Some guys will do anything to avoid shooting a free throw." And he laughed. Then I asked if he was okay. "I'm scared to death," he said. I told him to do whatever the doctors told him. "Coach," he said, "I promise."

I was sitting at home watching games on TV, and I saw the flash come across on ESPN. At the time I didn't see the film footage of him going down. I just heard that he'd collapsed at another game. Then David Spencer [the assistant who recruited him to USC] called from the hospital. He was in tears. "I don't think he's going to make it." Then he called me back and said Hank was gone. I just broke down.

Then I saw it on television. And I will never forget this. I saw him running up the sideline, they showed the high pass and the slam dunk, and then I saw him stagger, and then I saw him go down. He tried to get up. I can still see the look in his eyes. The look of a champ. The champ's been knocked down, he knows he's in trouble and he knows that if he doesn't get up off the canvas the fight is over. "I've got to get up." But, of course, he couldn't.

RANDY JABLONIC, *rowing, University of Wisconsin:* When I coached the national team, it was a joke. "Look out for Jabo." Don't let him come up to you. *Don't let him put his hand on your shoulder.* That's his way of saying, "Joe, I'm sorry, you're not going to make the team." It got to the point where I'd walk up to a table, just come up to talk, and everybody'd be ducking sideways so I couldn't put my hand on their shoulders. I can laugh about it now, but it's always tough to tell a kid that he's not ready to do the job.

FRANK LAYDEN, *Utah Jazz (retired):* Some guys are a pain in the neck. Or a constant discipline problem. It's not hard to cut them. Others you can't reach. And there were a lot of players that for whatever reason didn't want it bad enough.

ANSON DORRANCE, *U.S. women's 1991 World Cup soccer champions and the University of North Carolina:* I took the core of the existing [women's national soccer] team and brought it back together. What I wanted to do was win the first women's World Cup. We felt it was going to be played in 1990; those were the rumors. So what I started doing in '87 was put together a team that could win in 1990. We eliminated a lot of the senior players, who were still outstanding, and brought in a bunch of [junior] players who had potential but at the time the seniors were still destroying. Unpopular decisions. But from a coaching standpoint they weren't difficult decisions. After watching these youth players, it was pretty easy to select them. Well, I say it was easy, but in the back of your mind you always feel that, well, who really knows?

Our senior team could have beaten our youth team at that point—and the senior players knew it. To replace them with the core of this youth team was a difficult political choice. There was a lot of hostility, because no one was really proven. But I was always thinking of the future. The now was not important. By the time we got to China and the World Cup, all six of those kids were starting against Norway in the World Cup Final.

Having to tell the six women who were cut, that was the hard part. I had a conference with each of them. I owed each player the right to object, to let me know her feelings. I stayed up all night with one, trying to explain to her how, even though this was my choice in terms of player selection, it didn't indict my friendship or respect for her as a person or as a player. It was very difficult for me to make those decisions.

It's difficult to separate personal feelings for the players from the objective coaching decisions. Players don't see the two as different. They take it as a personal attack. "Are you mad at me?" or "What have I done to you?" That sort of thing. The relationship with this particular person has recovered, thankfully, but at the time it was just shattering. This was her dream. Think about it: I am empowered as the coach to make or break someone's dream.

What people don't see is the connection you have with the players you're cutting. It's totally exhausting. Because if you genuinely care your pain is similar to theirs. You have to be so careful in the words you select. They're hanging on every word, trying to read into what you're saying some shred of connection. It's a bizarre conversation. They're desperate to know that you still care. At the same time they're desperate to sort of trap you with your own words. It's that or "You made this decision months ago." It's a combination of protection systems that they turn on to try and maintain their own sanity while at the same time they're trying to remain connected.

FRANK LAYDEN, *Utah Jazz:* For the players it starts in junior high. That's the bottom of the pyramid. By the time they get to the NBA there's only three hundred jobs left. It's easy to cut a Tom McMillen.

He was a Rhodes Scholar; you know he's going on to something else. But you also have to cut players who everybody's been counting on. He's put everything into this and nothing into anything else, and now there's no job for him.

This may sound crazy, and it's not an original thought, but sports have done more harm than good for blacks. What happens is, we get a lot of athletes who get out of school who do not have diplomas. Even if they do, they don't have an *education*. And if they can't make it in professional sports, they feel like a failure—even though they're not—because they put all that time into just one thing.

I cut a player once, and he committed suicide. His contract ran out, and he became a free agent. At that time you had to match. You had to give him the same salary or he had to go. I'm general manager and coach. I say, "Go out and see how valuable you think you are and then come back." Well, he did that and didn't get what he wanted. I think a lot about that.

DON NELSON, *Golden State Warriors:* It never gets easy. Manute Bol was a friend. But for us to trade him was the right thing to do. It was a good basketball decision. Sometimes the nicest guys, the best people, may not be the best players, and they have to go. With the [Milwaukee] Bucks I traded Junior Bridgeman after he'd played there many years. I traded Marques Johnson and Harvey Catchings, good friends. They went in one trade.

There are parts of this business that are cold, and that might be one of them. We're trying to create a family atmosphere in a cutthroat business. On one hand we've got free-agent players and they leave you; on the other hand players have us, and we can trade or cut them at any time. Yet while we're doing all this business stuff you have to create a family, a kind of love situation, among the members of the team and even the front office. It can be very difficult.

ANSON DORRANCE: There's always a tension before the last cut. Then, once the cut is made, the next practice is euphoric. That practice pulls the players together. Because they made it. Players will do almost anything to win the approval of their coach. During the whole cut process they're not close, because they're afraid they're not going to make it.

There's a tension between the coach and the players that dissolves upon the final roster selections. All of a sudden all kinds of positive things happen. You develop a closer rapport because they trust you now. You sense their excitement about having made the team. You selected them.

BOB ASHE, *soccer, Catlin Gable School, Portland, Oregon (retired):*
I grew up in Belfast. In Ireland, coaches aren't as revered as they are over here. I was brought up playing rugby, where the coach was not allowed to coach, even during halftime. That puts the onus of responsibility squarely on the players.

I have a picture of one of my soccer players. I've kept it for years. He's in the middle of the field and he's looking at me and he's got his hands out as if to say, "I couldn't do anything about it." Every time he kicked the ball, he looked over to see if I would nod or smile or scowl. I kept telling him, "Take responsibility!" I watch basketball on television, the college games. Players are always relating to their coach. Am I pleasing the coach? Is he mad at me? There's too much emphasis placed on the coach over here.

There's an English coach named Graham Ramsay. He says in Germany they don't play organized soccer under the age of twelve; they play pickup games. After age twelve they start working. It keeps the kids open-minded and creative. Because of that they produce players with flair and creativity.

The system here is that you need the pressure and the strength, that it's good for a kid. But there's a subtle difference between drilling somebody to death and allowing the creativity to flourish. Over here a kid gets the ball and everyone shouts, "Pass! Pass! Pass!" A kid needs to learn there are times when he should be encouraged to take his own man and go at him and try to beat him. You're not going to develop any Peles if every time a kid gets the ball he thinks he has to pass. You have to allow a kid to do something with his skills. Maybe there's a whole bunch of Wayne Gretzkys out there that don't ever come to the fore because it's coached out of them before they can do anything.

This isn't the case in girls' high school soccer. Girls' soccer isn't as well organized. As a result, there are always a couple of girls who are just dynamite. We had a girl, Tiffany; she's at the University of Portland now. Tiffany was just amazing. She'd get the ball, and it was obvious she was going to move, do something. Your heart would go into your mouth watching her.

I wonder sometimes if we're not organizing the fun out of the game and that's taking the creativity with it. A lot of kids get very tired not being able to please their coach. But where do you start pleasing yourself? Maybe that's where great coaching comes in. The great coach recognizes that moment as it's happening and is able to release his player.

RON O'BRIEN, *diving, Swimming Hall of Fame Aquatic Complex, Ft. Lauderdale, Florida:* To work with Greg Louganis was a coach's dream. To work with the best there ever was, I considered it a privilege. I'd stand there watching these great things happen *in practice.* I got to see him, good as he was, continue to improve day after day, month after month, year after year. For ten years.

After he won both the three-meter and the platform in '84, we talked about the double-double in '88. Two gold medals in back-to-back Olympics. It had only been done once before, by Pat McCormick in '52 and '56, and never by a man and never by anyone in the modern era of the Communist countries. We talked about it once, and then I don't think we ever talked about it again. We both mutually chose not to talk about it, and instead we focused on the process.

The three-meter event [in 1988] was first. I talk to him before he does each dive, then after he comes back I give him a critique. I remember in the qualifying round he was getting ready for his two-and-a-half-somersault pike. I don't know whether you can call it a premonition, but I had this feeling he was going to hit the board. I remember thinking, "Should I tell him to jump the dive out?" I had to make an on-the-spot decision, and I decided not to say anything. He took what we call the "hurtle" to the end of the board, and I knew he was in trouble and he didn't realize it. After he hit the board, my first thought was, "Is it over right here?" I didn't think it was serious, but I could tell he'd gotten a heck of a whiplash. If the board had hit him in the back of the head, it could have knocked him out.

He got out of the water by himself, and the doctors put some temporary stitches in. Then I grabbed him and we took off down a hallway to another pool, where there wasn't anybody around. He said,

"I've worked too hard and too long not to try." We were doing what they call "bonding." Bonding together all the things we had been through together prior to that moment in the ten years of our relationship. Every adversity that we ever went through together, worked through together, was responsible, in some way, for getting us through that. We leaned on each other. We used everything we'd ever learned to get us through that situation.

I told him to jump in the practice pool. It was cold, and that kind of woke him up. Then he went out and did a great dive; he did the best dive that was done in both days of that competition. He qualified for the finals in third place.

But the next day when he got up I knew he was in trouble psychologically. He looked . . . I wouldn't say scared, but very tentative. He hadn't slept, and I sensed on the bus on the way over that he was not real confident. Normally when we warm up we have a set routine: He only does so many dives and then we get right out. But I could tell that unless I made him do that dive until he regained his confidence, he was going to be really questioning whether or not he could do it. I realized I was going to have to provide the aggressiveness. "Do another one! Do another one! Do another one! It looks good, but you've got to do this. Do another one!" Then I said, "Okay, you're fine. Put it on automatic." He blocked it out and went up there and did it. One of the best dives he'd done in years.

The platform competition was a reverse image of Greg's first Olympics in '76. Then he was the sixteen-year-old in the lead with one dive to go when Klaus Dibiasi, the defending gold medalist, beat him on the last dive. It's fitting that it came down to the same thing again, with Greg this time the veteran. Going into Greg's last dive, Xiong Ni had a 3-point lead. Greg needed about 8⅓s. The judging had been tough; there was a possibility he could do an excellent dive and not get enough points.

If you go back to the videotape, you'll see a shot of me looking up at the ten-meter platform and then bringing my eyes down to the water. I was running my own videotape replay of exactly how I wanted to see that dive, a three-and-a-half somersault. Every coach has his superstitions. I try to project a concentration level across the space between myself and my diver and actually send positive vibrations and dots and images to them just by the way I'm thinking.

Greg was already crying by the time he got out of the water. He didn't know at that point whether he'd won. He was crying because he'd just done his last competitive dive. That was his first emotion. When he got around the corner of the platform, the place went nuts. He looked up at the scoreboard and then he saw my son Tim pick me up and swing me around like a rag doll, and he knew he'd won. That was the moment.

We had been building to the double-double for four years. We had done everything we could not to acknowledge that it even existed. But underlying that, every day we'd gotten up and we knew there was something unique going on here. It was like there was this third person following us around everywhere we went. For four years we had submerged ourselves totally into the job at hand, the process, the day-to-day routine. So what I felt right then was relief, just this unbelievable relief. And it all came out in that one moment.

One-on-One: Reggie Joules

The first time I saw Reggie Joules, I was living in Fairbanks, Alaska. He was competing in the blanket toss at the 1979 Eskimo-Indian Olympics at the University of Alaska in Fairbanks. In the blanket toss, about thirty-five people clutch a walrus hide maybe twenty feet in diameter and use their collective energies to snap a person high into the air. It is a dangerous, breathtaking event, the signature moment of the Eskimo-Indian Olympics.

An Inupiak Eskimo from Kotzebue, Alaska, in the Northwest Arctic, Reggie dominated this event (as well as a couple of others) throughout much of the '70s and early '80s. That night he stood in the center of the blanket, bobbing gently. Then it started, the crowd counting in unison. One, two, three, FOUR. And there he was, in the air, rising gracefully to the ceiling. At the apex of his flight, Reggie dislodged a ceiling tile, maybe forty feet above the floor. Back on the blanket he looked at the ceiling, then turned and talked to his tossers. And then he was off again, up in the air, soaring toward the ceiling—where he replaced the tile, pretty as you please. Gold medal, Reggie Joules, by acclamation.

Over the years Reggie has served as player, coach, charge de mission, guiding light, and Elder at the Eskimo-Indian Olympics as well as at the Arctic Winter Games, a biennial sports festival for the people of Alaska and the Yukon and

Northwest Territories in Canada. He is forty years old, married with four children, and lives in Kotzebue, where he works for the school district. He serves on the board of directors of the Eskimo-Indian Olympics and coaches when asked. He still takes the occasional ride on the walrus hide, he says, to keep the young bucks in line.

My first recollections of life are from down at St. Michael's, south of Nome, where my grandfather was a teacher. Then he got transferred to Deering, which is just south of Kotzebue. In 1958, 1959 we moved to Kotzebue.

Every Christmas the community would stop what it was doing and gather at the community hall. They'd have this big Eskimo games tournament. The community hall would be packed. There wouldn't be any room at all. But it's not the athletes that I remember best; it was the Elder who ran the games. He ruled with an iron fist. Most of the time I remember that the Elder was Woody Goodwin, Sr., who carried a lot of weight in the village. He was a good provider, and people respected him for that.

So many of the [individual] games are tied to one's ability to provide for the family. Especially for the male. Theirs was a life of hunting and fishing and gathering. You had to be strong, you had to be strong long, you had to be quick, you had to be agile, with a good sense of balance. The games reflect this kind of demand.

There are all kinds of games. The one-foot high kick—you try to kick a fur ball by hopping on one foot and then kicking the ball with the foot you're hopping on and landing on that same foot. Or the two-foot high kick, where you jump off both feet. The seal hop. The kneel and jump. Or the four-man carry, where four people hang on you and you see how far you can carry them.

I never competed in these games until I was a senior in high school. I went away to boarding school when I was fourteen and I didn't come home until Christmas my senior year. I had an older sister who had married into one of the families of Point Hope, so I went up there. She informed the people that I was coming to town, and even before I arrived I'd been selected to be on a team at the community hall.

I learned a couple of things that night. I found out that I had some natural ability. I had never done the high kicks before and I was pushing the champ. But the big lesson was that even though it was competitive, everybody was willing to coach me—even the people I was competing against. That made a lasting impression on me. It's the reason I got into coaching. When I started competing, coaching

the others was the natural thing for me to do. It didn't make any difference to me whether the guy I helped beat me.

When I graduated from high school in 1970, I decided to compete in the games in Kotzebue on the Fourth of July. I won the two-foot high kick and placed second in the one-foot. Back then, the Chamber of Commerce sent the winners to the [Eskimo-Indian] games in Fairbanks. I didn't do much that year, but I got hooked. The next year I started collecting medals.

It was always the coaching that kept me [involved in the native games], even when I was still competing. I coached Lady Larue from Bethel [the premier woman one-foot and two-foot high kicker in the early '80s]. She was a heck of a gifted athlete, real hot stuff, the easiest athlete I ever worked with. I loved her attitude. It was always "fresh start, can do."

It's so much fun to be with the younger folks. Maybe you'd be watching them, and then you'd have the pleasure of showing them that they could do it and watch them grow from there. It reminds me of this one girl. She was at a clinic, just standing there. I asked if she was scared because the boys were bigger. I said, "Look, I'm shorter than all of them and I can kick their butts six ways to Sunday." She ended up taking third at States.

The Games gave me an avenue to express myself as an Inupiak person.

By the time I was ready to go out hunting, my grandfather was too old to take me. When I got married my friends insisted that I learn to provide for my family in the traditional way. Because I was involved in the Games by then, I could see the relevancy of how they fit into and were meaningful to our culture.

I'm a small part German and five-eighths Inupiak and there might be some Laplander in there. When you're of mixed blood as a kid, you're in no-man's-land. It was the Games that gave me a sense of belonging. They cemented my identity. That's why it was always pedal to the medal. Competing in these Games, coaching these Games, they changed the direction of my life. They opened my eyes to what I could do. Of who I was and what I was all about.

SEVEN

Winning and Losing

Boiling hot dogs. Bobbie Schultz has put a dozen years between herself and those boiling hot dogs, and still she can't forget them. She'll be outside, at a baseball game maybe, and she'll catch a heavy, steamy whiff. And just like that it's all those years ago at the New Jersey state field hockey championship game. Out on the field her girls from Shawnee High in Medford are getting beat by Wayne Hills High. Behind her on the bench is that pot of boiling hot dogs. And standing on the sidelines is Bobbie Schultz, one trapped coach.

"I remember thinking I was going to get sick," Bobbie Schultz recalls. "I went in overconfident and we lost. We never got off the bus. I knew once the second half started and we still couldn't penetrate that it was over. I felt nauseous, just nauseous." Final score: Wayne Hills 3, Shawnee 0.

"I was unable to think," she says. "I was too emotionally involved in what was happening to look for a way to cure it. It was horrible. I got so wrapped up in the fact that we weren't playing well, that I wasn't coaching them well, that it took me two months to figure out what I could have done. It took me that long for my mind to clear enough to see." Never mind that Bobbie Schultz has won seven state titles. She has yet to escape those boiling hot dogs.

Winning and losing; losing and winning. Two sides of the same coin. Give it a flip and take your chances. "There is nothing to compare to what coaches do," insists Bob Lucey, the football coach at Curtis High in Tacoma, Washington. "Once a week you step out there in front of all these people and try to get somebody else who's doing the same thing you are." Someone will lose and someone will win. "And one of you could end up looking *real* bad. You risk that all the time."

CHUCK NOLL, *Pittsburgh Steelers (retired):* I was speaking to a group of executives, and one of them came up to me. He was a vice president, a big executive, and he said, "You're lucky. You've got a scoreboard." At first I didn't follow what he meant. "After it's over, you've got a scoreboard to tell you whether you're right or wrong. Most people, they're never sure."

BARBARA JEAN JACKET, *1992 women's Olympic track & field coach; Prairie View A&M (retired):* I was born back in 1935 in Port Arthur, Texas. My mother was a single mom. Eva Mae Getwood Pickney. She raised three kids all by herself. Port Arthur took care of its own. Port Arthur made me tough. We had a saying in school: Everybody had to pass on 10th Street and Lincoln. They had a mailbox there, and if you got mad at somebody you said, "Meet me by the mailbox." And we'd fight.

To quote my uncle, he said that losing wasn't in my vocabulary. There weren't any girls that lived on our block to play with. I was the only girl out there playing football. I could hit, too. There was this one lady that told my mom that I wasn't ever going to be anything. I made up my mind right then that I was going to be somebody.

MIKE MARCOULIS, JR., *basketball and baseball, Freemont High School, Oakland:* I went to my father's funeral that day and coached the game that night. It never crossed my mind not to. I just wanted to be back coaching, be with my friends, with my players. My father would have done the same thing. He was a coach for thirty years. We'd shoot baskets; we'd play catch in the backyard. I played for him in Babe Ruth. As I got older we used to talk a lot about why he did this, how he did that. Coaching that game was something I was determined to do. Like the other coach said after the game: "I know why you coached this game. I can see your father's fire in your eyes."

DICK VERMEIL, *Philadelphia Eagles (retired):* One of my strengths is also one of my faults. I always believed I was responsible for the loss. I probably carried that too far, because it gnawed away at my inner, deep confidence. We'd lose a game on a fumble, and I'd be mad I called that play. That kind of rationale whips you. I'd say it to the press: We didn't do a good job. That floors the media, completely disarms them. But say it enough and you start to believe it.

I think it goes back to how you were raised. Being too driven. My dad owned a garage right next to the house, and it was there seven days a week. I was around him all the time. He was a very intense, vocal guy, demanding. I mean, he was on your ass continually. I think it did help me a lot to get pushed like that and to have a lot demanded of me at an early age. But it also gnaws at your confidence. You never knew if you were good enough. You never knew if you did anything good enough to satisfy him.

JIM VAN HORN *(was a volunteer basketball assistant at Allentown and Lafayette Colleges, both in Pennsylvania; he owns a sports-marketing company):* As a young kid I was fortunate to play on a top high school team with a high school all-America. I don't think that as a high school kid I had any desire to be an NBA player. I didn't have any intention to go to college. I just liked basketball. Then my senior year, all of a sudden Dean Smith walks in the door and asks me if I'd like to go to a college in North Carolina. He was at our school to recruit Larry Miller [the all-America], but he wasn't kidding; he had come looking for Jim Van Horn. He recruited me to Elon College, where a friend of his coached. And all of a sudden here was an opportunity to move on.

When my career came to an immediate halt—I got hurt my freshman year—I think what happened is that part of my life stopped. People always talk about the frustrated high school athlete, the guy who became the fanatical Little League coach. Why is this guy so fanatical? It's because something in all these people stopped one day. It stopped *personally.* They had fallen in love with something that gave them the ability to be singled out as somebody important. And then it stopped.

After I got hurt, I went to Allentown College, which at the time didn't have a basketball team. I graduated and got into business, and I realized that I wanted a piece of that back. I became an assistant at

Allentown [which now had a team]. I was just helping out. But I got the bug again.

JIM SHORT, *wrestling, Simley High, Inver Grove Heights, Minnesota:* I named my first son after the kid who beat me. John. When he was born, his mother asked if I wanted to name him after me. I said, "No, I want a first-place name." John had beaten me in high school. I wrestled him five times. In the finals at States we had another good battle, but I lost 3–2. It was definitely a bummer, no question about it. It was devastating at the time, but what it does is it gives you a lot of resolve to make a name for yourself. All I wanted to do was put something back into the sport as a coach, come back and win some individual state titles and a state team title.

I don't want to say that [state-final] defeat was entirely my motivation, but it's been at least 50 percent of it. They never remember who was second—it's true. I was not going to be satisfied with being a second-rate coach. I was going to do everything to be the best coach I could. [In 1985, twenty years to the day of Jim Short's state-final defeat, his son John won a state wrestling title.]

BILL MUSSELMAN, *first coach of the Minnesota Timberwolves (now with a CBA team in Rochester, Minnesota):* I have to have competition. Sometimes I'll leave for the airport late, just to see if I get there in time. I'll play PacMan until I beat the highest score on the board. I play somebody in racquetball, I'll let him beat me the first game. Now he thinks he's better than me. Now I'm having fun, now I've got some competition, now I've got to rise to the occasion.

I've always loved challenges. I wonder what makes me like that? Like, when I lose a job, it's okay. A lot of guys would panic. I never panic. If I'm out of a job I know I'll get a job. It creates a new challenge. A lot of it has to do with my mother, I think. My mother had cancer. She beat it. I went home for her birthday. She's seventy-eight. We went out and shot hoops.

Are you born competitive? I don't know. But for some reason I have an unbelievably competitive nature. As a kid, I used to eat and sleep sports. A great day was playing ball all day. I loved it. It's the same with coaching. My mind can get away from the problems of life. Maybe it's escape.

I had a tragic accident happen to me early in life. One of my best friends I went to high school with and then on to college, we were playing in a pickup game. I was running down to the other end and I hear this thump. I turn around, and he's dropped over of a heart attack. Guy was twenty-one years old. He died on a basketball floor. That had a great impact on me.

My brother got into a serious accident his senior year in high school. I came home one night and he was in the hospital with practically every bone in his face broken. I was playing college football, and he's in and out of the hospital getting plastic surgery. I'd go over to see him before games. It would get me fired up.

There's times in your life when you realize that there's not a lot of time in your life. Through sports I've seen it all. Life's not easy. There are going to be ups and downs. Don't ever let the downs in life get to you. I will not let anything get me down. I battle life.

STEPHANIE VANDERSLICE GAITLEY, *basketball, St. Joseph's University, Philadelphia:* It was the fourth grade, and my mom coached against me, and they won the championship and I came home and cried and I didn't talk to her all night. Dolores Tripoletti stole the ball and she made it 6 to 4, and I went home and cried. I had never thought about losing before, never thought what it might feel like. When it finally happened I took it real hard. And my mom was the other coach! The competitiveness began then. It began in the fourth grade. It was already in my blood.

TIM WILKE, *girls' basketball, Lowmira High, Wisconsin:* There's times when I wake up at 3 in the morning and feel like jumping out of bed and watching a tape. Doing something. I've got this friend, he's a coach, and he's as nuts as I am. On game nights, sometimes he'll come over at 1:30 in the morning and get me out of bed, and we'll talk for hours. It's crazy. But I love basketball.

JIM ZULLO, *basketball, Shenendehowa High, Clifton Park, New York:* The thing that kept me coaching was that I wasn't very good. The game was so fast! I'd catch a mistake, and while I was thinking about how to fix it, they'd scored and now somebody else was making a mistake. I stumbled along, did well enough to get the job where I am now. They had never won; it was the graveyard of coaches. I lost my first year, and it drove me nuts. I decided to do it till I got it right.

I was at Shenendehowa ten years before I won a championship. It took me ten years! I couldn't win, and I didn't know why. I almost got fired a couple of times. There was intense pressure from myself. I wasn't good enough. We were never able to beat the really good teams for the longest time. Once we lost in overtime on a half-court shot. It killed me, but I was determined I'd keep doing it until I won a championship.

Winning breeds winning. We've won nine straight league championships now. I think I'm supposed to win and my kids think they're supposed to win. The other team, *they* think we're supposed to win. That's a big help. And the referees, they think we're supposed to win, too. In the last minutes of a game there's a real psychology going on. The other team doesn't get the call because we're supposed to win. Absolutely.

SUZIE McCONNELL, *basketball, Oakland Catholic High, Pittsburgh (member of the 1988 U.S. Olympic gold-medal basketball team and 1992 bronze-medal team):* It took me a long time to get over that game. [The 1992 Olympic loss to the Russians, which eliminated the U.S. from gold-medal contention.] I do a lot of motivational speaking—to kids, high school students—and I talk about it. Winning the bronze as compared to winning the gold. What it comes down to is expectations.

Winning another gold medal is what motivated me to make the comeback. In 1988 I was a completely different person than I was in 1992. [In 1988] I was right out of college, I wasn't married, I hadn't had a baby, I didn't have a career. My son was born in October of 1990, and it was in February of '91 that I decided to make a comeback. I hadn't picked up a ball, I hadn't run in two years. It was a long process.

I've always been very competitive, especially with myself, even in the classroom. I have always expected myself to do well. I expected to win [in the 1992 Olympics]. The toughest game I ever had to get motivated for was the bronze medal game [against Cuba]. We'd had our sights set on the gold. It was a close at halftime, maybe a 2-point game. It was the only time Coach [Theresa Grentz] ever yelled at us. At that level you're dealing with professionals, self-motivated people. You shouldn't have to raise your voice. But I think she could see it all slipping away. Going home without any medal at all. It made me realize how much I hate to lose.

This year we lost the WPIAL [Western Pennsylvania Interscholastic Athletic League] title to Upper St. Clair, 51–47, and then we had to jump right back into it to get ready for the States. It was just like when we lost to the Russians and had to jump into the bronze-medal game. I talked about that with my team before a couple of the games [in the state tournament].

I thought about it again when I walked out for the [state] championship game at the Hershey Arena. I didn't want the reputation that I couldn't win the big one. That was my fear. In 1988 I'd won a gold medal but I wasn't a starter; in 1992 I was the starting point guard and we didn't win it. This was another big one, and I didn't want to lose again. [McConnell's team won.]

BILL WHITMORE, *athletic director, Concord school district, New Hampshire:* When I was [head coach at the University of] Vermont, every kid I coached graduated. But we also had to play Villanova, Michigan, Notre Dame, Dayton, North Carolina, North Carolina State, Tennessee, Vanderbilt. We needed the money to pump up our program. I killed myself to be mediocre. We beat Rick Pitino three times in one year. We beat Ohio State when they were ranked two or three in the country. We went to Notre Dame and lost by 8. I thought we won the game! But there isn't an asterisk next to that L on my record saying, "He did a hell of a job." I wanted to win. I wanted to win more. It would be like being a surgeon and you're doing the best you can, except that 50 percent of your patients die.

NAN AIROLA, *volleyball, Providence Catholic High, New Lenox, Illinois:* I've never taken time off, even when I was pregnant. I pushed, pushed, pushed. I just love it. I got more into it as the years went on. Being pregnant and raising kids, all that, I never lost the competitiveness. As a first-year coach I was crazy. I'd get sick. I'd sit in my office and sweat. One time when I was pregnant I took off a week. Another time I lost a baby during the season. The season had just started, and it was the end of the pregnancy. It wasn't because of the season. It was just too much. I remember battling through that.

ROY CHIPMAN, *basketball, University of Pittsburgh (retired):* I was insulted and sort of depressed that the camaraderie among the coaches, the farther up the ladder you go, deteriorates. There's almost like this silent war going on.

FRANK LAYDEN, *Utah Jazz (retired):* Everything's a bitter fight now. In college it's the recruiting that separates everybody. In the pros, it's all the games. Very seldom do the coaches shake hands.

HUBIE BROWN, *New York Knicks (retired):* You all have the same goal, and only one person reaches that goal every year.

STAN MORRISON, *basketball, San Jose State:* When I'm at a clinic I always listen to the other coaches. In a clinic environment coaches say things they would never say anywhere else. Everybody gravitates to their areas of strength. Go to a cocktail party, and all the man-to-man coaches are in one corner and all the zone coaches are in the other. It almost gets that crazy.

JIM SATALIN, *basketball, Duquesne (retired):* A lot of times you'll see a coach pick as his best friend among the other coaches the guy who always loses to him. He's a good guy, but he's also a good guy because he's beaten him.

STAN MORRISON: The closer you are to a coach, the more competitive it gets. I really enjoyed coaching against Gary Colson at Fresno, Jerry Pimm at UC Santa Barbara. I have great respect for those guys. I enjoyed coaching against Ralph Miller at Oregon State. Certainly Lute Olson at Arizona. I enjoyed Larry Brown when he was at UCLA. Those guys were on top of their game. If I could get players in the same neighborhood, I felt I had a good chance to go after them.

DICK MacPHERSON, *New England Patriots (retired):* One of the toughest games I had to play when I was head coach at Syracuse was against West Virginia and Don Nehlen. He's one of my best friends. We'd been coaches together coming up. We changed diapers for each other's kids, all that. I hated to play him. We didn't talk the week before. I couldn't wish him well before the game because I had to think of my program. There was no joy in beating him, and I hated to lose to him. I'd rather it be somebody over there I don't know.

DAVE LAFFERTY, *girls' basketball, Vinson High, Huntington, West Virginia; boys' basketball, Ceredo-Kenova High, Kenova, West Virginia:* There's this one coach who's known to be a real gentleman when everything's going right. When his team starts losing he'll do anything to win. Cuss his players, cuss my players, anything. It went all over me. I got all fired up. "Come on down, anything you want." He didn't move.

STAN MORRISON: There are schools that are infamous for making sure everything goes wrong when you're on the road. Your shootaround on game day? You get there and they say, "The faculty has the gym now." You either have a major scene or leave. The locker rooms are either freezing or boiling. There's no supplies, no towels. They don't knock on your door when there's five minutes left in the half. "Game starts in thirty seconds!" If your team is small, you want a lot of air in the ball and tight rims to kick the ball out on long rebounds; if their team is tall they'll loosen the rims and take some air out so they can win the jumping contests. Death by a thousand cuts.

NICK HYDER, *football, Valdosta High, Georgia:* The coach who says his team is going to be the sorriest has the best team. One time this one coach said his offensive team was so sorry he could put them on the ten-yard-line without any defense on the other side and they wouldn't be able to score against a light drizzle. Then another coach said, "My team's so sorry that when the crowd yells the vibration knocks them down."

JIM SHORT: Every coach downplays what he's got. Some of that's phony, but in some respects it's a way to keep from becoming a jerk. When you've got a good team, it's real easy to be a jerk.

Coaches were jerks to me. We started our program with kids who had never wrestled before. I used to come home after a meet when we'd get drubbed 40–7 and I'd put on Roger Whitaker. He's mellow music and I needed that. I'd sit on the couch, and my wife would sit next to me, and I'd say, "I don't know why I'm doing this."

We had losing seasons for at least five years. When I got to the top I vowed I would never be like some of the coaches I'd coached against. One coach told me, "I don't think you can give us any competition." Maybe he was being honest, but he was being a jerk, too. Sometimes honesty is not the best policy. Shutting up is the best policy.

I vowed to get that team. And I did. We ended up humiliating him—you can't tell your kids not to pin their man. Everybody has his day; everybody gets beat. That coach taught me a valuable lesson: Someday we'll get beat; in the meantime, don't be a jerk.

HARRY VANDERSLICE, *Little League baseball, Ocean City, New Jersey:* It was during our championship game for the eleven- to twelve-year-olds. Our pitcher's on the mound; they have the bases loaded. Their coach is coaching third base, and suddenly he yells to our pitcher, "Let me see the ball." Our kid throws him the ball. The coach steps aside, the ball rolls into the dugout, and two runs score.

Man, I was hot. But I don't believe in showing your temper in front of the kids, so I waited. Three years later I'm playing the same coach again. He had his big kid pitching. There were two outs and the bases were loaded, and the guy we have up has struck out five times already.

I called time and told him to do *exactly* what I said. "When the pitcher goes into his windup, drop your bat." He gets back in the box and drops the bat when the windup starts. The pitcher stops, the umpire calls a balk, the runners are advanced, and we win the game. Just like that. This coach comes running over. I'd waited three years. "Me, tell a kid to do something like that?" I said. "You've got to be kidding." Then I said, "Payback's beautiful, isn't it?" That's the way I rationalized it.

DERRIL KIPP, *girls' basketball, Maine West High, Des Plaines, Illinois:* Let's just say I was in over my head the first year we went downstate—that's what they call the state championship. It's breathtaking. I didn't know the court was ten feet longer than our floor. I couldn't figure out why every time we pressed they'd get a layup. Even after the game was over I didn't know. That first year the girls were up the night before, all excited, making flowers instead of sleeping. You know—those tissue-paper flowers to decorate the bus. We go down a day and a half early now.

The second time I thought we had a good shot. Then two of the girls got salmonella. We put one to bed at the motel, and she's getting worse and worse. She tried to get up and fell over. We take her to the hospital, they look at her and say she has the flu and put her on antibiotics. Remember the big case they had with the salmonella in the milk? She was the first case and the worst one; she almost died.

We won the first game without her. Then my point guard got salmonella. We brought up freshmen and held the ball. I think it was 4–2 at the quarter. Everybody was booing, but we had no choice. We had them beat. We lost 27–24, and we were up with two minutes left.

Winning a championship, a lot of it is luck. Once you get to that situation, unless one team is far and above the best, the team that's lucky wins. We went downstate five times before we won. And then the year we won, it was pretty much by luck, by making a last-second shot.

BOBBY CREMINS, *basketball, Georgia Tech:* It was the most depressing moment of my life. I wanted to win so much. Not just for myself but for my teammates and for my coach, Frank McGuire, and for the fans at South Carolina. They are incredible fans. And then everything was spoiled.

That year, 1970, we were undefeated in the ACC going into the ACC tournament in Charlotte at the old Coliseum. We played North Carolina State in the ACC championship game. It was a tie game, and John Roche threw me the ball, and I went to get it and Ed Leftowitz intercepted and laid it up. I didn't know know how to handle [the loss]. My best friend tried to console me, but it didn't do any good. I had to get away. He had a friend who had a place up in the mountains of Asheville, so we went there. Us and a couple cases of beer.

I got a little revenge in 1985. We won an ACC championship in Atlanta. I thought back to that game I lost as a player. "Well, I got a little bit back." Then we played for the [ACC] championship again in 1990, and this time we're in the same city. Winning it then, back in Charlotte, that was full redemption. I remember after the game we were on the team bus driving back, and ironically we drove right by the old Coliseum.

I told the bus driver to slow down and I said, "I got you back, you son of a bitch!"

That loss back in 1970 made me a better coach. That loss really did me in. Basketball is my whole life, and I wanted to win it *so much*. But I've learned because of that moment. Every coach, every year, is going to have to go through the tough losses. Every year it'll happen. When we made it to the Final Four in 1990, I didn't feel real bad after we lost. When I walked into the locker room after the game, I couldn't believe how the kids were reacting, how they were hugging each other, how they were saying what a great year it was. "We got here! We lost, but we *got here!*" There was a time as a coach when I would have said something, but not anymore.

PAT HEAΓ SUMMITT, *basketball, University of Tennessee:* [Summitt's Lady Volunteers made seven trips to the Final Four before winning a championship, in 1987.] There was a time when I was so driven to reach that goal [an NCAA championship] that maybe I didn't have the grand vision. We were doing things right—graduating players—and we had discipline. We had great opportunities to travel, and there were wonderful experiences for our student athletes. But I was so driven to push it to that next level that maybe I didn't stop and enjoy all the other things. This energy from within, that desire to be the best. I've had it from the time I was a little kid. Whether it was playing my dad in checkers or competing on a basketball court. I hate to lose.

There was a point where I thought we'd never get over the hump. That was a real concern. In '84, when we played Southern Cal for the championship, we led that game for thirty minutes. I can remember thinking, If we can get over this hurdle and win this thing. . . . Quite honestly, I thought about retiring. Later that summer I was going to coach the Olympic team and I was thinking: national championship and gold medal, let's do something different. [Not winning the NCAA championship] brought me back.

What happened was I finally got to the point where I felt that we did have one of the top programs in women's basketball. I realized there is more to this job than winning a national title—if you don't realize that it's very shallow thinking. And I finally knew [a national championship] was going to happen.

That's why in 1987 it was such a sweet victory. We were not expected to win; there wasn't any pressure. It was very special. And we got the monkey off our backs. It was completely different than winning the [Olympic] gold medal in 1984. I was too exhausted after that to even feel any celebration inside or any thrill of winning—there is so much pressure at that level. But this [1987] was a tremendous high. I was so excited for our players, and our program, the whole school. There were a lot of tears. The pressure I felt all those years when we were knocking on the door but never won, plus the responsibility I felt as the Olympic coach, I mean, all of that was over with: Okay, now I can get on with being the coach at the University of Tennessee. [The Lady Vols won again in 1989 and 1991.]

P. J. CARLESIMO, *basketball, Seton Hall: [Carlesimo's 1989 team went to the championship game of the NCAA tournament.]* In the NCAA it's lose and go home. You're day to day, game to game. Play until you lose, then put away the uniform. You can't handle it any other way.

Now you're in the regionals. We beat Indiana on a Thursday and now we're playing Vegas on Saturday. We beat Vegas and it's great. *We're going to the Final Four!* But then almost immediately it's "Who are we playing? *Who are we playing?*" Get the tapes, here we go, bing, bing, bing! What time are we leaving? Where are we staying?" You get to the Final Four and there's practice, meals, tutors, press conferences, family, friends, tickets. You don't have time to go, "Wow! This is the Final Four!"

It wasn't until after we beat Duke [in the semifinal] and we came out to scout Illinois-Michigan and then we're going back to the hotel and it's Saturday night, and now it starts to sink in that on Monday night we're playing for the national championship. It sneaks up on you. There's this party on Sunday night that's essentially a New York City thing. By then we were as prepared as we were going to get. It must have been midnight; the kids were asleep. So we went to the party.

We're driving back and we're looking at each other and laughing because we're playing for the national championship. You gotta laugh. You've got to pinch yourself. "Do you believe this? We're going back to the hotel and tomorrow we're going to play for the national championship."

The championship game, that's a strange one. It's the only game you play all year where you know there will be nothing else. The season's over. Today. Up till then the idea was to keep playing. But that's not the way it is the last night. We're going back home to New Jersey tomorrow, and we're either going to be national champs or we're not. That's a very unique feeling. Everybody wants to be in this game, but you're the one.

You can't walk on the floor for the Final Four your first time and tell yourself it's just another game. [In the semifinal, Duke, led by Danny Ferry, jumped in front 29–8 midway through the first half. The Hall won 95–78.] Maybe it helped Duke that they had been there before. But they played great for the first ten minutes and we played lousy. We were really struggling. I just wanted us to *play*. That's your worst nightmare: not playing well. You work all year—in a way you've worked your whole life. And maybe this is the only time you'll get there.

You could be Michael Jordan and you still want that first shot to go down. That's what happened to us. We couldn't get it down. I took time-outs. There was nothing to tell them, nothing to change. Danny Ferry was playing great. There was nothing we could do. It didn't matter what the score was. It didn't matter how much time was left. I just wanted us to start playing. People have said to me, "That's not an easy way to think when you're in the national semifinal," but that's honestly what was in my mind. *Just play.* After one time-out, we scored. Then Darryl Walker hit another jump shot, and it was like, "Okay, we're playing." [In the final, Seton Hall lost to Michigan 80–79 in overtime; Rumeal Robinson made two foul shots with three seconds left in overtime for the win.] If Rumeal misses those free throws, who knows? When you get in a game that close, silly things happen. A lucky shot, a great play, a tough call. It could be anything. You don't really have control. People have asked me, "Would you do anything different?" Sure. If I know Rumeal makes those free throws, I tell our kids not to go near him. But it's a stupid question. Because basically, no, I wouldn't do anything different. Because I can't. We were prepared. Our kids played loose and hard, and we got beat.

DICK VERMEIL: I allowed it to happen. The Super Bowl, for one reason or another, was sort of an anticlimax to the NFC championship game against Dallas. It had taken us five years to get to that point [the

NFC championship]. We'd been on a crusade. Beating Dallas, as intense as that was, it was like we already had the feeling that we did it. We never talked about going to the Super Bowl. It was always *win the NFC championship game.* The end result is we go to the Super Bowl, but that whole year we never had as our goal to go to the Super Bowl. I couldn't picture ourselves as a Super Bowl team. But I could picture ourselves beating Dallas in the NFC championship. If I had it to do over again, I'd approach that whole year differently.

JERRY REYNOLDS, *basketball, coach turned general manager, Sacramento Kings:* The better you are, the more you are ultimately doomed to failure. There will always be a game that you don't win, and that becomes the big game you could never win.

JOHN WINKIN, *baseball, University of Maine:* I can tell you every pitch of every key loss I've ever been in. In '47 we won a state Legion championship, and then we went to Torrington, Connecticut, and reached the regional final. We had to wait four days because of the rain. I remember practicing in the halls, waiting. And then we lost in the eleventh inning, 1–0, on what should have been a double play, and we failed to execute and they scored. You never forget, never.

DON NELSON, *Golden State Warriors:* You enjoy the wins during the off-season. The losing's too hard on me. I don't mind the traveling, the road, all that. It's putting all your efforts into winning and then not being successful. It's too much. You go like hell to win thirty-five games and there's still forty-seven losses. It's too much.

DICK VERMEIL: I'm a very emotional, overintense guy. But I believe I handled the [1980 Super Bowl] loss real well. I was down and disturbed and mad at myself, but I don't remember it carrying over for a real long time. I didn't dwell on that loss and I don't think I ever have. Now, I can remember losing during the regular season, and geez, it would kill me. It's one of the reasons I got out of coaching. The loss was so devastating that I wasn't doing a good job refocusing for the next game. But the final game of the year you don't have another game to prepare for. It's all of a sudden, Pow, you lost. You're emotionally drained—me especially. But you don't have to gear it up the next day.

GEORGE KARL, *Seattle Supersonics:* My first year as a pro coach I'm with Cleveland and we start off 2-19. They were hanging me. A lot of nasty stuff was said. I'd be driving to the game, and I'd have these urges to stop the car or turn around or just keep on driving right on by.

HUBIE BROWN: [On coaching a losing team:] There are two ways of doing it. One way is you give them time off, you shorten practices, you don't prepare. You take the losses and ride with it. Do that and they call you a "communicator." Or you can coach every game like it's your last game on earth, even though there's no playoffs, no high school tournament, no NCAAs. You come to every game totally prepared. That, my man, is hard to do. Do that and they call you all kinds of things.

DON NELSON: Coaching's a great job—if you *have to* compete every moment of your life. I guess that's what drags you in. I like to compete at anything. The killer instinct. I don't know why I got it, but it's in me.

FRANK LAYDEN: There is a fear. It's a fear of failure, of people not liking you if you lose.

JOHN KEMMERER, *basketball, Riverdale High, Fort Myers, Florida (no longer coaching):* The greatest thing about being a coach is the winning. Some people say that with me it was better than sex. Coaches can talk all they want about working with the kids and all that stuff, but if they do, they'd be lying. You hear it all the time: "We had a good season, we worked hard, good kids—we won two ball games." That's nice. Why work with kids and lose? Losing draws you down. Winning is the ultimate. Why the hell would you want to coach and not win?

RIC SCHAFER, *hockey, University of Notre Dame:* The year before I got here, the team was not successful. I came back as head coach just bubbling. I wrote to all the players before the season. And everything fell into place. We won twenty-seven, lost four, and tied two. We had eleven games tied or losing going into the third period, and we won them all. Attendance quadrupled. I'm the hero. I get coach of the year. Me. Ric Schafer. Notre Dame coach of the year!

Then—you know there's a "then" coming—the next year I'm the leading candidate for goof of the year. In my optimism I overscheduled.

Biggest mistake I ever made. But it was easy. It is not hard to get teams to play Notre Dame. And we got hammered: We started off with an 8–2 loss; two games were 11–1. We lost to Michigan 15–5. We lost to teams that we should have beat.

Losing breeds on itself. It's an awful disease, and we had it. You've got to fight off the gloom. Inevitably, there are going to be those moments. You can only mourn for so long. I didn't help. I made some bad mistakes. One was coming out in the school paper and saying, "There are glaciers in Alaska that move faster than some of our defensemen." *That* was a mistake. Then I made a second blunder. We were preparing for Michigan, and I told the press, "We're going to square our jaws, bare our teeth, jump in the trenches, and give it everything we got. But we'll bring a white hankie, just in case." Comments like that do plenty to disassociate a coach from his team. It is *the* mistake of coaching— putting yourself at a distance from the team. When things are going great, it's easy to put yourself front and center. But when things are going poorly, you can't disassociate. You've got to be prepared for whatever happens.

I spent most of the season trying to patch things up. I was an ornery son of a gun. Frankly, I was a jerk. I was so caught up in bringing us up a level. I'm glad I got that out of the way. I hope I learned my lesson.

MIKE MARCOULIS, JR.: You win fourteen games in a row, then you lose one and all of a sudden you feel you can't cut it. The problem with winning is you always have to be worrying about winning the next one. There's just this brief period of time where you can enjoy a win. The satisfaction of winning wears off a lot quicker than the disappointment of losing. It's not fair.

JOHN KEMMERER: One year we only lost one conference game. We lost by 1 on a 3-point shot. The second time we beat them by 40. But for three weeks until we played them again, I was miserable. And we won eight games in between. I'd go home, I wouldn't want to be around my wife, I wouldn't want to be around my kids. Go home, have a drink, go to bed. Sometimes I didn't eat. That's miserable.

ROY CHIPMAN, *basketball, University of Pittsburgh (retired):* It's manic-depressive. One day you're up here and two days later you're down here. Pick up the paper one day and you're a great coach; lose the next game and now you're a lousy coach. Your psyche is constantly asking: Are you happy or are you sad? When we won I couldn't get to the office soon enough the next day. If we lost I'd slink in through a side door. I was always battling my fears with basketball.

MIKE MARCOULIS, JR.: There was a period where, for a couple of years, at a certain point during the season, my eye would start to twitch. I'd feel this muscle get going in my eyelid.

JERRY REYNOLDS: I was the interim coach a couple of times. The only full year I was 27–55, and I was miserable that whole year. From the time camp started until the last game it was . . . for lack of a better term, it was like I was one big boil on your hind end.

JOHN KEMMERER: I had a 2–22 season once. You do not go 2 and 22 and be happy. I got run down, I got sick. I was drinking like a fool. Just so I could go to bed—you know, not drunk, just mellow. The doctor told me I was anemic. He put me on iron pills and vitamins. My platelet count was about half what it should have been. I came down with a lung disease, which I have today. It's a form of tuberculosis. They put me on steroids to control it. They put me in the hospital for a while. A lot of it was stress. I've never been real good with dealing with things like that. I don't miss that feeling. I hate it. You never get over it.

GENE VOLLNOGLE, *football, Carson High School, Los Angeles:* One of my worst defeats was 31 to 0 back when I was a B coach in 1955. The fellow I coached against, this past year he helped coach our B team because his son was our B-team coach. First thing I said was, "I still remember that 31 to nothing, and I still want to get even."

ED CHEFF, *baseball, Lewis–Clark State, Lewiston, Idaho:* We've played ten straight NAIA national championships; we've lost three. The very first team was probably the best team I ever had. They were 69 and 5. We got to the championship game, a double-elimination thing. We had to win one, and we lost two. We played Lubbock

Christian down in Lubbock, Texas; 7 to 5 in the second game. We had the bases loaded in the ninth with our two best hitters coming up, and we got beat.

I asked the guys if they wanted to change and they said, "Head out." We had a couple of vans and a motor home. When we got to west Texas, at an all-night place, and we stopped to eat, I asked if they wanted to change. "Keep going." The next day we found a spot, like at a trailer camp or something, up in Wyoming, and the guys took showers and cleaned off the dirt and washed away the loss. Then we drove straight through to Idaho.

CLEVELAND STROUD, *basketball, Rockdale High, Georgia:* We're on the semester system. At the end of the first semester, I lost five players to grades. That left me with ten. Then another player contracted mono; another broke his foot. So at the end of the regular season I brought up some players from the JV team. Turned out one of these players was ineligible—unbeknownst to me. This kid played in the first game of the subregion tournament. We were beating this team by 20 points, so with less than a minute to go I put this kid in with some of the others. That's all this kid played in any of the games leading up to the state championship, which we won.

With him playing in that one game, we had to forfeit all the games we played beyond that point. I didn't know about any of this until we checked grades for spring football. We'd won the state championship, received all the accolades. We're only about eight thousand people, so it was a big deal. The Atlanta TV stations came down. I used to be the janitor at the school, so it made a real good story. I was eating all this stuff up. Then all of a sudden, here's this kid who's ineligible.

It was so insignificant. It was the fourth film I looked at before I found him. My first inclination was, if I don't say anything, nobody will ever know. I can keep everything that we've earned and go from there. That videotape could have disappeared. All that went through my head.

I couldn't sleep; I wasn't eating much. If I tell somebody, they're gonna think I'm a fool. But I made up my mind that I had to tell the principal. Even he asked me, "What do you think?" I told him, "Hey, I done what I should do." He said, "I don't think we have a choice here." And I said, "We really don't." Then I apologized.

The principal had to notify the superintendent, and he notified the Georgia High School Association. They wrote a letter back saying we would have to forfeit the title. The superintendent told the principal; the principal told me. I asked if I could tell my players before it was made public.

There was a little bit of anger, not toward me or the kid, but they thought the penalty was harsh, considering the circumstances. There was some real bitterness, but I was real proud of them. They held up real good. The leadership that led us to the state championship showed up that day.

Well, we stood up to some ridicule. But then people started talking about honesty and integrity. I live next door to a family who has a daughter who's a reporter with the *New York Times*. She got it on the front page. It snowballed from there; *20/20* wanted to do a documentary. One accolade after the other. It got to be a big thing.

I can't put my finger on what people were responding to. The only thing I did was try to do what I've been teaching over the years: Tell the truth no matter how much it hurts. Things usually happen for the best, and this has worked out for the whole program. My kids know what I expect, and they know I'm not blowing hot air. They know I mean business, and I think they appreciate that. Kids are seeking discipline; they're looking for someone to lead them. Kids look to their coach, and he can take 'em either way.

WANDA ANITA OATES, *boys' basketball, Ballou High School, Washington, D.C.:* I don't care too much about winning and losing. In fact, I'll coach to lose. There are lessons that young people have to learn. If they won all the time and never experienced losing, then how are they going to overcome adversity in life?

I say I throw games; I have not always coached to win—it's the same thing. The players caught me one time and they got mad. We had this team beat; it was 30 to 8 at the end of the first quarter. I said, "I know I can win this game, so now it's time to see what we got." I did, and we lost by 10. The boys were so mad! I told them it's not always about winning. "You'll learn by the end of the season." Sometimes they understand; sometimes they don't. But we won the East Division, and I knew who I could count on and who I couldn't.

ART COLLINS, *downhill skiing, Reno High, Nevada:* I've had a lot of people ask me, "Don't you ever get excited? Don't you ever get upset?" Essentially, my answer has always been, "Well, they haven't started shooting yet." I guess I don't get stressed until the bullets fly.

I spent three years in Southeast Asia, from '66 to '69. Vietnam taught me that you've got to live life for today. You need to have a positive attitude. Negative attitudes, you don't survive. Everything has to be put into perspective. Coaches get too stressed and worked up, and they lose perspective of what they're involved in and what they're doing. I've seen the streaks of light. If you've seen tracers, you know the streak of light.

JEAN ROISE, *basketball, University of North Dakota, Williston:* One thing that surprised me when I got into coaching was that I enjoyed the kids, win or lose. After we won the state [at Grand Forks–Red River High] it was great, but it had been just as much fun when we were 3 and 15. It was always the kids who made the difference.

NAN AIROLA: I don't have this great need to win a state championship anymore. When I was younger that always had to be my goal. I could get obsessed. I was crazy. What changed it all was we had a big season, and I noticed that not everybody was talking about it. I realized that maybe, just maybe, volleyball wasn't quite as big a deal as I thought it was.

JOE NEWTON, *cross-country, York High, Oak Brook, Illinois: Track & Field News* said that of all the runners participating in high school track and field, only 3 percent are going to put a foot on a track at a college. And of those 3 percent, only 1 percent are going to run for four years. I looked at that and said, "Am I going to coach for that 1 percent, or am I going to coach for the kid who can't break ten minutes for two miles and help him win a state championship so he's got a dream come true for the rest of his life?"

A high school coach is dealing with kids for just a moment in their lives. Each one has his own potential. My job is to allow him to come out and do the best with what he's got, every day, and win a few championships along the way and leave here feeling like he's accomplished something. That's how I coach. Get them to commit to excellence.

Some coaches use their runners like robots, trying to build up their own records. It's ego. Some coaches keep waiting for that diamond to come along. You may never get that diamond! I've never had a super-big-time guy. You have to coach what you got and get them to do the best they can, and then maybe you can do some winning. In the thirty-two years we've been going to the state meet, we've got seventeen firsts, seven seconds and four thirds. That's twenty-seven out of thirty-two times we've gone down, and they've gotten a moment in time that will stay with them forever. Guys come back all the time. "Where's the trophy, Coach? I want to see my name." They treasure their moment forever.

ANSON DORRANCE, *head coach, U.S. women's 1991 World Cup soccer champions and the University of North Carolina:* It took me by surprise the way I felt at the World Cup. Obviously, it was a dream come true and an incredible opportunity to be involved in the first one. But to win it . . . it wasn't the sort of elation I think most people would think you'd feel after this kind of event. It was a completely different experience than coaching in college. The pressures I felt were very real and nerve-wracking. I never felt that stressed in college, even when we won our first national championship. I never felt the pressures people expect you to feel, because my attitude toward athletics has always been very casual.

I don't believe in committing suicide if you lose or crowning yourself king if you win. Most people who've spent any time analyzing winning and losing realize that neither is that big a deal. Effort and discipline, the elements involved, are important, but not the thing itself. But the World Cup was different. I was representing a large, imposing constituency. The last thing you want to do is let your country down.

During games I felt a tremendous sense of urgency. After games I'd have a tremendous headache. During all the NCAA championships, even when a game was close, I could still crack jokes. I was always able to find that ironic distance from the game itself. It was like I could watch myself, and even when I'd get upset, kicking water buckets and throwing my hands in the air and ranting and raving, I realized that what I was really doing was performing for myself. I'd watch myself doing all that and be able to say, "This is hilarious!"

At the World Cup I never found that distance. I never was able to get away from it. I don't know how to explain the way I like to coach without trivializing the quality, because I think it's a good quality to have. "Reckless abandon" is a good way to put it. Reckless abandon is knowing there's danger and yet it doesn't affect you. It's a quality I've had in every other arena I've ever coached in. But I didn't have it at the World Cup, and that irritated me. I was immersed in every single successful and unsuccessful pass, every single good and bad tackle, every great and weak shot. It was like I was this guy who'd bet a hundred million dollars on the outcome. All the things that I thought were important about athletics were overshadowed by something that I knew wasn't that important—and yet I'd made it that important. I hated being governed by something as ridiculous as athletic success. I couldn't control the fact that if we lost I would have been shattered.

We opened with Sweden. We beat them 3–2, a harrowing game in which we were leading 3–0. The second game we beat Brazil 5–0 and I felt comfortable. The next game, against Japan, I never felt comfortable, but we won 3–0 and that put us in a great draw. The quarterfinal, against Taiwan, we won 7–0. Our best performance was the semifinal against West Germany. Following that game I felt on top of the world. I felt all my fears were behind me. We were peaking at the right time.

The final was against Norway. We scored late to make it 2–1. That put me into an incredible panic. The game was ours, and I didn't want to lose it. There was no relief. Should I substitute? This player is getting tired; I have two players warming up. I'm turning to my assistant and saying, "I've got to pull this player out. Who should I put in? Maybe we should ride this sucker out." If we don't make this substitution and that player causes our downfall, I'd blame myself forever.

Winning was just tremendous relief. The players are all running out on the field, and I just sit there, everything draining out of my body, the emotion just falling out. The players are dancing up and down the field, and I'm hardly moving. I don't even feel that good.

Don't get me wrong. There were a lot of things that were fun, a lot of little elements that caused me to appreciate this event. One of the most memorable was after we won we got back to our floor. We were on the same floor with Sweden, the team that we had barely beaten in the first round. They had their medals—they'd finished third—drawn in a pattern: CONGRATULATIONS USA. It was a wonderful gesture of respect and friendship.

A lot of those kinds of things. Different players expressing to me how much all this meant to them, a lot of personal vignettes. When we won I tried to find my wife and family; everybody was there. All those things add up. But no real feeling of celebration.

I flew home backwards: China to Zurich to London. The trip was exhausting. I was in the Zurich airport with Tony DiChicco, my goalkeeper trainer, and Roger Rogers, my administrator, and we had a great postchampionship celebration. Wonderful feelings of friendship.

I finally got home. Nobody was there, because my wife had flown the other way and was hung up in Seattle. I'm alone in my own house. I have this incredible night's sleep—I was totally exhausted and I slept for fourteen hours. The next morning I take a shower. I put Phil Collins on the CD, crank it as far as I can, and dance around the room in my underwear. That's the first time I felt like I'd won.

■ EIGHT ■

Monday-Morning Quarterback

It's all said and done. He's second-guessed himself a million times, he says, but he's over that. And he's never felt sorry for himself, not ever. He just had to realize that if a person makes some good decisions in his life, then he's bound to make some bad ones, too, and in the long run that was a bad one.

What it is, Jim Criner says, is that he should never have left Boise State for Iowa State. But here's the way he had it figured then. He'd won a Division I-AA national football championship at Boise—with only four full-time assistants. Moving to Iowa State, into Division I, would give him eleven full-time assistants. *Eleven!* "I thought all that help was going to allow me more time to do what I liked to do," he says. "But it ended up being the opposite. At Boise I had to coach the offensive line. I got down in a three-point stance and knocked some heads. I had a hands-on relationship with my players. I didn't have the time when I moved to Iowa State, and I missed it from day one."

Isn't it ironic, Jim Criner says. He made it to the top of his profession, and then he couldn't do what he did best, couldn't do the very things that had gotten him there. "Most of what a head coach does is coach his coaches and help with the game plan," he says. "Moving to Division I took me off the field and put me behind a desk."

There was always *something*. An interview, a booster meeting, an alumni breakfast. The hounds are baying on every level of the coaching ladder. Maybe it's parents in high school. A few moneyed alumni in college. The impatient owner in the pros. And everywhere, it seems, there is the press. And, of course, the fans.

"I turned down a lot of jobs when I was at Boise," Jim Criner says. "Boise was the kind of place where we could have lived the rest of our lives. It's something that my son and I have talked about. He was a high school athlete when I was at Iowa State. He could see the frustration that I felt. He made the comment that when he decided to get into coaching he was not going to be as ambitious as I was. He was never going to let what happened to me happen to him. He just wants to *coach*."

FRANK LAYDEN, *Utah Jazz (retired):* I always told the team, don't worry about the peripheral foes—the wives, the fans, the friends, the press. If you're going good, they're going good; if you're not going good, they're not going good.

JERRY REYNOLDS, *basketball, retired coach turned general manager, Sacramento Kings:* I can't say it was ever fun. I don't think I ever really enjoyed coaching in the NBA. We didn't have a winning team—that's part of it. But there's also the "happy factor." Regardless of what you do, there's always X number of people who are unhappy. Somebody feuding with somebody else. The media, this, that—it's always *something*. Call it "the crap syndrome." The coach has to eat crap about six days a week.

JACK PARDEE, *Houston Oilers:* I understand the Golden Rule: An owner doesn't have to have a reason. Jack Kent Cooke came into Washington and he wanted to make changes. I had to get out of town; it was just too painful to be in the area.

SAM RUTIGLIANO, *football, Liberty University, Lynchburg, Virginia:* Seventy-eight and '79 were my first two years as head coach of the Cleveland Browns. It's late November 1980, and we beat Pittsburgh in Cleveland, 27–26. We're probably going to win the division. A major step up. After the game I went up to the owner's office. The owner's wife, Pat Modell, says to me, "Congratulations, Coach." I didn't even get a chance to say, "Thank you," when she says, "But we must beat them in Pittsburgh." On the drive home I say to my wife, "I am never going to grow old gracefully in this job."

BUTCH VAN BREDA KOLFF, *basketball, Hofstra University, Long Island:* I worked for Charlie Finley for one year; he had the Memphis Tams in the ABA. He was desperate, and I was available. He didn't know anything about basketball. That's why we got along.

SAM RUTIGLIANO: When I made it to head coach with Cleveland, I enjoyed it immensely, but it wasn't nearly as fulfilling as the effort it took to get there. I was an NFL coach of the year. In August of 1984 I was given my fourth five-year contract. Eight weeks later I was fired. I thought I'd be able to weather the storms. But there's no bunker, no safe spot for anybody. Bill Walsh, Don Shula—all the great ones—every one of them is being tapped on the shoulder and there's somebody saying, "What have you done for me lately?"

CHARLIE THOMAS, *basketball, San Francisco State:* My first job as a head coach we started off with twelve guys; at one point we were down to six. We played the defending NAIA national champions; down 4 at half and we got beat by 9. That was a major accomplishment. A school from Nashville beats us by 40. We're getting destroyed in the second half when the president of our school comes out of the stands and hands me a bag of popcorn. "If you're going to get beat, you might as well enjoy it."

We started coming together. We finished 11 and 19 and got invited to the National Little Colleges tournament. Then I started recruiting, and the president went bonkers. He cut my phone off, said I was spending too much money. He made my assistant coach the athletic director. Crazy stuff. Same guy who brought me the popcorn. I thought he understood, but I guess not.

ABE LEMONS, *basketball, Oklahoma City University (retired):* When I first went to [the University of] Texas it was a gold mine. They had everything you needed. Won the NIT in '78 with the best record of any team to ever win it. When I went into Texas and the Southwest Conference, they didn't care whether anybody had basketball. Football was dominant; still is. If you're going to create something new, you're going to make waves; when you do that you make enemies.

Now, [football coach] Darrell Royal, he helped me some. And there was a guy named Frank Irwin. He helped me a lot. He was bigger than the president. He was a political advisor to LBJ. He ran the school from the shadows; he hired and fired. The most powerful individual I ever knew.

Well, what happened was my support kind of died out around me: Darrell quit; Neal Thompson, the faculty rep, he resigned; and then Frank Irwin died. There were a lot of heavy hitters at Texas, and all you had to do was get one of those guys down on you and you're gone. I didn't get fired because Mike Wacker got hurt. [Wacker was Texas's star player; he sustained a season-ending injury.] They'd have gotten around to it anyway. Once they get on your trail, there's no way to know your enemies. I'd never been around those kind of people before. You've got to watch for the guy with the smile and the invisible knife.

OLLIE BUTLER, *basketball assistant, Cal State–San Bernardino:* In thirty-three years of high school coaching, I had one incident on the court. And I had the worst goddamn administrator ever. A principal who'd been cut off my team when he was in high school. Can you believe that? Came back and became my principal, and he set out to get my butt. No doubt about it. He made that statement. Eventually, that's what happened.

The game was tied 51–all, with one second to go. We called time-out and set up our usual play. Well, my guy and his guy are locked up, and so my man shoves his guy and they call the foul on my guy. They go down and make both free throws and beat us 53–51. These two referees had just refereed our game on Monday—this was Wednesday. We got beat by one, 69-68, and they'd made another lousy call—a guy tried to block a shot and slapped the backboard, and they didn't call it. Now it's Wednesday and I'm walking off the court and I said to one of the refs, "Two times in one week is too much." He just mumbled something and that was the end of it. Then one of my players yells at the other referee, "You cost us the game!" Well, this referee comes roaring down on him and shoves my kid. My player punches him right in the mouth. And then all hell breaks loose. Our principal was incredibly happy.

BILL MUSSELMAN, *first coach of the Minnesota Timberwolves (now with a CBA team in Rochester, Minnesota):* When I coached the Tampa

Bay Thrillers in the CBA, the owners said they wouldn't buy the team unless I coached it. One of the owners, I rode to work with him every day. He told me: "I want to learn this game. I want you to talk basketball." So I did. There is an advantage to working for an owner like that.

AL BORGES, *offensive coordinator, Boise State, Idaho:* I read my press. Sure I do. Most coaches do. If they say they don't, they're lying.

ROY CHIPMAN, *basketball, University of Pittsburgh (retired):* Everybody asks, "Don't you miss coaching?" I do. There's not the same thrill in business. The thrill of victory. I don't get that anyplace else. But business doesn't come with the down side. If I lose an account this afternoon, two hundred thousand people don't know it.

TOM HOUSE, *assistant to the general manager, Texas Rangers (and former pitching coach):* Marshall McCluhan said we were all going to be the product of our media. We've got a very hungry media. Jose Canseco comes out of Madonna's apartment at 4 in the morning and everybody knows it. That makes the sports world a very small place.

ROY CHIPMAN: I told them at the beginning of December that I was retiring at the end of the season. I suggested we not tell anybody until then, but the chancellor called a press conference and announced it. We beat Tennessee, Texas A&M, and Louisiana. We won the Sugar Bowl Tournament. We came back and beat Georgetown. Then we went to St. John's and lost in overtime. That's when it started. By the time we got back to Pittsburgh it was like we'd lost by 60.

Talk about a lame-duck coach. Everywhere we went, the media focused on me. "Why are you leaving?" They buried the team. The kids didn't get any ink at all. They were getting called late at night, in the dorms. The kids were never a pain in the neck, but psychologically it destroyed us. It started out that my leaving was the reason for a loss. Pretty soon it became the reason for everything. Everybody began to believe it. After a while it became reality. It was just a mess.

FRANK LAYDEN: I miss training camp. No pressure, you have fun. But I don't miss the bad calls. I don't miss getting up early and going on to the next city. I don't miss the one hundred games. And I don't miss the one hundred pregame interviews and the one hundred after-game interviews. The same stupid questions every day. "How's it going, Coach?" Blah, blah, blah. It was like having to talk about *Gone with the Wind* every single day.

TOM HOUSE: Sports are cruel. People are interested in what the athlete can do, not who he is. No one cares if an athlete is dysfunctional—that doesn't have anything to do with his being a jock—he's got to put up the numbers. Who a person is is just as important as what he is. But nobody has time for that.

JOHN NICKS, *Olympic-level figure skating (Tai and Randy, and Tiffany Chin):* Coaching at this level is so much different from when I started. The pressure of media and money. The media coverage is much more intense, much more knowledgeable. "Why did so-and-so leave out her triple jump?" It used to be "Why the green dress?"

The media is willing now to challenge the coach, they're willing to challenge judges' opinions. And I think in both cases we deserve those challenges. It keeps me on my toes. The media is super-important to our sport. I won't even call it support; it's *involvement,* both good and bad. I much prefer it to the old scene.

KERRI HEFFERNAN, *Boston Beantown Women's Rugby Club:* Acclaim can backfire. Every time the *Boston Globe* or the *Boston Herald* writes an article about women rugby, it's always the same old shit: Why do women play rugby? You get so tired of it: They're pretty— even if they have scabs on their knees. It gets so old you don't want to hear the question anymore. Sometimes I'd rather they didn't even know we played. Leave me alone.

DICK VERMEIL, *Philadelphia Eagles (retired):* I got tired of answering the same questions. I tried to be honest and specific. I just wasn't bright enough to give different responses.

TOM HOUSE: You have to let them do their job and you have to do your job with them, but it can't be at the expense of the player or the team. You have to be able to tell a story without giving it away. I would have no chance of handling that well. To me there are always so many more factors involved in a specific act or a move or performance leading up to a game or a specific play than the media could ever hope to talk about. There's no way they can bring out all the factors that caused a success or a failure. I'd never be able to say all the things that led up to it.

MIKE PRICE, *football, Washington State:* I've come to realize that they'd like to have the team they're covering win every game, too. That way everybody can be happy.

JERRY REYNOLDS: I was treated pretty good by the media. I deserved some criticism—I can't say they were wrong. But I took it too personal. I'd read where some fan called me a stooge—which may of course been true—and I'd be saying, "That son-of-a-bitch . . . I'll punch him." The guys that last are able to laugh at those things. You have to leave the game in the locker room and go to the next one. I couldn't do that.

But it was always honest emotion, and I think my players and the press knew that. I might make a fool out of myself, but they knew it was sincere. When I was at West Georgia I kicked a chair and broke my toe. It was a big play and a big call. They were bolted down. My foot hurt so bad I could have cried. I have this partial plate, and sometimes when I get mad and start yelling I spit it out. My wife used to say I did things that were very embarrassing, jumping around, whatever. The only thing I can say is that was the way I was. I'd really get involved in the game. That's one thing I liked about it. It puts you right out there for everybody to see.

DICK VERMEIL: My first year, I cut a guy early in camp and one of the writers really got after me. A front-page picture of the player being cut and a caricature of me with an ax in my hand. I didn't want him to make the football team. All I wanted was to give him a chance to be on the field for a few days, and he was out of there. I knew what he really was. But this reporter didn't. I jumped all over his ass in front of the media in the lunchroom. I shouldn't have done that. We met later, and off the record I told him why I'd done it. We're friends today.

CHUCK JORDAN, *football, Conway High, South Carolina:* When we were 7–1, a lot of people were saying, "Yeah, well, it's just a matter of time." The thing you've got to realize as a coach is if you're hearing those things, you can't discount them. Because your players are hearing them too. It doesn't always matter what the truth is; it matters what perception people have about that truth. Let's be realistic. I'm a grownup. I pick up the paper and see, "Conway: The Team to Beat," and man, I swell with pride. "We must be pretty good!" Wait a minute. *I'm* the coach. I'm supposed to know how good we are. If it's having an effect on me, it's having an effect on the kids.

BOB WOOD, *tennis, University Liggett School, Grosse Pointe Woods, Michigan:* Publicity can kill you. Everybody has to buy into it. Everyone has to know his role. Everyone has to *enjoy* his role. Everyone has to know who's going to have his picture in the paper and who is not going to have his picture in the paper. The guy who's going to, he's got to handle that. The guy who's not, he's got to handle that. Everybody has to handle it.

When we were turning into one of the top high school tennis teams in the country [thirteen consecutive state titles, a then–national record], a freshman came in and played number one. He was a little German kid who lived in the community but who had not gone to our lower and middle school. The year before we had won the state title, but we'd done it without a great player. This ninth-grader comes in and shoved everybody down. We were moving it up a notch. The Detroit papers jumped all over it.

I allowed it to happen. I was young. They came in and did a couple of big stories on this freshman. For a couple of weeks after that the rest of the kids on the team had their noses bent out of shape. Now I understand why. Maybe I allowed it to happen because vicariously I was living through this kid—he was the first kid who ever beat me. I forgot about the rest of the kids who'd won a state championship the year before. To the kids' credit—not mine—they overcame it.

JOHN WOODEN, *basketball, UCLA (retired):* They passed a rule that you had to permit the media in the dressing room after the game. I never favored that. I didn't think that was the place for them. And they only want to talk to a few players anyway. I thought it was not in the best interest of our team—and that's my job, isn't it, to do what I think is in the best interest of our team? When they passed the rule, the chairman of the committee made the statement, "That will take care of Johnny Wooden." I'll say frankly that I was hurt by that statement. I always felt as I was as cooperative as any coach in the game.

HUBIE BROWN, *New York Knicks (retired):* Understand the situation. You've lost a heartbreaker and there you are and you're surrounded and you're soaking wet and the questions start coming. Are there times when you're short-tempered? Of course. You're a human being.

JOHN WOODEN: I never felt pressure from the crowds. What I hated to do—and this was very important—was that following that great game against Louisville [the 1975 NCAA semifinal: UCLA 75, Louisville 74 in overtime], I had to go face the media, with a hundred cameras in my face and everyone popping questions. It had never bothered me that much before. I thought, if this is beginning to bother me now and I'm worried because it's something that must be done, I better get out.

I always went to my team first. I went into the locker room after that wonderful game and told them regardless of how we did [in the championship game] Monday night, that this last team I ever coached gave me as much pleasure as any I ever had. Then I went to the press room and I waited until an appropriate question was asked, and I told the press the same thing.

JOE RAMSEY, *basketball, Millikin University, Decatur, Illinois:* After two years at Oklahoma and now sixteen years at Millikin, I've run across a lot of people on the Division III level who are better pure coaches than some of the coaches in Division I. Whether they'd be successful handling all the other stuff that goes with Division I, I don't know. Just because you can coach doesn't mean you can do all the other things.

GLEN MASON, *football, University of Kansas:* I get to the point sometimes where I'll just walk in and say, "I'm not doing anything else." You're involved in recruiting, and that is highly competitive—it's a game with its own set of rules. You're involved in PR and fund-raising.

Every civic group in the world wants you to talk—breakfasts, lunches, dinners, the whole shot. You better talk with your players. If you don't watch out, all too often as the head coach the only time you get players in your office to talk to them is when something's wrong. Bring them in when something good is happening.

GARY ZARECKY, *basketball, Foothills Junior College, California:* When I finally got to the Division I level [at United States International University in San Diego], I figured it would be mostly Xs and 0s. I found out that's a very small part of the game. It's become a huge corporate business that hides behind a college mascot. You've got to be a North Carolina, a Syracuse, a UCLA. They're the ones who build the monumental facilities, these Greek coliseums to honor sports. Maybe fifty schools can do that. The other 246 [Division I] schools can't. Some of those top-50 schools I played against, the coaches smile at you. They don't even know what their budgets are.

I am in awe and I am full of envy and I would love to be there. But I don't respect these coaches the way I once did. I don't look at them anymore as these great X-and-0 basketball masters. They're public relations icons, marketing geniuses, businessmen. To be honest, the best *coaches* I faced were many of the unknown coaches at those 246 unknown schools who had horrendous handicaps to overcome but were doing a great job with their kids. All the coaches nobody will ever hear of.

DON NELSON: When you're the head man, you have a lot of people who will do things for you. From players to fans to assistant coaches to trainers, everyone's telling you how great you are. You have to be careful. It's nice to feel you're good at what you do, but that's the limit of it. Don't ever believe that it's really you.

RIC SCHAFER, *hockey, University of Notre Dame:* I'm the hockey coach at Notre Dame. Sometimes I still can't believe it. I went to school here, played hockey here. Now I'm the coach. It's great. But I'm just the hockey coach at Notre Dame. Sometimes I have to laugh. Every summer there's a fund-raiser for the athletic department, a golf tournament. Who does everyone want in his foursome? Lou Holtz, everybody wants

Lou Holtz. You should see the looks on their faces when they realize they're playing with the hockey coach.

JOHN WOODEN: One of my finest coaching jobs up till then was the 1959–60 season at UCLA when we finished 14–12. We had to win the last game of the season against USC. I felt as good after that 14–12 as I did after the 30–0. People judge you, but you have to judge yourself and that's what really matters. Success is within yourself.

BOB LUCEY, *football, Curtis High, Tacoma, Washington:* Sometimes a coach has things going on with a kid that nobody else has a clue about. You might have a kid who's just gone through a situation with an alcoholic parent. But they're up there in the stands saying, "This kid sucks"? Hey, there's something going on that's a heck of a lot more important than football. And you know what? It's none of your business.

P. J. CARLESIMO, *basketball, Seton Hall:* If people thought of college players as their sons or daughters, they'd think differently. But they don't. They see uniforms. They think *all-American.* If they thought of these kids as their yo-yo son who oversleeps or who does stupid things, they'd say, "What else did we expect?"

RON GREENE, *basketball, Calloway County High, Murray, Kentucky (also coached at Loyola–New Orleans, LSU–New Orleans, Mississippi State, Murray State, and Indiana State):* People think coaches are public property. To have moving vans pulled up in front of your house, to have signs put up in your yard: "Coach won't be home tonight because he's in the bayou in cement shoes." I'm not asking for sympathy; I made my decisions. But my family paid for them. It's tough on families. I'm not sure that the losses didn't contribute to the deaths of my mother and father. People talk about stress causing strokes. Both of my parents died of strokes. They were seventy-some years old, and they couldn't understand the things that were being said about their son.

DICK VERMEIL: I went after a guy in the stands once. "Vermeil, you son of a bitch, go back to UCLA." I jumped in the stands after him. Chuck

Bednarik [an honorary assistant] caught me by the foot—I was already up in the stands. Fans don't realize how it feels.

TONY LaRUSSA, *Oakland A's:* You've got a one-run lead in the ninth inning and there's a man at second and third and there's two out and you need one more and your best pitcher's facing their best hitter. Your temples are pounding, your heart's beating, your stomach's rolling, your legs are weak. The whole ball of wax. It's hard to appreciate that unless you've sat where we sit.

BILL CURRY, *football, University of Kentucky:* I call them "The Fellowship of the Miserable." The people who are constantly pointing out why it's going to be a miserable day. They're everywhere you go. They tell me why I can't succeed at Kentucky, why I couldn't succeed when I was at Georgia Tech, or why I shouldn't have been the coach at Alabama.

The Fellowship of the Miserable has decided the outcome of their efforts [ahead of time] so they can always be correct. "I told you it was going to be a rotten day." There's a risk in saying, "We're going to win the championship." They'd rather be right than take the risk.

Every coach has to battle against them. Sometimes they're the people who love you the most and are trying to protect you. Like after my second year at Georgia Tech. Our record was 2–19–1. A good friend of mine came in, a famous sportscaster. He said, "Before I turn this camera on, surely you're not going to continue doing this. You're destroying what could be a fine career." He meant well. But I said, "You don't know me. The last thing I would do is quit now."

BUTCH VAN BREDA KOLFF: My third year in Detroit we started out 6–4. The year before we'd been 45–37, but we hadn't played well at the end. Dave Bing, Jimmy Walker, Bob Lanier—those were my burned-out days. That third year there were these two black guys who sat behind the bench. Every time I put a white guy in, they'd start: "There he goes, putting in his son again." My son played for me later. I let them get to me. I should never have allowed that. So I left. I got in the car—took my dog—boom, drove down to the Jersey shore.

LaDONNA WILSON, *basketball, Austin Peay State, Clarksville, Tennessee:* It's the little things about coaching that I'd like people to know. Seeing students improving and gaining self-confidence, the way they grow up while you've got them. Those things can be so rewarding. But that's not the stuff fans see.

DON NELSON: There is a philosophy that says you should never worry about the fans. I disagree. The fans are as important as anything else. I like to please them, I like to communicate with them, I like to get to know them. I like to have a special relationship with them. Fans float with the success of the team, but if you level with them and you don't lie to them, they'll have a better chance to respect you. You can't let fans interfere with your making good decisions, even if you're going to be unpopular. But at least you can level with them and explain it and not lie about it.

DICK VERMEIL: I still think the Philadelphia fans treated me way beyond my expectations coming in. They were losing when I got here. I spent a lot of nights in the community—not getting paid—all kinds of clubs, talking about the way we were going to do things. I shook hands with more NFL football fans than any coach. I did it because I knew it was going to take some time to win. I didn't want everybody to start saying, "Same old thing." I wanted them to recognize the little changes. I wanted to bring them in to what we were doing. Fans want to see effort. It's maybe the one thing they really can evaluate.

BILL CURRY: [Curry coached Alabama for three years, 1987–89, going 7–5, 9–3 (and a No. 17 ranking) and 10–2 (No. 9 and a 33–25 Sugar Bowl loss to national-champion Miami.] I've always been interested in illogical hatred. I've always tried to understand racism. I never could, but I understand it much better now, having been the object of illogical hatred. Some people [at Alabama] hated me no matter what we did, no matter how we conducted ourselves, no matter how much we won. I would walk into a room and the feeling of dislike was palpable. And I would think, "My gosh, these people don't even know me." I learned how that sort of thing can wither and drain you.

There were death threats from day one. You have to make a decision: Are you going to live subject to your fear of those kinds of people, or are you prepared to walk out in front of seventy-five thousand people and go about your business knowing that somebody might have a rifle and a scope? It wasn't a hard decision. If you're ever even once controlled by fear, then you'll always be controlled by fear. But you're darn right you take them seriously. I never worried about it, but every time I walked on the field wearing a crimson sweater, I thought about it.

There is an obsession bordering on the religious that the coach at Alabama must be of the direct lineage of Paul Bryant, not unlike the search for the Messiah in the Judeo-Christian world. And I am not using that analogy lightly. Walk into a home in Alabama to recruit. If it's a white home, very often they'll have three pictures on the wall: FDR, Jesus Christ, and Coach Bryant; I don't have to tell you which one is the largest. In the black home it's Martin Luther King, Jesus Christ, and Coach Bryant: and I don't have to tell you which one's the largest. This is a religion.

My third season we beat LSU to clinch a share of the SEC title. A friend of mine, an engineer from Alabama, went up to a member of the board of trustees and said, "Isn't this wonderful? It's like old times!" The game was down in Baton Rouge, and our fans are drowning out the LSU fans. "Roll, Tide, roll!" It was beautiful. According to my friend, this guy said, "I don't care if he wins eight national championships, a Georgia Tech man is never going to be our coach for long. This guy is history." We were 9–0 at the time.

RIC SCHAFER: All I know is I want fans there.

GREG CARPENTER, *girls' basketball, Concord High School, Vermont (now at St. Johnsbury Middle School):* Parents don't attend athletic events these days. It's kind of universal, from what I see. Parents don't turn out. Both parents have to work. I think they're finding it much harder to be as involved with their child as they'd like to be. When I was playing, I know it was important to have my papa there. I wanted parental approval, and athletics was one way to get it. Even now, I'm seeking that approval.

SANDRA CHILDERS, *softball, Marion–Adams High School, Sheridan, Indiana:* One night this father was standing behind the fence just throwing a fit. His daughter was better than that, on and on. When my girls went back on the field I turned around and said, "Hey, if you can do better, get out here. I don't have a kid on this field." Every parent heard it. And that was the end of that.

KURT ASCHERMANN, *youth league sports, Sparta, New Jersey; author of* **Coaching Kids to Play Baseball and Softball** *and* **Coaching Kids to Play Soccer:** We had an umpire once who had a confrontation with a kid in one of our older leagues. Two weeks later this umpire was coaching in the younger league against the younger brother of the kid he'd had the confrontation with. Their father challenged this guy to a fight in the parking lot. The police were called, and then the father laid down behind this guy's car and claimed he'd been run over.

BOB LUCEY: The kids who are the happiest have the parents who are just thankful their kids have something positive to do after school. They're not interested in what's going to come out of it; they appreciate everything that's going on right now. Too many parents don't understand the process. When parents get into it for their son being a major college athlete and they really get hung up on that, it's real tough on the team. What happens is the kid gets into himself. Maybe the parent's been coaching them, too. Kids can't play for two coaches. It'll ruin the kid.

RICHARD CICIARELLI, *baseball, Midlakes High, New York (retired):* I had three top-notch catchers that year; one was a senior, two were juniors. The senior was my starter. One of the juniors was on the varsity as a catcher since he was a freshman, so he was my number two. All three were too good to sit, so I caught my senior and played the other two in the outfield. The father of the number three catcher was upset and he brought a sign to the game: "Why is the best catcher playing in the outfield—.316 average last year—great speed." Something like that.

Coaches learn to ignore those people. But it did bother the father of the boy who was catching. There was an argument at the game. To stop further arguments, our school invoked our policy about signs on school property. The ACLU got involved and it became this big controversy over freedom of speech. The baseball got lost.

MIKE MESSERE, *lacrosse, West Genessee High, Camillus, New York:*
We have a problem, we deal with it. I've had players I wouldn't let try
out because of their behavior who went on to be three-time college
All-Americas. We've had outstanding starters, the best players on the team,
who have had to leave after the second game. You've got to take a stand.

You take some heat from some parents: "You're going to lose."
But we don't. Some parents go to any lengths to get their kids back.
Parents, right or wrong, back their kids. I say if he's wrong, he's wrong,
and deal with the consequences. Kids get away with murder because
we don't want the parents to come in.

People don't want their kids to fail. Well, maybe a kid needs to
flop on his face once in a while. Nobody wants to yell at kids anymore.
I say it depends on what you're yelling. If it's constructive criticism and
you're making a point, getting their attention, what's wrong with that?
"You're embarrassing him." You know who's embarrassed? The parents
are embarrassed, not the kid. The kid knows he screwed up.

Here's what you're really doing when you're trying to get a kid to
perform. What you're saying is, "I believe in you, I'm not giving up
on you." When you say, "Don't worry about it," when you don't say
anything, then I've given up on that kid.

LEE BATTAGLIA, *Crystal Lakes Gymnastics Training Center, Illinois:*
I've seen a lot of individuals go through the ranks. I've taken kids, nine-,
ten-, eleven-year-old kids, and brought them up and put them on the
national team. When I see the potential, I'm thrilled. But then I say to
myself, Does he have the other stuff? The discipline? And will his parents
commit the time?

Take the kids from the parents. That's the ideal situation. Raise them
like your own. It's one thing to make the national team; it's another thing
to make the Olympic team; it's something all together different to become
a world or Olympic champion. I would love to take some six-, seven-,
eight-year-olds and just pull them away.

I realize I'm talking about two different trees here. I'm a born coach.
I also realize that if I were a parent, I wouldn't want that to happen to
my kid. That's not the American Way. I'm telling you what you need
to do to produce great gymnasts. It doesn't excite me as much as it used
to when I see somebody with the kind of talent it takes, because I look

at that person and say, there's something that's going to stop you. I've seen too many kids with talent who are gone now.

You can say the Russians perverted the sport. They'll take thousands of kids and then narrow them down. They test body parts, flexibility, structure. They get their top twenty-five out of that thousand, and they put them in the gym and they start working. It's an unnatural existence. If their muscles rip, their bones go, they're gone. Good-bye. There are going to be just a few sole survivors, but those are your world champions. The Soviets were good. And there's still China. It's scary. Who's going to beat them?

I know I wouldn't want that to happen to my kid. What if he gets injured? There is always the risk of injury, of falling. I'd be the same type of mother and father that I don't like. I'd want my kid to swim in the summer, play soccer in the fall, do some gymnastics in the winter, and play baseball in the spring. It's very difficult. I'm between a rock and a hard place. I've grown very negative. I want to tell all the parents, "Stay away; it's none of your business." But it *is* their business—it's their kid. But this is not the way to make a world champion.

JO FOWLER, *track and basketball, Owensboro High, Kentucky (retired):* I don't think parents take a daughter's sports as seriously as they do a son's. On my girls' varsity I had a girl who was one of my starting five. Her brother was on the boys' varsity. One day the girl didn't take out the garbage or something, so for punishment her mother didn't let her go to the game. If that had been the son, she'd never have done that.

I had one mother talk her daughter into quitting the team. The daughter was crying one day, and she said, "Mom doesn't understand why I want to be working this hard." This girl didn't come out for track the next year, and she got killed in a wreck running around with her friends.

I can't help but think. It comes to my mind every time I hear a parent say—and I still hear it occasionally—"I don't understand why my daughter wants to do this." Something constructive. I just think that if that girl had stuck to her guns, that she might be alive today.

DORIS HARDY, *athletic director, Riverside/Brookfield High, Illinois:* We had an athlete who was drinking. I was the assistant AD then and the basketball coach. I had no choice. I turned her in, and she was kicked off the team. She also got kicked off the track team. The parents sued. They contended she lost any chance for a scholarship. They said the school hadn't given them enough information about what would happen if a kid did this sort of thing.

I was crushed. I'd spent all this time with their daughter. There were rules and regulations; it was no surprise. First you take it personally; then you get angry. And then you change your phone number because you get tired of the calls. You get really irritated. After a while you figure you don't need this kind of grief anymore. You ask yourself two questions: Who's the adult here, and IS this the hill you want to die on? This wasn't my hill. Their suit didn't fly.

CHUCK JORDAN: A kid who played quarterback for us the year before, we decided to move him to a different position. The kid we took out was black and the kid we put in was white. Certain individuals made something out of that; thirty of the sixty kids on the team walked out. Probably the best team we've had. We went 1–11.

Because football was such an important thing in this community, all of a sudden we had a group of people using one decision to make a much larger statement. We were being used and our kids were being used. I still resented it. The funny thing is, my first year at Conway I benched a white quarterback and put in a black quarterback. I caught the devil about that, too.

It was the most difficult year of my life. We'd get beat 36–0. I talked with the governor of South Carolina five times. The Human Affairs Commissioner, this guy, that guy. I had to do so many things other than coach. I thought about quitting. But this is what athletics has taught me, and it's why athletics is so important for kids today: There comes a point when you're running those wind sprints and you say, "I'm tired of this crap." But you keep going. That's what I felt in that situation. A lot of it had to do with my faith in Christ. I wouldn't be fair in not mentioning that. I resolved that this was what the Man Upstairs wanted me to do, and I had no choice but to do it.

We had the top defensive player in the country. He broke the boycott and practiced with us. But he was threatened by his own community and went back out. We had six or seven seniors on that team who would have been college athletes. One of them ended up getting in, the great linebacker. And the only reason is because I went to bat for him. The kids that suffered worse were the kids who didn't play that year and came back the next year as seniors. That next year, for the first time, we did not have anyone get a scholarship.

All along the motto of the boycott was that it was being done to help the kids. That's a smoke screen. They were being used; we were being used. Conway football was being used to make a bigger point. I resented that. It was done at our football program's expense and, more importantly, at the kids' expense.

I can see how the black kids on our team are going to have a tougher time achieving what they're capable of achieving, because of our society and the way things are. I had a problem with the way the adults who organized the boycott went about things. They used the dern people they were trying to help. I always knew the kids had no choice. I know in my heart that the kids suffered. I've had kids come back and tell me that. One kid's a marine now. He was over in Saudi Arabia, the Gulf War. Before he went over, who's the last person he comes to see?

NINE

Home & Away

His wife would call to tell him what happened. Maybe his son had hit a home run. Frank Layden hadn't seen it, of course, because he was a coach and he was at some other game. "'Scott hit a homer today,' my wife would say," Frank Layden recalls. "And I missed it. I wasn't there. I spent my time with other people's kids. I was always at somebody else's game. I didn't see him play much when he was in high school—I was coaching at Niagara then. When I was in the pros, I think I saw him twice. I missed birthdays, graduations. That's a tragedy. You can't get it back."

It remains one of the abiding ironies of the profession. On the one hand, coaches speak eloquently of the traditonal values. God, family, country. On the other, they appear willing to sacrifice all to the gods of their game. It's as if they can't help themselves and are willing to hold their lives hostage to their competitive urge, their love of the game, their need to win.

Always, you must feed the monster. One more meeting, one more recruiting call, one more look at the videotape. Get to your desk by 6 A.M. and there's a coach in the conference who got to his by 5. Leave for home at midnight and there's another coach still looking at tape. You work half your nights away from home. Sometimes you sleep in the office. All this to win a game that, you constantly remind your players, isn't the most important thing in their lives.

"Coaches lose their sense of priorities, no doubt about it," Frank Layden says. "Coaching saps your energies. It consumes you." The road exacts its own toll. Bus to plane to bus to hotel to bus to gymnasium. "After the game, where do you go?" Frank Layden asks. "You go to the bar to hash out the game. You start banging down the beers. That part of the game is depressing."

There's no one holding a gun to a coach's head and telling him he must coach. Or is there? "I had ten years of high school coaching, ten years of coaching college, and thirteen years of pro coaching," Frank Layden says. "My wife was delighted when I quit."

JOE RAMSEY, *basketball, Millikin University, Decatur, Illinois:* I think a lot of people were skeptical when I applied here, because I was a Division I coach coming down. How serious could I have been about staying? But I'd decided to get some place where we could let our family grow up. I'd spent two years as a grad assistant at Southern Illinois. That's where I played. My last year as an assistant, SIU won the NIT with Walt Frazier. The next year I went to Robert Morris Junior College in Carthage, Illinois. Our '67 and '71 teams finished third in the nation; another team finished eighth. Those credentials got me to Oklahoma.

I went there in 1971 as an assistant to John MacLeod. When John took the Phoenix Suns job, I left Oklahoma and went to Kansas State as an assistant. But the fellow that Oklahoma named after John left had a heart attack, and I was named the head coach. I was thirty years old, and I felt I could take on anything. We were 31–21 in my two years. That's not terrible. But at the time, the job of promoting basketball in the state of Oklahoma was overwhelming. With more experience, maybe I would have done things a little differently. We had a lot of demands other than just the Xs and Os. You had to be available. At Oklahoma you've got the chairman of the board of Phillips Petroleum calling you.

My second year we were ranked fourteenth in the nation. Then my second-leading scorer blew out a knee. That made it very difficult for us to play at the same level. There were some people calling for a change. There was another assistant coach who had pursued the head job at the same time I did. I don't think the ship ever got smoothed out. Maybe my youthfulness didn't allow me to sort through things as well as I might have.

I told them I'd move on if they weren't happy, and that's what happened. I could have stayed on the Division I level, but I wanted a chance to concentrate on the things that I enjoyed most—the working with the kids, the coaching end of things—rather than all the extraneous stuff.

This was the only place I applied. We wanted a place where we could emphasize our family. I've been here for sixteen years now. Our kids have had the same classmates from the first grade. We're in a nine-team league and we're consistently in the upper division. We've won the conference championship twice and been to the NCAA Division III tournament three times. We were ranked seventh in the nation once. I have no regrets about the decision to come here.

Now, with one of my kids graduating from college and the other in college, I might enjoy having a shot at it again. I'm only forty-eight. Sometime before I'm through coaching I'd like to experience it again, see how I would handle it this time around. In Division III a basketball game is not nearly the event it is in Division I. The hoopla, the attention, the excitement of the big crowd. Stepping into the arena with fifteen, sixteen thousand people. That's what you coach for, that's a real part of the drive. I guess I still kind of miss that.

SAM RUTIGLIANO, *football, Liberty University, Lynchburg, Virginia:* I know coaches who've put their family second. And then they turn around twenty-five years later and say, "My gosh, my daughter's married," and they don't have anything. I don't believe in "quality time." That's a lot of crap. The only thing you have is time.

DON NELSON, *Golden State Warriors:* Everything costs; you pay a price. Going through a divorce is a price. Missing some awfully good years with my children is a price. I have four wonderful kids. But it's their mother who gets the credit for that, not me. The game is more important than the things that maybe should have been important. I'm the guy who did things wrong, I'm sure. But I suppose I'm also the guy that's been successful because of it.

SR. LYNN WINSOR, B.V.M., CAA, *golf, Xavier College Prep, Phoenix, Arizona:* I walk every morning from 5 to 6. There's a group of Sisters here who go out together. We have Mass at 6:30. It's a quiet time for all of us to be together. I grab something to eat and I'm over at school by 7:10. We get out at 2:15. The golf team usually leaves at 3 to go over to Camelback Golf Club, our home course. We work to quarter to six. That's practice days. Match days, sometimes we don't get home until 7:30 or 8.

I try to be home for dinner at 6. The evening meal is really important, the time to be together. After dinner we have evening services, and I want to be there for that. There are fifteen Sisters in our convent. It's a great group. One of the other Sisters coaches basketball, and a third is the ticket taker at all the games. The principal doesn't miss a game. And the rest of the nuns always show up. They're our built-in fans.

I want to spend time with the Sisters. The Sisters are my family. But it's difficult. I remember one time after I had missed dinner four nights in a row, I came in and one of the Sisters said, "Oh, it's good to have you home. We missed you." I've heard that from time to time. But I also know that I'll come back from a golf match and it'll be late, and I'll walk into the kitchen when everybody's getting done with dinner, and everybody wants to know how we did, what happened, all that. Everybody wants to share my happiness.

JOE TORRE, *St. Louis Cardinals:* Any manager who says he doesn't take it home isn't really into it. I was broadcasting with the Angels for five years, and I think my wife enjoyed that time because she got to go home with the same guy every night. Now I'm managing again, and the moods change.

WANDA BINGHAM, *volleyball, Churchill High, San Antonio:* The guys I've gone with usually say, "I can't take this." Once the season starts, I'm very involved. I'll be out with someone and I'll be thinking: "Should I play her here? Should I play this kind of rotation?" I find myself drawing little circles, looking for different situations. I do that all the time.

Not getting married was more or less a choice. If I were a man I don't think I would have to have made that choice. But I guess I'm used to that sort of thing, though: When I grew up, women were always sitting back—less pay, fewer opportunities, less everything. I don't think about that too much though, really, because I enjoy the volleyball so much. I'm happy with what I'm able to do. I like to water ski and snow ski. Maybe later on, when I can't do those things, that might be something I'd have to think about. I know that having my own children is ruled out, but these kids are my kids, you know? I don't think I've missed out on that.

I kind of fell into this. There was one guy, he came to some of my games. He told me he couldn't stand it; it made him real nervous. We started doing less and less together. Before we realized it, we weren't seeing each other anymore. It wasn't something we chose to have happen. But it was during volleyball season and the team was doing really well. It's annoying that sometimes the understanding isn't there.

JERRY POPP, *track and cross-country, Bowman High, North Dakota:*
I've got three kids. They were all born in the late spring. I get teased about that. It's always been the last week I'm home before school starts, if you know what I mean.

TOM BROSNIHAN, *basketball assistant, West Side High, Omaha:*
I was at Creighton University from 1970 to 1982. I did the recruiting. My kids were young, and I know it was hard on them. It was hard on my marriage, too. I got divorced last year. Being an assistant is a tough life. I enjoyed it, but it's a tough life. I do think that when I came off the road I gave my kids good time. Make the time good when you do come home. Show how much you really do care. I've always thought my children knew that, and as a result they didn't have any problem. At least I don't think they did.

I'm sure my ex would disagree. I'd be gone twelve, thirteen days—maybe more—a month. That took its toll. Once I was close to getting the Southern Illinois job, but my wife didn't want to leave Omaha. She said as the head coach I'd never be home. So I was limited. I've always not blamed her, but it's still a matter of not getting to the big time. I don't say that with regret. Maybe it was the right thing. A lot of guys have wonderful families and they're doing it. My family was good too; it just didn't work out.

BILLY BARNETT, *six-man football, Dell City, Texas:* Coaches don't lay it on the line. They're afraid to show any feelings. But yeah, I've had coaches say to me, "Me and my wife, it's gone." That's all they'll say.

SAM RUTIGLIANO: I was in the locker room getting ready for practice the week before we played Florida State. I was then a coach at the University of Maryland. I was talkin' small talk with the head coach, Lou Sabin, about how my wife got a great deal on carpet. He gave me one of those "Ps-s-st! Come here!" Then he says, "Don't buy the carpeting." "What do you mean?" "I just got a phone call," he says. "Got an opportunity to go with the Denver Broncos." I looked at him. He said, "You want to go?" I said, "Yeah, but you're going to have to tell my wife!"

LINDA LEAVER, *Brian Boitano's skating coach:* Brian was in one of my beginning skating classes when I first noticed him. At the end of each class we tested everybody to see if they were proficient enough to go to the next level. They had to do a simple two-foot spin. Brian spun so fast he fell down. I told him to slow down, that he didn't need to spin that fast. But he wound up and spun so fast he fell down again.

In his first private lesson I found Brian highly coachable. He wanted to please me so much that when he did a jump, instead of letting his head go around with the turn, he kept his eye on me as long as he could to see if I liked the takeoff. Then, at the last minute, he'd flip his head around to see if I approved. He loved to skate, to try new things. I went home and told my husband that I had this terrific new student, only eight years old. He said, "You always think your students are good." And I said, "Yes, but this one's going to be a world champion."

When Brian was twelve years old he developed "jumper's knee." His doctor suggested that he be casted and that he might not ever skate again. His parents consulted several doctors and chose one who didn't cast him and recommended that Brian stay off the ice at least six months. He was out nine. During that time, my husband completed his Ph.D. from Stanford and was looking for a job. He received a fantastic opportunity on the East Coast. I said, "Give me five years. Please." We had moved for the Navy and his schooling. "Brian can be a world champion." He believed in Brian and he believed me and he took a job locally.

That five years turned into a long time. When I look back, things like that seem amazing, but at the time they were perfectly normal. I believed so strongly that Brian would be a great skater, and that I wanted to work with him, and here he was, injured and not even on the ice. I had an absolute belief that Brian would be a world champion.

SAM RUTIGLIANO: I moved nineteen times; my kids went to twenty-three different schools; I bought and sold eleven houses.

HUBIE BROWN, *New York Knicks (retired):* You have to be married to a very strong woman. Because she's the one who has to start from scratch making friendships. She's the one stuck getting the right schools for the children, the right church. She's the one who has to suck it up and survive on the amount of money you're bringing in as an assistant. The new coach moving ahead, you walk into an instant situation with the new team, the coaches, the office staff. You're on the road recruiting, seeing America, getting out, using the expense account. You just can't make it, unless you're married to a horse.

HARRY VANDERSLICE, *Little League baseball, Ocean City, New Jersey:* My son was playing. He was seven years old—he's thirty-seven now. We're in the stands and I'm saying, "The coach gets along with the kids, but he doesn't know baseball." All of a sudden I'm this big mouth. And my wife says, "Well, if you're so good, why don't you take it up?"

I coached for thirty-two years—I still work with the pitchers—and I still think she set me up. We used to go to Shibe Park [Philadelphia Phillies] on dates. We'd come in on the train. I remember the first game, I asked her to hold my scorebook while I got hot dogs. There was a man on first and one out and I'm telling her the guy at the plate hits the ball and the guys out there are outfielders and these guys in here are infielders, all that. When I come back the other team's up and she hands me the scorebook, and there it is marked down: "6–4–3." And I'm feeling like a real idiot.

CARLTON LEWIS, *football, West Point High, Georgia:* My wife was killed. . . . Somebody run her off Interstate 85 into the river. We didn't find her from Friday till Wednesday. She was going down to buy a country ham, and on the way back somebody hit her on the right rear fender and knocked her over the bank and into the river, and she went under. It happened during football season. My daughter, she was thirteen, she'd gone on the bus to Jackson to see us play. We always had a bus to take students, and she was on the bus and wasn't in the car. I missed the next week looking for [my wife]. We buried her on Thursday, and I went out Friday night and I coached.

DARLENE KLUKA, *Ph.D., assistant professor in health, counseling, and kinesiology, University of Alabama at Birmingham (and retired volleyball coach):* What has it cost me? It cost me a significant relationship, and I lost my boy in the transaction. What has it cost me? I would have loved to have kept my family intact. I would have loved to have had a larger group of children to "take care of me" as I grow older. I came through when it was extremely difficult. And today it still is extremely difficult for a female to devote 100 percent to the job, 100 percent to the family, 100 percent to yourself. It took quite a toll. If I had it to do over again, would I do it? Yes. But I would make a few changes along the way.

I would have chosen to do less as a professional—not *be* less, just do less. Then I could have tried to have some type of home scenario. I look at male coaches, and they have wives who stand in the background and take care of the home fires. I was not afforded that luxury. It's quite a balancing act, being a wife and mother and full-time coach and a good professional.

BUTCH VAN BREDA KOLFF, *basketball, Hofstra University, Long Island:* You don't make a sacrifice. You do but you don't. The family comes to all the games. We have pictures of the kids when they were little. We'd go to Berelli's afterward and get spaghetti. It's almost the opposite of a sacrifice. You've got your children around a collegiate atmosphere. What better way is there? They don't ever think, "Am I going to college?" And they're around nice guys. It's almost easy to bring kids up well.

In Princeton, we lived in an apartment. We'd lose a tough game on the road and we wouldn't get back until 2 o'clock. But I'd know there'd be things pasted on the door. "Don't worry, Daddy, the sun is shining." So you're not there but you are there. They're all a part of you.

It's all worth it. The pluses far outweigh the minuses. You go to a Final Four and they go with you. We lost to North Carolina in overtime in the tournament one time, and the whole team went out afterward and then got back to the hotel and went in the pool. My kids are in the pool and we're passing a basketball around, and the kids are having a great time. The average child doesn't get that kind of stuff. They still talk about it: "Remember that time we were all in that damn pool."

DORIS HARDY, *athletic director, Riverside/Brookfield High, Illinois:* I've had to make lots of sacrifices. *Lots.* I had to make some major decisions about the life I wanted to lead. There's no way I could have gotten married and had a family and done as much as I have professionally. You just say good-bye to a personal life, and that's the choice you make. And no regrets, okay?

I never sat down and said, "Okay, Doris, here's road A and here's road B—which one you taking?" I gradually moved in that direction as things happened in women's sports. You become a head coach, an assistant AD, you move into the department chair. One thing pushed into another. And then you wake up one day—this just happened to me—and say, "My God, you're going to be fifty! What happened to your life?"

Of the original group of women in the Chicago area who got girls' sports started, I was the last to stop coaching. I used to have a whole group of friends who coached. We'd get together and have a drink and complain. That part I miss. Now, either the women coaches are too young, or they're guys and they've got their own families. There's a price to be paid either way. If I had gotten married, had children, there would have been a price that way, too. I wouldn't have done some of the things I've done. But that's life. You make choices.

SALLY BAUM, *tennis, Goucher College, Towson, Maryland:* I was going to be the next Sonny Jurgenson. I had no clue at age eight that I couldn't do that. I'd play for hours, punting the ball to myself. I'm a Redskins freak, still am. My dad would help. We'd do anything you could do to throw and kick and hit. It wasn't what a girl did, but I loved it. Nothing was going to take its place; not boyfriends, not . . . anything.

I knew I was going to coach. If you're doing anything with coaching, you're going to hear about Slippery Rock [University in Pennsylvania]. I was a hard-core athlete in college, just like in high school. I played lacrosse and field hockey. I graduated from high school in 1972, the year before Title IX. It took a couple of years to get instituted, so it wasn't until my senior year that Slippery Rock offered scholarships to the freshman class. I'd look at them and say, you're not good enough to be on scholarship.

A couple of years' difference and I would have been a scholarship athlete. I would have stuck with basketball. I hit for 32 points a game in high school. I would have been a point guard, a John Stockton type, a long-range bomber. Basketball would have been my life. I would have gone through the ranks just like the men have done: become an assistant, then be a head coach, do all that. But there weren't those options then.

I would have been somewhere in Division I, being a point guard, going to the Final Four. I can just see it. Boy, to get to the finals! The Olympics. One time, let me do it. You have to feel that it could've happened. Even if I hadn't made the team, at least I would have had my shot.

But you know, I think it's better for me that things turned out the way they did. I'm much happier this way than I would have been the other way. To fall into that competition thing, the dog-eat-dog and survival thing. Forget it. I don't know whether I would have gotten married. And I would never have had the boys—I've got four boys. I would have gotten caught up in all that basketball-is-my-life stuff. Absolutely.

That would not be the life for me. But had I been eighteen back then, back in '73, and not twenty-two, I tell you, I'd have ended up like that. I would have grabbed for that brass ring. You have to go for it. The only reason I didn't is because it wasn't there. You have to wonder how many like me are out there. And how many of those kids who came after me who did get caught up in it would have been happier doing something else.

STEPHANIE VANDERSLICE GAITLEY, *basketball, St. Joseph's University, Philadelphia:* I was at Villanova as a player my sophomore year; Frank was done college—he went to Albright. He came up to

Villanova to play a pickup game. He came in with another good-looking guy, and I thought, Hmmm, two tall, good-looking guys. It was real casual. Then, after we lost to Rutgers, the last game of the season, and the tension was off, I wanted to see him. We went steady junior year, got engaged senior year, and got married after graduation.

Frank's a unique individual. He's done a lot of things for me that a lot of guys wouldn't do. I think he realized there's only like 290 Division I coaching jobs. I can still remember walking around the University of Richmond campus when I interviewed. It's the prettiest school I've ever seen. And he said, "You better get this job." At that point we had not decided that we wanted to coach together. What happened was when we were in Richmond and Frank was in sales and I was coaching—he says this himself—he got jealous because I had a job that I loved. So he became a volunteer coach, and we were fine with that. So much of this job you take home with you anyway.

I had to come to grips early on with "Could I handle this? My husband as my assistant coach?" I had to get over the insecurity of that. And Frank went through "What are my friends going to say? They'll think I work for my wife." And then we both went through some stages in our lives. His father passed away. Life's too short to worry what people think. Frank had a sales job and we had all this money and we were still miserable.

I've been a head coach now seven years. Frank has been my assistant all seven, with the last three years on a full-time basis. It all meshes together. Frank is not intimidated by the fact that I'm the head coach. There's a nice chemistry, and it works. At Richmond, people were concerned everybody would think it was really Frank. That didn't faze me at all. I am extremely confident. Frank is a very dominating person, very vocal and demanding. But I never feel I have to get over top of that for the kids to know I'm the head coach. When a decision needs to be made, they see me.

I think the kids look at Frank and say, "He must really love it if he's going to be an assistant to his wife." I think they respect that. Frank doesn't mind being the fall guy, getting on kids and getting in their faces. He knows that's not me. And after the kids sit back and realize that's what he's doing, they understand it, because they also know that he would do anything in the world for them.

I remember one game when I was still at Richmond. It was against James Madison. We were 22–4, it was the last game, and we were going for an undefeated league season. By halftime we're down 10. It was ugly. In the second half we're making a run and there's a whistle and Frank freaks and gets a technical. And then I yell at him: "What the hell are you doing?" It was the wrong time to take a T. We lost the game.

Frank thought he was responsible, and he came into the locker room and told the team. Then he split. It was Alumni Day and I had to go meet all of them. As soon as I could I called my dad. I was crying, I was so upset. "Dad, I'm so worried about Frank." You could see it in his face in the locker room, he looked like a puppy dog. My dad was real worried, because he had a card game going and he got himself away. "He'll be all right, honey. I'll talk to him."

Frank came back that night, and it was my turn to pick him up. The next day we practiced and came back full steam. The conference tournament was at our place and we had the same team again, and it was the same scenario all over again, except this time we won. It's probably the most exhilarating game I've ever been involved with in my life.

I know I'm lucky. I found Frank, I got my master's, got married. Our boy comes to practice. The new baby [Gaitley was pregnant during the interview] will be with me. Our opener is December 1. By then I should be huge. I don't foresee being out very long [after the baby is born]. The first time I was back in three days. We have to give the kids one day off a week, so maybe I'll only miss two days. I can always sit and shout.

I've been coached by men and I've been coached by women. I don't feel there's much difference. But I always use in my [recruiting] pitch that they'll be playing for someone who went through all the things they're going to go through. I've had the good games; I've had the bad games. I've had the boyfriends; I've had the cycles. I've had everything they're going to experience. I think that I portray something to them. You can be a mother, you can be a wife, you can be a coach, you can be a professional. You can have it all.

[Gaitley had her baby the week before the season opener. While her mother babysat, Gaitley coached. Her doctor saw her on television, called the arena, and told her to go home. She didn't.]

JOHN KEMMERER, *basketball, Riverdale High, Fort Myers, Florida (no longer coaching):* I coached for fifteen years and I walked away a winner. I was ready to get out. I didn't want it to affect my marriage, but it did. I'm going through a divorce now. I tried to avoid all those things, but I guess I waited too long.

I can remember when my first daughter was two years old, I came home early, and she started crying because she didn't know who I was. I'd wake up at 4 and be gone from the house by 6 o'clock. It was dark when I left and it was dark when I got home. I'd fix myself two, three drinks, eat, and go to bed. My family didn't come first. I used to say it did, but it didn't. That's how I handled things, and I handled them wrong.

I've seen coaches who handle it right. I guess these coaches have control over their lives. If they're married, they have control over their marriages. They got what they want; they must love it. But I have to wonder how happy they really are. My ex-wife and I have talked about this. How we could have carried on our marriage the way things were. I set a pattern that we stayed with. I'll bet these guys have the same type of marriage. They never got to that point in time, like we did, where you finally realize your life could be a whole lot better than it is.

KATHY RUSH, *basketball, Immaculata College (retired):* In '72, when we won the first title [Rush's Immaculata teams won the first three women's NCAA championships], I was pregnant with my older boy. In '74, when we won our third, I was seven months' pregnant with my younger boy. In 1975 I coached the Pan Am team, which was also the World Championship team. We picked the team in June, practiced in August, and in September we went to South America and then Mexico City. I arrived home in November just in time to start the college season. In June of '76 my husband and I split up.

In '77, when I got out of coaching, I said I'd taken a lot of time away from my children, so I was going to take a year off. And it was "Wow! This is what normal people live like?" I went out to dinner on Friday nights: I did things on the weekends, went skiing. "This is great! Let's take one more year." Now it's fifteen years later.

JIM SATALIN, *basketball, Duquesne University (retired):* There are coaches out there who would get off the bandwagon right now if they could just figure out a way to do it. There's a lot of coaches who wish they were doing something else.

Coaches come in here to play Syracuse. [Satalin does local TV commentary.] Big-time, high-powered coaches, they all say the same thing: "You look relaxed, you look better." It's obvious they still want to coach, but there's this other side of them saying, "It must be nice to go to a basketball game and not have your stomach get chewed up."

They'll ask me if I enjoy what I'm doing. Do I enjoy not coaching anymore? I still love the game, and I love the TV work. I get to shoot the breeze with the coaches, go out and have a couple of beers. I love all that, but in terms of the actual coaching, and recruiting and dealing with school administrators and those kinds of things, no, I don't miss any of that in any way at all. And then I tell them: "And you know what, I don't think you would either."

BILL WHITMORE, *athletic director, Concord school district, New Hampshire:* Coaches have amazing egos. That's one thing I really didn't like. They just thought they were better than everybody else. They'd cheat on their wives. A lot of them were alcoholics. No substance, and yet they'd preach it. I always kid people. I say I had a choice of three things when I coached. Number one, when I was on the road, I could drink. Number two, I could pick up women. Number three, I could drink coffee. There's so much pressure, you need a vice. I drank coffee.

ANONYMOUS: Addiction-wise, I abused alcohol right from the start, when I was 16 years old with my buddies. I've since found out after I had my problems that almost every one of the people I grew up with has had a problem with either drugs or alcohol. Someone told me two years before [treatment] that I was an alcoholic. I laughed at them. "What do you mean, I'm an alcoholic? Look at how many games I've won. Look at how much money I'm making." The fact is I had a terrible problem that almost killed me.

There's a lot of stress in coaching. But there's stress in every facet of life. No one put a drink in my hand. No one put a gun to my head and made me drink. It was completely my own doing. I have to look at myself. It would be too easy to say, "It's because of my mother," or, "It's because of my job." That's the type of excuse I would never have taken from my players, I can't take it from myself.

Every addict figures out ways to maintain things, to enable themselves. I had maybe seven, eight speeding tickets, but I never got one when I was drinking. I would never drive fast when I was drinking. It was when I was going to get a drink, that's when I'd be speeding. They told me in treatment that statistics say you drive 175 times drunk before you're arrested.

I was a classic case of denial—minimize, rationalize, intellectualize. I did all that. *I was a successful coach.* You know, as an addicted person, you're never satisfied with anything. With me it was always, "Don't these people know that I can coach? That the kids I have can play?" The weakness is wrapped right around the strength. I would say I am a very driven person. Look at my record—every step of the way, my teams overachieved. But instead of being grateful, I was resentful: The system is so unfair; there are a lot of coaches more well known than me who don't coach as well as I do. All of that may be true, but it's still the talking of an addicted person.

The weakness is wrapped right around the strength. Take less and make more out of it. There's nothing wrong with that. It's the American way and all that—work harder and make your life better. That's coaching. The lifestyle lends itself to that. The next win, the next test; get satisfied and you lose. I'm coming to grips with that, continuing to understand. What it is and the fact that it never goes away, that it's always there, calling me.

I know coaches who are alcoholic. A lot of them don't know it. Some of the most talented people I know are addicted people. Success has many fathers, failure dies an orphan every time. When I was winning, an awful lot of people were coming around and calling. After I got into trouble it was a whole different ball game. *That* is a sobering experience.

I look back now, and thank God. It was the best thing that could have happened, because I had to hit bottom. In the program, you name it, claim it, and then you dump it. The pain, the shame, the guilt. You have to take responsibility for it, but then you have to put it behind you. Yesterday is a cancelled check, tomorrow a promissory note, today is cash on the line. All I'm promised is today.

Things have gone very well for me since I've gone into treatment. I'm talking with some people. I'm looking forward to getting on with my life. All I know is right now I'm feeling better every day. And I have to wonder: If I did all I did while I was medicating myself everyday, what can I do being sober?

One-on-One: Anonymous

An unintended though not unforeseen consequence of the NCAA's takeover of the AIAW (Association for Intercollegiate Athletics for Women) in 1982 is that the number of women coaching women has plummeted. An unintended—and, again, probably not unforeseen—consequence of this shift is the increase in sexual harassment of female athletes by male coaches and inappropriate behavior by both coaches and athletes.

The coach, by the very nature of his position, is a powerful figure in an athlete's life. The athlete, by the very nature of her position, is conditioned to please her coach. But where do the lines get drawn? And who gets to draw them? Boundaries blur; signals get easily mixed. There is much debate as to how widespread this problem really is. Meanwhile, it remains a situation that smolders with incendiary potential.

I had just been named athletic director. He was on sabbatical. Soon after I took over I started to have these women student athletes come to me asking, "Will this coach be back?" I had ideas things were going on. But I heard things second- or third-hand: A gal had had an affair with this coach. They went to a party and ended up in bed. Then she found out he was married, had two kids. She was ready to kill the guy.

I also knew through the grapevine about [another] girl who'd had a relationship with him. She knew he was married, everything. She was head over heels for this guy. She felt he would leave his wife, but of course he didn't. His wife found out and started coming to practice. He dropped her, and she left school. It blew her mind.

This girl was willing, so far as I know, but there were others who weren't. They'd come to me and say, "He'll put his hand on my knee"; "He'll run his hand up my leg and I don't like it." I said, "Do you tell him to stop?" And they'd go, "Well, yeah, but I don't know if I can say no."

It can be really tough when you're a woman with a male coach. He controls the scholarships, who's on the team, who travels to away games. Who plays. Everything. Women, I think, are by nature very trusting. They're more open; they like affection. They like to give hugs and get hugs. But where does one thing end and another take over?

This coach was very manipulative. He was *very* good-looking. And very charming. You could get swept up in it. Especially these young girls. It was interesting. There never seemed to be any unattractive women on his team. That may be neither here nor there, but it was very obvious. Initially, this guy was a real mover and shaker. But there was kind of diminished returns. Every year the numbers [on his team] went down.

When I was just a coach, it would've been real difficult for me to tell another coach what he should do. I was pretty sure what was happening, but I couldn't prove it. It will always come down to a he said/she said situation. There was a lot of rumormongering. You had to be real careful about who you believed and what you believed.

But then I got the title [of athletic director]. Until then, there was no woman in a position of authority. When [the women who complained] came to me, their concern was, "If I say what's going on, is there anything that can be done about it?" I told them I had to know exactly what was done, and asked if they would be willing to stand up and say it. But until a situation happened with me, there was nothing I could substantiate.

The athletic staff, the male coaches and the female coaches and the secretaries, we were all at a party. We did a lot of social things. This coach is there, so is his wife. I go to the refrigerator to get a beer, and all of sudden this guy is right behind me. "Hey, did you see that outside?" he said. "Come on out here." We go outside, it's real dark. And he starts . . . peeing. Yeah, peeing! Then he grabbed me and put my

hand on his penis. And I said, "You dumb asshole! I should go in there and tell your wife." "Don't do that, don't do that," he said. "I'm just having fun." And I start thinking, what if I was a seventeen-, eighteen-year-old girl on his team right now?

After that I brought everything forward. We were in a meeting planning the year. They were all men. It's one of those things where you don't know where to start. "I've got to come right out and tell you that I've had complaints from some women student athletes about this coach. He's been having affairs with these young ladies." They all looked at me. "That's not happening. He's got a beautiful wife and kids." The old scenario. Well, this guy with the wife and kids was messing around, and what are we gonna do about it? "Do you know what you're doing? You're playing with fire." I was given a month to prove it.

I tried to get in touch with the gal [who had expected the coach to leave his wife]. I had no idea what perspective she was coming from. Was she coerced into this relationship or was it a willing give-and-take? She absolutely would not talk to me. But there were a couple of gals who had been on his team who had transferred. They had really looked up to this coach. I tracked them down and talked to them. He had gone to their house. It was about 11:30 at night and he'd been drinking, and he was honking the horn, hollering for them to come down. One of them did.

She was a very naive gal. I mean, she had dated very little, wasn't sexually active—when you're in a college setting, you know the ones that are and the ones that aren't. Or at least you hear things and have a pretty good idea.

He had intercourse with her that night.

I told this girl that she had to put this all in writing, and that if it went to court she was going to have to stand up and say it. She goes, "How do I know anything will happen?" And I said, "You have my word on it." So she wrote me a letter. I read it, and, my God, I started crying. What this girl went through with this man. Then I got so damn mad I wanted to kill the guy myself.

The first thing I did was copy the letter. Early on, two administrators told me to cover my ass because people were out to get me. I kept the original at home. I didn't want people getting into my office at night. You can call that paranoid, but I was going to protect these people.

I took a copy of the letter to the dean—the former football coach. He'd been in total denial. Then he read the letter and goes, "I had a feeling this might be going on." Right. He called up the [school's] lawyer and read it to him. "Is this grounds for firing?" The lawyer says, "The guy's history." The next morning they called this coach in and read him the letter and asked him, "Did this happen?" And he says, "Oh, yeah. And my wife knows about it." Like, "So what?" They gave him two choices: resign or get fired. He immediately said he wouldn't fight it and resigned.

It was kind of a sour-grapes ending. We accomplished what we wanted, but he's off the hook. That left a bad taste in the mouth. The university didn't make anything public. That was the deal. People would say to me, "He's not coming back?" And all I could say is, "Right." We were never able to bring it to a conclusion.

I did speak to some of the girls one-on-one. They were very happy—almost surprised that the system had worked. But no sooner would they say they were happy when they'd ask me where he was. I have no idea. "Where will he go now?" "Who will be his next victim?" All I could say was there was nothing we could do about that. We resolved the problem we had. That was the best we could do. *[The narrator has since left the college where these events took place.]*

TEN

Getting Fired

It wasn't her idea, she says. If she had her way, she'd still be out there every spring, running behind her girls and onto the grass for the start of another softball season. But a few years back, Andrew Jackson High School in Chalmette, Louisiana, became a magnet school, one that didn't offer the traditional team sports. After twenty-two years, Rose Misuraca Scott was no longer a softball coach.

It happens to all coaches. There comes the day when there is no game. They burn out, quit, get fired. They're told the money isn't there, that the organization is going in a "new direction." Someone tells them how much they're appreciated, then asks them to clean out their desks. Sometimes they are pulled away kicking and screaming. Sometimes they run away gleefully, free at last. The differences are similar (as Yogi Berra may or may not have said), but sooner or later— and usually sooner than later—they wake up and suddenly there is no game waiting for them. No routine to get them through the day, no rituals of tradition. No grinding in the pit of the stomach, no thumping of the temples. There's . . . nothing.

Rose Scott keeps her hand in. She's the athletic director, after all. And she teaches some P.E., which means she still gets out there every spring, back onto the grass and dirt of the softball diamond. But it's not the same. "I miss the smell of the field," she explains. "There's a different smell when you're smelling it with a P.E. class than with a team after school." What Rose Scott means is she misses the talent.

You know: The girl at the hot corner who can go to her right and get the ball to first on a rope.

Talent. It made everything sharper. "You can smell the grass anytime," Rose Scott says, "but how does it smell when it's first cut?" That's the difference; that's the talent. "How does the dirt smell when it's turned over for the first time? How do you explain that? It's just sharper. It's new, it's exciting. You can smell it. You can feel it. You can almost reach out and touch it. It's just this smell that fills up your nose. It can get hold of you." And never let go.

P. J. CARELISIMO, *basketball, Seton Hall:* Digger Phelps coached Fordham my senior year. I was supposed to start law school the following year. But Digger left Fordham, and I got a chance to be an assistant coach for five hundred dollars. I can say now things worked out. But look back five or six years after I got the Seton Hall job, and you would have been saying I should have gone to law school. Three years from now, who knows, things might change again. Coaching's great—I love it, I wouldn't do anything else. But I know I've been very lucky. And that it could all change quickly.

There are a lot of successful coaches who are out of jobs right now. Your stock goes up and down very quickly. What have you done for me lately? Go back eight, ten years and look at the Final Fours, and you'll find people who are no longer coaching. They've had to go the pro-assistant route, go to Europe, or they're out of jobs. Coach a major university, make good money, be an NBA head coach: It doesn't always work out like that.

I've got a really good situation. But when I took the job in 1982, it was not perceived to be a good situation. Four or five years ago my job was in jeopardy. I can say that if we hadn't got to the NCAAs, I'd have been out. Then who knows?

SAM RUTIGLIANO, *football, Liberty University, Lynchburg, Virginia:* When I was coaching back in Lafayette High School in Brooklyn, there was a coach who'd tell me, "Between a pat on the back and a kick in the tail is six inches." That's coaching. Too many coaches make the business their god. That's a big mistake. You will never, ever be able to count on it. There will always be someone to tap you on the shoulder and say, "Hey, you're finished." Like they did with me.

TOM HOUSE, *assistant to the general manager, Texas Rangers (and former pitching coach):* Baseball is a vicious game. If you're past your prime it shows pretty quick. I don't want to be some guy leaning on a fungo bat. This is a real precarious existence.

JIM SATALIN, *basketball, Duquesne University:* Bill Foster told me once that you should never stay more than five years at the same school. After that they appreciate you less and less, no matter what your record is. You become part of the same old thing. He was absolutely right on the money.

JOE TORRE, *St. Louis Cardinals:* You learn to recognize the signs. People in the organization don't talk to you. People don't visit. Nobody returns your calls.

HUBIE BROWN, *New York Knicks (retired):* You can get fired because of your win–loss record. You can get fired because of your style of play, even if you win. You can lose your job in a merger—that's happening a ton at big-city high schools. Another way is to create an incident— punch somebody, grab a kid. The last way is to take a stand.

FRANK LAYDEN, *Utah Jazz (retired):* I loved being the coach at Niagara. I'd played there. I'd probably be at Niagara today. . . . All I wanted was some kind of guarantee, some kind of long-term contract, some kind of tenure. But I used the critical words: "or else." Never say that. I said I'd leave or else, and they planned my good-bye party.

HUBIE BROWN: When you take a stand, you must be ready to go before you do it. Don't threaten the athletic director, the principal, the head of the boosters, the superintendent because you think your past record, your past accolades are bigger than the system. Before you do that you better have another job.

K. C. JONES, *Seattle Supersonics (retired):* You got twelve million coaches out there, everyone lined up to take your job. But the approach while you're coaching is to focus on what's between the lines. That's why getting fired [by the Washington Bullets] was a real jolt. Being fired for the first time—there's no way to handle it. At first I felt bad. Later on it felt disastrous. It snuck up on me. I didn't know it took such a toll, until some months later it was "Wow!" And I recognized that the thing took a much greater toll, had much more of an impact, than I had thought.

JIM SATALIN: My last two or three years at Duquesne were tough. We weren't winning a lot and it was very frustrating. I had come to Duquesne from St. Bonaventure, where I'd won a lot. I was one of the bright young coaches, and then I went to Duquesne and it didn't work.

The first year was good. Duquesne had lost everybody from the previous year, but we won twelve games and I was coach of the year in the Atlantic 10. The future looked pretty good. Then four players got caught in a rape situation. They couldn't play on the team, but we kept them on scholarship. They were all acquitted, but then two of them were kicked out of school and two of them had to sit out another year. We lost two years of scholarships and it ruined the program.

The firing: It didn't come particularly out of nowhere. The last couple of weeks there were a lot of hassles, and a couple of the media people were involved. So it wasn't a shock. But still . . . it's like a death: Even though somebody might be sick for a long time, when they die and it's final, it's still terribly shocking, terribly disappointing. Looking back, it's something that probably won't ever leave me. No matter what anybody tells you.

I was at the school, and they called me in. The one thing I wanted was to keep my self-respect. I wasn't going to beg for the job; I wasn't going to let them say I resigned. "Play one way or the other." I walked out of that office and went over to the athletic office, and it hit me again. There was a guy there, a friend, a janitor, and I asked him to pack my stuff. Then I went to see my attorney. "There's going to be some statements made," I said, "and I want to make sure I make the right statement." Then I went home.

My daughter was in eighth grade then, and I had a boy in the fifth. We got everybody together, and I said, "I want you to know that it's going to be all over the news that I was fired today." They started crying. I think in the back of their minds they thought we probably wouldn't be staying in Pittsburgh. That hurt as much as anything. They really liked it there. We had great friends. To me, Pittsburgh is still home. The only reason we did leave is because I didn't know if I could stay there. It might have been too much to read about the team every day, to hear about this guy doing a great job, that guy doing a great job, or what a difference this year as compared to last year.

As it was, we stayed a whole year. I became very embarrassed. I didn't want to be seen on the street. It was like I was a failure, and I had a tough time living with that. And I was worried about the kids. People can be mean. They say things, even inadvertently.

I'm from Syracuse. My father still lives here, and I have a brother and sisters here. Friends were able to get me a good job as a sales manager at an insurance agency, making a little more money than coaching. I got into some TV work for the university, and here we are.

I can look back and say that getting fired was a blessing in disguise. That doesn't mean it wasn't excruciatingly painful. I lost some self-esteem, some self-respect. It was devastating in the sense that I don't know whether you ever get over that initial feeling of hurt.

TONY LA RUSSA, *manager, Oakland Athletics:* Getting fired [by the Chicago White Sox] was a real test. I'd always asked a lot of questions of managers, coaches, baseball people that I respect. I felt I had a good framework for handling the good times/bad times. Just because your job is in jeopardy, you don't change the person you are, you don't change your decisions, you don't try and cover your butt. It was a good, tough experience. I held true to what I'd been taught, and when I walked I felt I'd done my best.

But when you put eight, nine years into one organization, you don't just get fired, you can't just leave. We had a real family-type thing there, from the people who worked in the ballpark up to the front office. It's one of the reasons we got to where we did. It really bothered me that that was getting disrupted.

I remember we did a road trip in '83, the year we won the division. I'll never forget it. We got beat at home two out of three by the Orioles. The last game was real emotional. That's the game I threw first base. The umpire took away a two-run homer, and we ended up getting beat by one run. So now we're going on the trip. New York, Texas, Kansas City. Kansas City had a good ball club, and the Yankees were still the Yankees. Texas was our big competitor, and we had four with them.

Their advance guy watched us for about a week and reported back to [manager] Doug Rader that we were "winning ugly"—you know, a blooper, an error, something. We sweep the Yankees. Great series; won one game 1-0. Then we go to Texas; we had a four-gamer with them. One of those games was a little strange, and that's when Doug said to reporters, "They're winning ugly, and one of these days it's going to come crashing down around them." We won three of four. It was beautiful.

So now we've won six of seven, and we go to Kansas City and win two of three. We had to keep it going, and we won eight of ten. Our lead went from four or five to maybe seven or eight, and Texas is coming in. The fans really caught on. They had "WIN UGLY" signs all over the place. Though the truth is that it's never an ugly win. I don't care what it looks like. You can win 10–0 and it's never easy, it's never ugly.

A couple of years later, it was just unfortunately the wrong combination of people. Ken Harrelson should have had his own manager, and instead he had me. It didn't work; a change had to be made. But I still felt real bad. In fact, when the A's first called me two or three weeks later, I asked for more time. I was interested, but I wanted to take over the next spring or at the end of the season. They said September 1. I said no. I wanted time. I would have liked to have let Chicago go first. [La Russa took the A's job less than a month after being fired.]

GARY BLACKNEY, *football, Bowling Green University:* Going to Ohio State to coach under Earle Bruce was like going to Mecca. It was the pinnacle of college football coaching. That's how I viewed it. We won over 85 percent of our games; we won probably the same percentage of bowl games; we graduated over 75 percent of our student athletes. We did *everything* right. And yet we got fired. That was mind-boggling.

SAM RUTIGLIANO: I've been in that room when an entire coaching staff is fired. They look at each other, they look at themselves and say, "What can I do? It's the only thing I know." You have no place to turn and you're dead in the water.

GARY BLACKNEY: It was after we lost to Iowa, the Monday before Michigan. The AD called an emergency meeting. You don't do that the week of the Michigan game. Everybody's asking . . . "What's going on?" Then we found out: We were all getting fired. We were 5–4–1 that year, but in my other years with Earle [Bruce], no season was ever less than 9–3. It's still the biggest shock.

SAM RUTIGLIANO: I walked away [from a staff firing at New England] saying to my wife, "Only a dumb mouse has only one hole to escape from. I am never going to be in that situation again. Once I hit the magic number between forty-five and fifty-five, I'm either going to be where I want or I'm going to be out. I'm not going to sit around waiting for somebody to tap me on the shoulder."

JIM CRINER, *assistant with the Sacramento Surge in the WLAF; prior to that was fired at Iowa State:* I was lucky to have a plan. For me it was fly fishing. I wanted to own my own shop. I was lucky enough to purchase the number one fly shop in the country, Bud Lilly's Fly Shop in West Yellowstone, Montana, in the corner with Idaho and Wyoming.

That's the bad thing about football: It's a disease. It's what makes you a good coach, but it's also what gives you a narrow field of interest. As a result, you don't develop abilities in other areas where you could be just as successful. Coaches are too into what they're doing. They put in an unbelievable amount of time. I've had friends who were outstanding coaches, who had worked very hard throughout their careers. They had a bad year and they got fired. All of a sudden there wasn't a coaching job available. They start selling insurance because they have to support a family, and they're miserable.

STAN MORRISON, *basketball, San Jose State:* He came into my office at USC on a Tuesday before we were to leave on Wednesday for a Thursday-Saturday road series in Oregon. They wanted to make a change after the season. Just like that. Getting fired completely sucks. Emotionally and physically it was debilitating. We'd won the PAC-10 the year before. I'm coach of the year. I told my wife, "We're going to Hawaii." We checked into a condominium on Sunday at 2 in the afternoon. I went to bed and woke up at noon on Tuesday. When I'm on vacation, which is rare, I go hard. I ride every wave, dance every dance, jump off every cliff into every pond. This time I never left the condo. Then I said, "Let's put our lives back together."

BUTCH VAN BREDA KOLFF, *basketball, Hofstra University, Hempstead, Long Island:* When I got the [New Orleans] Jazz job they were 1–15. We win my first game and suddenly I'm 1 for 1. Next time I look we're 5 and 42. We were on the ropes forever. But we end up winning twenty-three—going 18 and 17 in our last thirty-five games.

We were looking forward to the next season, but 38–44 wasn't it. Pete [Maravich] was out for twenty games, and without him we were 6 and 14. The next year we had an even better team, and then they go and change the hierarchy. They took the guy from promotions and made him the general manager. Knew nothing. Made the trade that got us Gail Goodrich for a first-round draft choice—Magic Johnson. But we're winning anyway, we're 14 and 12, damn near 16 and 10. And I get fired.

I got this phone call to come to the office right away. My wife's not home, so I leave her a note: "Must go to the office, may be fired." I go in and they got some hatchet man from California and some other guy, might have been a lawyer. They told me. I said, "I'm not saying a word." But I did ask who was going to take my place. Elgin Baylor. And then they said, "Do you think he's a good choice?" Elgin's my boy, so that was fine. But I just look at these guys: "You're asking me?"

I called my wife and told her to get hold of our daughter and to meet me down at Joe's, a little bar we used to go to. I get there, and people are saying, "What are you doing here?" "I got fired." The guy that did the firing, he had cops at the game because people were throwing things at him.

And some enterprising guy, by 5 o'clock that afternoon, he had these handkerchiefs printed up with BUTCH on them. I ended up at another joint after the game, and he was there. Said he tried to sell them for six bucks but they didn't go over. So he dropped to four bucks and, man, they all went. I was a four-dollar cry in New Orleans.

JIM CRINER: I was attracted to Iowa State because they were the worst program in the country. It was an opportunity to shake up the football world. We got to where we beat everybody in the conference—Missouri, Kansas, Kansas State, Oklahoma State—everybody but Oklahoma and Nebraska. And one year we led Oklahoma 10−6 with fifty-four seconds to go, and twice we had chances to beat Nebraska. The program was on the brink.

And then the fourth year the wheels fell off. When I took the job, the athletic director asked me to keep a guy that I ultimately fired because I found out he had violated rules. And I hired another guy who I didn't check out as closely as I usually do. He knew the system, and it was the easy way to get somebody. He violated some rules, and by the time I found out he was already gone.

The guy I fired, he made some accusations to the NCAA. So in the middle of trying to run a season, I become a detective. I hired an attorney and a guy to do some investigation. We were able to reverse everything. What we were accused of got thrown out. But Iowa State got tagged.

The guy who quit before I could get to him, he had used a university credit card to buy gas for kids. No one knew about it. We start going through the files, and suddenly we find it. We had recruited some junior-college kids who had signed with us and came there to live. This guy tries to find the kids an apartment. They were black, and he couldn't find one. So he put them in a motel. But they weren't recruits, they were there to go to school, so that's a violation. And the fact that he drove them around was a violation.

I get back, and the kids have been in the hotel for five days. They didn't have any way to pay the bill, so I paid it. That's what I did wrong. I paid the bill. If I had done what the NCAA wants me to do, I would have kicked them out.

Eventually, the NCAA saddled us with thirty-four violations. We were never accused of anything major, and some went back to previous coaches. And the way it works is this: One coach driving three guys in a car, that's three violations. The press, the majority of them kept the accomplishments of the team separate from everything else. But you can never totally divorce yourself from it. Every news conference there were always the questions. I probably aged ten years in that one six-month period. The guy who had hired me retired. The new president washed his hands of the whole thing. He'd been telling boosters the same thing he'd told me: He was going to stand behind us until the season was over and then decide. But it never got that far. And I never did get direct word.

DOUG BARFIELD, *football, Opelika High, Alabama:* Everybody needs to get fired once. It makes you appreciate and understand things.

I grew up in south Alabama, about eighty miles north of Mobile, in Grove Hill. I played ball at Southern Mississippi. Then I coached a year in Grove Hill, five years in Mobile, and two years at another high school. Then my college coach called me back to Southern Miss. From there I worked my way up the ladder.

I was ambitious. I went to Clemson, then was hired at Auburn as an assistant and spent four years under Coach Shug Jordan. He was a legend. When he resigned, I took over. BOOM! We started out rough, but after four years we were 8–3. But we were never unified. When you win you can overcome that, but we never beat Alabama. They had a gentleman over there name of Bryant. Well, nobody else beat him either.

The fifth year we changed presidents and we lost a couple of close games, and we ended up 5–6. We lost a big game early to Tennessee. The place was filled, and they whacked us: 42–0. The worst licking of my career. We never recovered. We go down to LSU and drop a pass in the end zone. Same thing at Mississippi State—down on the two-inch line and we don't get in. At Auburn you always finish up with Georgia and Alabama, and we lost both by pretty close scores.

There's a fine line between winning and losing. You need that edge, and we didn't have it. The harder you try, the worse it gets. The media gets in there, things get to building, and pretty soon you're fighting City Hall. It was toughest on my family. My kids were in college then, at Auburn. My son was one of our managers; my daughter transferred to Mississippi State. I pressed for a decision. Our A.D. recommended a new four-year contract. The new president—along with the board, who knows?—didn't want that. As Frank Howard said, "I resigned for health reasons: The alumni was sick of me."

I stayed away [from coaching] for seven years. Then a situation came up—a new consolidated high school down in my home county. I needed five years to get twenty-five years of retirement. Plus, I thought it would be a challenge for me at my age. I missed the camaraderie, the competition, the people. I missed the smell of the locker room after the game—it's such a great place. To be with all these guys who have worked hard and planned and accomplished. To see those faces in the locker room after a game is one of the great rewards of coaching.

Now I'm at Opelika. My wife and I discussed moving back here, in the shadow of Auburn. We'd always liked it here, the town, the church, the people. We made our peace before we came. Nobody likes to think they failed at something. What you have to do is look at it rationally and analyze it. Yeah, I regret it. But it's not something I'm going to harbor and carry around with me.

I always thought I would be the one who wouldn't lose perspective. I needed straightening out. I was spending too much time worrying about football. We feel strongly about our faith, and my family is very important. At Auburn I let them slip to second and third. In retrospect, maybe I thought football was too important.

I love athletics, or I wouldn't be back in it. But I'm having fun now. Auburn was the big time, no doubt about it. We were very close to doing well there. We just didn't quite get it done. I guess the thing is, I don't long for that anymore.

PAT GRIFFIN, *associate professor, social justice education program, University of Massachusetts, Amherst (former swim coach):* I had an opportunity to either become the aquatic director or get my doctorate. I went back to school. There are so many things about being a woman coach that men coaches don't have to think about. You have to be a diplomat, you have to be a fighter, you have to know your rights in terms of Title IX. You need to know specifically, *in writing.* You have to know the sex discrimination laws. You have to be prepared to stand up for what you're entitled to, because I don't think there are many athletic directors who are going to give it to you. Women have to fight for everything they get in athletics. And it wears you out.

BILL WHITMORE, *athletic director, Concord school district, New Hampshire:* I enjoyed the teaching [while basketball coach at the University of Vermont]. Getting that six-foot-ten kid who can't play, but by the time he's a junior you've got something. He was a glue horse and you turned him into a thoroughbred. Because you worked together, you sweated together. I loved the strategy. I remember once we were at a tournament, and the only time we had to prepare for the next game was after the first game, so we stayed up all night watching films. Looking for weakness, how to stay away from strengths. That was fun.

The rest of the business is a traveling show. You get home from practice on a Sunday night and you've got ten calls to make to recruits, and they all tell you they've just talked to five other coaches. The next morning you're at the airport, and for two weeks you're on the road. I recruited one kid for a year. I saw him sixty times. I saw his team win one game 115–30 in a Jewish community center. I'm sitting there saying, "He's six-foot-eleven, he's six-foot-eleven."

You know the business. If you don't win, you get fired. If you have a better opportunity, you leave where you are. You move to the next win. Maybe that one gets you closer to an NCAA championship or the hundred-thousand-dollar job. My wife and I said, "This is crazy."

SAM RUTIGLIANO: I believe in a higher power. You've got to have a wife and a family you can go home to who can tell you to take out the garbage. Or you can sit with them and eat pizza, and that's all you want to do with your life. Those are the guys that survive. The ones who don't are the Type-A guys who personalize everything. Every game is a crisis. They get so focused on what they're doing, on what people expect, that they never sit down and assess where they're at. They get lost in the pressure of the moment. And when it's over and done it wasn't any fun.

DICK VERMEIL, *Philadelphia Eagles (retired):* Toward the end of my career I got way too intense in my dealings with the officials. You're after 'em, you're on 'em, you confront 'em after the game. I damn near hit a ref after a game in Dallas. He'd missed the most vicious illegal hit I've ever seen in a pro football game. I was embarrassed, but that's why I went after him. It was inexcusable. The guy could have had his neck broken—I don't know how he ever got up. The ref got loud, and I got louder. It's all part of why I got out of coaching. I could have accomplished more by not being so intense. I knew I was getting wound too tight and I knew I had to take a break. I recognized some things; my wife recognized some things. The wins weren't satisfying me, and the losses were killing me.

[Vermeil often slept at Veterans' Stadium during the season.] I made a lot of mistakes like that. I'm a compulsive worker. If I went to bed at 2 in the morning in the office, that was two more hours of sleep that I got than if I went home. That's the only reason I did it. The mistake was because I thought that way I kept adding another hour to my day. Another hour, another hour.

I kept looking for another detail that would help us win. I kept finding ways to take the next step, the next breakdown of film, the next evaluation. The more I knew, the more I was exposed to even more unique ways of preparing for the game. I'd discover something while preparing for a game, and it would add an hour to my total preparation. That automatically became part of my next week's preparation. I had this thought at 2 in the morning last week, so this week I'll keep looking until 3 o'clock. Pretty soon it was 5 o'clock in the morning.

ABE LEMONS, *basketball, Oklahoma City University (retired):* Get out of coaching for even one year and you lose the feeling. When I got fired by Texas, I decided to redshirt, make them pay me. You forget how you used to hit those Rolaids, how you stayed awake nights worrying about your team, wondering why it's always the good player who's the only one who ever gets hurt.

PAT MANCUSO, *football, Princeton High, Cincinnati:* I'm sixty-three, been at this thirty-seven years. What am I going to do if I retire? What am I going to miss? How am I going to fill the void? That concerns me.

JOHN E. LEE, *football, Walpole High, Massachusetts:* I've talked with retired coaches, and they all say the number one thing they miss is the limelight. I walk downtown here and everybody still knows me. I like that.

JOE TORRE: When I was a broadcaster, traveling anonymously was kind of nice. But being a manager pampers you. You pack your bag, take it to the park, and that night you find it in your room. It's great. It's easy living. You get a suite every place you go. A basket of fruit, a little wine—well, Budweiser, actually. You never have time for that stuff, but it's still nice. People pay attention. What you say has credibility.

People wait for your answers. Whatever you do happens right now. I love it. Everything is *live.*

JENNINGS BOYD, *basketball, Northfork High School, West Virginia (Boyd coached Northfork High to nine state titles, including a national-record eight in a row):* I missed coaching terribly. [Boyd retired from Northfork in 1981.] Wait, let me say that for a while there I was so happy to be away from it I couldn't believe it. But before the end of that first year away, I missed it so much I had to quit going to the games. [Boyd returned to coaching at Bluefield High in West Virginia; he retired again after three years.]

RICHARD CICIARELLI, *baseball, Midlakes High School (retired):* Coaches stay young because they hang out with kids. Get away from the kids and all of a sudden you're an old man.

MIKE MARCOULIS, JR., *basketball and baseball, Freemont High School, Oakland:* My father died in December. In January I went to the principal and said, "I don't know if I can do this anymore." But he said, "See if you can stick it out."

So I stuck it out. I worked the summer leagues, and the next year started and I'd never gotten any time off. There was a lot of frustration, a lot of grief. And then it was the season, and I was working with these kids, and five of them were ineligible, and none of them are responding, nobody was getting along. I woke up one morning and said, "What the fuck am I doing this for? I'm quitting." I called my sister and told her. "I can't go back. These kids, they get to me. I need to get out of Oakland. I need to get out of here. I need to get *out.*" The next morning I told the principal. "You wanna talk about this?" "No."

I sat around for a day, and then a friend stopped by. "What are you going to do?" Well, I had this bright idea. "I'm going to start a kennel." I love dogs. So I told him I wanted to open up a kennel, work with dogs. I have this dream of having some land with dogs running on it and I'm taking care of them. This friend goes, "Huh, okay, sure. Talk to you later."

Well, I start thinking. Do you *really* want to run a kennel? I sat there and got more depressed. I was more depressed being away than I was on the day I left. I missed it. It's hard to get away from. The kids are addicting. You think you can get away. Then you see some new tenth-graders and they're fresh and you see that athletic potential. Hey, maybe we can have a pretty good team. I think it was ninety-six hours later when I called the central office to see if they'd filed my papers. It was on a Saturday, and the kids were playing their last game. "I'm coming back." The guy said he'd see me at six. By game time, I was there.

JOHN WOODEN, *basketball, UCLA (retired):* I didn't miss the games or the tournaments or any of that folderol. But I missed the practices, the working, the daily planning. I missed it right away.

PAT GRIFFIN: I don't miss the coaching part at all. I miss being a coach. I miss being called "Coach." I loved being able to say, "I'm a coach." Especially as a woman. Athletics had always been such an integral part of my life, first as an athlete, then as a coach. When I stopped coaching I had no official tie with the athletic world anymore. For the first time in my life, I was not on a team or the coach of one. It took me a while to figure out what I was. Sometimes I'll be out with a group of friends who still coach, and they'll all be talking about their teams and complaining about this and talking about that, and I always feel sad that I can't talk about it anymore.

BILL MUSSELMAN, *first coach of the Minnesota Timberwolves (now with a CBA team in Rochester, Minnesota):* The thing I miss[ed] more than anything is that everywhere I've been there have been these basket-ball fanatics that kind of surround you. When I was in Albany [in the CBA], there was a guy who was on the board, we'd go get something to eat and talk basketball. There was a PA announcer—after the games we'd sit and talk, rehash the game, talk basketball. Those are the things you miss when, you're out of it. I've never coached for the money. It's the other things: The thrill of the game, back and forth. Finding a way to get some points for your team. The Xs and Os, the preparation. Talking basketball, running into basketball people. I love it.

MARGE RICHTER, *organized the Orlando Rebels, a women's fast-pitch softball team, in 1954; she coached until 1985, when the team*

disbanded: There was a time when I thought I would die if I wasn't coaching. I couldn't conceive of not spending my summers doing that.

We played our home games in Varner Stadium. We sold season tickets, and there was a minor league club with the Twins and we outdrew them. But we were really a traveling team. Our closest competition was in Atlanta. We played in a league with teams from Connecticut, Massachusetts, and Pennsylvania. We were like one of those old barnstorming baseball teams. We'd get in the motor home and go play in the Houston tournament, then go up to Topeka, Kansas; Illinois; and then St. Louis. We'd go up into Canada, the Midwest, the Northeast, all over.

I was never just the coach. I had to make all the travel arrangements, raise all the money. We collected cans and newspapers, cleaned the Citrus Bowl after rock concerts. We had to get the program book out, sell advertisements, beg. I loved to practice, and I had the old-type player who loved to practice, too. The game was the icing on the cake. We played thirty games in a season in the early years, up to eighty-five later on. We won at least 80 percent of our games—I only ever had but one losing season—and we won the national title in 1981.

It was my whole life. And I probably overdid it. I mellowed in the later years, but there was a long time there where it was the be-all and end-all. I could never understand why it wasn't for everybody on the team. Times change. I used to have kids who were thrilled to sit the bench for two years before they got to play. But it got to where it was, If I can't play, I don't want to be here. They didn't have that intensity.

So when it was all over, I didn't miss it as much as I thought I would. Maybe because we finally won a national championship. We were always perennial threats, and we finished second and third and fourth a bunch of times. We won the title in an upset, beating the Brakettes, the team that wins it all the time. The tournament was in Houston, and we had to get right back in the motor home after the game and head back. When we got to Orlando a police escort took us to city hall. They put out a special edition of the paper.

But then it ended. Varner Stadium deteriorated. They knew they were going to tear it down to make a parking lot for the new arena, where the Magic play now. I drove by after it was demolished, when it was still all lying there. I kept the pictures. I hate to look at them.

SHERYL JOHNSON, *field hockey, Stanford University:* I was on the national field hockey team for fourteen years. I was a forward, and then for seven years I was an infielder. I just retired. I played in the most international games of anyone on the U.S. team. I was on three Olympic teams: '80, '84, and '88. In '80 we didn't go. In '84, I remember walking through the tunnel into the Coliseum for the opening ceremonies. It was exactly what I always thought the Olympics would be. We also medaled at that Olympics: We got the bronze. The Seoul Olympics, in the Olympic village—that was a dream come true.

I was an assistant coach at Stanford for one year; this is my seventh year as head coach. I figured when they hired me I'd be able to play and coach, and I'd be all set. I was definitely going for the '92 Olympics. But field hockey is truly an amateur sport, so once Stanford deemphasized field hockey and I got laid off, I couldn't pay my bills. It was either pay the bills or travel with the national team. I decided to pay the rent.

The athletic department was in debt and they had to make some cuts. Men's and women's fencing, wrestling, and field hockey. They made it even for the men and women—they were very clever about that. We had other cuts in '85 and then again in '89. Originally they took away the scholarships. Then they took away the operating budget, then they took my salary, so I became a full-time phys-ed instructor and I coached on the side. Then they took my job away completely. It was hard for me to target my anger, because it's always a committee that decides these things. The person who tells you is never involved in the decision. "We know you're doing a good job. You could have this job forever." Then in the next breath, "We're letting you go."

If I hadn't had all the good experiences through my own playing, I probably wouldn't understand how important it is to keep this going. Other people should have the opportunity I had. There are so many high school kids [in California] who play. It's such a great sport. If it gets dropped at the college level, there will be all these kids who never get the next opportunity. I've basically become a professional fund-raiser. That's the trick: They let me keep my job and stay with the program, but they told me I'd have to raise all the money. I'm fighting constantly to survive. We've done bake sales and car washes. We park cars for different events, take tickets. We do flea markets. Our biggest fund-raiser is the goal-a-thon: People pledge money based on the number of goals we score during the season. It's a lot of work. The other coaches who are in the same boat have to do the same type of work. The bigger sports have secretaries; they have student help. I don't think those head coaches are licking any envelopes.

Here's a doozy: We clean the stadium after football games. *We clean up after another team on campus*—the irony is not lost. It's degrading, but we need the money. And we usually have a winning record. We work all day Sunday. A dead squirrel in potato salad, baby diapers. It's gross. We try not to look. Broken glass, people get cut. You develop a sense of humor when you're picking garbage for eight hours. We called ourselves the "Trash Heroes" for a while. We even had T-shirts made up.

It builds character. The coaches from the programs that got cut, we've talked about it. Because our kids have to work so hard for what they want, they're actually more successful. It's a joke with the administrators: You want a winning record? Cut the funding. The football team's fully funded; they know the money is there. If that were taken away, would the football players work as hard as the field hockey players to fundraise so they could play? No. They'd transfer to another school.

At the regional playoffs in Iowa, our team had lost the day before, and we were watching the second game. Some people from Iowa who had gone to Stanford walked up to some of my kids. Well, the kids were bummed because they'd lost, and they weren't very talkative. When I got home, there was a letter in my box from one of those people in Iowa saying they were really embarrassed because they were Stanford grads and they had friends with them, and the team was really rude. They sent a copy to my athletic director.

I read that letter many, many times, and it took me about a month to write back. When I started writing, it all came out. That these kids had raised money all year to get to that game, they had to clean football stadiums and wash cars. "You don't know what they went through to get there, and then they lost, and they deserved one day to mourn."

We work so hard to keep it going. It's a good program; it's a great sport. Making it to the playoffs, even though we got beat 7–2, my kids went out to play the best they could. They fight so hard for this sport! If it just stops, all that effort's been wasted. [Johnson's field hockey program remains a self-funded varsity sport.]

ELEVEN

Fouls

What we need to remember, he says, is that kids aren't stupid. Even the little kids, the six-, seven-, eight-year-olds, the ones running around on the manicured Little League field wearing the major-league-replica uniforms that are two sizes too big. Once upon a time, these kids decided to play some baseball because it looked like it might be fun, says Ed Etzel, a psychologist and assistant professor in the West Virginia University department of intercollegiate athletics and school of physical education. It would give them a chance to run around, bump into old friends, meet new ones. Now here they are, it's game time, there are three hundred people in the bleachers, the place is *packed,* and their coach is yelling that they'll never sign a million-dollar contract if they keep making plays like that.

Tell them something they don't know, Coach.

"There is, unfortunately, an inordinate number of young people— adolescent and college-age people—who aspire to be professional athletes," says Ed Etzel, West Virginia's former shooting coach and a 1984 Olympic gold medalist in the small-bore rifle. "You have a better chance of being struck by lightning. That mentality has trickled down into youth sports. It can become real cutthroat real early, and that spoils it for a lot of kids." We've structured our entire athletic system solely to develop the one outrageously talented athlete capable of hitting the World Series home run, and to hell with everyone else.

So why does it always shock us when we realize (yet again) that these games we play at virtually every level have become a bit of grim business? After all, have we not taught our children well? "The kids who are really skilled are the ones who stay with it," Ed Etzel explains. "Those who aren't, they're cut, they quit, and they're probably not going to participate again." And even those lucky enough to be skilled enough are weaned early from the idea that sports is supposed to be an inherently pleasurable experience. "When you get beyond creating environments for kids to have fun, to be with their friends, to participate and improve their skills, when you go beyond that and emphasize the outcome of the competition, that's when things start getting strange," Ed Etzel says.

And stranger and stranger. The fanatical Little League scene. The overzealous high school atmosphere. The drive for the scholarship. Out-of-control college recruiting. The win-at-all-costs mentality. Performance-enhancing drugs. The million-dollar contract. Though it is impossible to draw a straight line directly from one to the other, it is plainly evident how we get ourselves from there to here. Kids aren't stupid, Ed Etzel says. And they can learn only what we teach them.

KURT ASCHERMANN, *youth league sports, Sparta, New Jersey; author of* **Coaching Kids to Play Baseball and Softball** *and* **Coaching Kids to Play Soccer:** There are lots of people who like the toothpaste out of the tube. And I can see why. I'm an assistant coach for my son's Little League. We were playing against this five-foot-nine kid who blew smoke. I devised this strategy that had us bunting and running and making them throw the ball. At the end of three innings— a kid can only pitch three innings—we were down 5–4 and about to face their number two. I had it. I had designed this perfect strategy, and then the wheels fall off.

It's Saturday night, and it's under the lights. There's a big crowd. And now here I am, the guy who's spent the last twenty years telling people not to get caught up in this stuff, and I'm as caught up as anybody. I've written books about it, I lecture, I give clinics. Like the parent who abuses his child. Something just snaps. I was *that close*. It was our head coach who pulled me back. I was kneeling down in the runway in the dugout. The kids could see I was disgusted. He came over and told me to go sit where I always did. "They're only eleven years old," he said. "I know and where'd you hear that?" He said, "I think it was at one of your clinics."

TOM BROSNIHAN, *basketball assistant, West Side High, Omaha:* I was coaching junior varsity baseball, and we were practicing, and the coach of another JV team shows up with his team ready to play a game. There'd been a mix-up. Then this other coach and I said, "Well, let's play." The kids didn't understand. "We don't have umpires," they said. So we said, "Let the catchers call balls and strikes, and we'll call the bases." My kids said they didn't have their uniforms, they'd have to call their parents. "Don't call anybody, play the game." There was no pressure, no uniforms, no mom and dad in the stands. The catchers called the game, we won in the bottom of the ninth, and there weren't any problems at all. It was baseball like when baseball was baseball. Just play. I think we've lost a lot of that over the years.

KURT ASCHERMANN: When we were kids, we went out and played all day long, all summer long. We didn't have PacMan; we didn't have MTV. We found four guys and we went down to Veterans Park and we played all day. Two on two, scores of 174–173. I'll bet I batted a hundred times. In Little League a kid will play two games a week and with batting practice maybe bat twenty times a week. I batted twenty times an hour. Winning wasn't that important at Veterans Park. If I got beat today, so what? Tomorrow I win 180–179.

ANSON DORRANCE, *U.S. women's 1991 World Cup soccer champions and the University of North Carolina:* My father was an oil executive. I was born in Bombay, and we lived there for three years. Then we moved to Calcutta and then to Nairobi, Kenya, and then to Addis Ababa, Ethiopia.

At the boarding school I attended in Switzerland, I played every sport they offered. I was passionate about athletics. I never got bored. When I got to [the University of] North Carolina [as a student] in 1970, the first year I was ineligible to play soccer, so I jumped into their intramural program. Roy Williams, the basketball coach now at Kansas, was my intramural manager. He asked what sports I'd like to compete in. I said, "All of them." He thought that was funny. "We take this seriously here." He put me on all the teams, and that year we won the campus intramural championship, and they awarded me the Intramural Athlete of the Year.

Too often when we're young our coaches and our parents put a ridiculous priority on the outcome of the game. But that's not why kids play; it's why adults "play." When you're young all you should do is get out there and have the best time you can. Only after your athletic personality is formed should you compete. You need to be old enough to understand that what competition does is develop excellence, and to become excellent you need to develop inside a competitive caldron.

When I was in Kenya the big sports were rugby, cricket, and soccer. When I went to Addis Ababa, the sports were soccer and this rock-throwing game. I don't remember the name. The idea was you've got this flat stone and you try to whack this cat-o'-nine-tails, cigarette-clipped cardboard out of a circle from about fifteen yards. We all became experts at throwing rocks.

In Kenya I went to one of those schools for British imperialists. It's a very healthy athletic atmosphere. Everyone playing. That's one of the difficulties for a lot of American athletes—only the extraordinary athletes compete. Singapore's where I had my first real coach. A soccer coach from what used to be Ceylon, which is now Sri Lanka. His name was Kahzi Nhaffa—I have no idea how you'd spell it. The image I retain of Kahzi Nhaffa is of him smiling, always smiling. My childhood memories of playing are very positive; my memories of the people who trained me are very positive. I don't ever remember being embarrassed by a coach or being personally attacked. I guess you could say all my experiences were very wholesome. Maybe that's why I'm still involved.

GENE VOLLNOGLE, *football, Carson High, Los Angeles (retired):* We've had kids transfer in from Texas. Football-crazy Texas. These kids are football players. And they tell me, "We've had all the football we want, Coach." And they're fifteen years old.

JACK WHITE, *Pop Warner Football, Canton, Massachusetts:* I've seen what a championship game does to a kid. I've seen young fellows come running off the field with tears streaming down their faces, sobbing so hard they can't breathe. They won't talk to anybody. Or they'll apologize to me because they didn't win. If I had control, I wouldn't have championships. But of course, the American concept is that there has to be a winner. We've lost the point of kids' sports with all these championships.

JOE NEWTON, *cross-country and track, York High, Oak Brook, Illinois:* We were practicing on the track, and the sophomore football team had a game. Look at these little guys. They come out, their goddamned helmets all but backwards, their pants too big, and they're just having a great time. Isn't it sad that when they get good, all the fun goes out of it? I loved being at the Olympics [as an assistant manager in 1988, the only high school coach ever named]. It was a great experience, a real thrill. With the elite guys it's about egos and money. I was happy to come home and be with my Mighty Mites, who like to run because they like to run. They're our last amateurs.

TOM HOUSE, *assistant to general manager, Texas Rangers, and former pitching coach:* It was 1971, and I'd been in the big leagues with the Braves for maybe a week. I threw a breaking ball that I thought was a strike. The umpire calls it a ball. All I did was shrug my shoulders— just a little body language. All I was trying to say was "Where was the pitch?" It wasn't anything that anybody noticed in the dugout. But it was eye contact between a veteran umpire and a rookie pitcher.

Well, the umpire takes off his mask and comes charging at me and yells, "Listen, you blankety-blank rookie, don't you ever challenge my balls and strikes. I've been umpiring since you were shittin' yellow in your diapers. Do it to me again and you're gone." I was twenty-five, maybe twenty-six. I'd been up maybe a week. It was a real wake-up call.

I think what was happening, in a way, was that you had an old-school umpire and a new-school athlete coming face to face. That was the transition time between what used to be with players and umpires and what is today. Back then there was maybe a bit more respect for umpires, a little more acceptance of their decisions, their authority. I started to become more aware of that toward the end of my playing career and as I was climbing back as a coach through the minor leagues the last ten years. Ego and money go hand in hand—and not necessarily in a complimentary way.

ABE LEMONS, *basketball, Oklahoma City College (retired):* Once you start making money, putting intrinsic value on things, it ceases to be a game. It's like the first time we ever had to lock our house in Oklahoma back in the '30s. We didn't have anything anybody would want to steal. Then we bought a radio, so we had to lock the door.

ED O'BRIEN, *basketball, Bishop Verot High, Fort Myers, Florida:* We had a man give me, the school's fund-raiser, five thousand dollars. Two days later he writes a letter to me, the basketball coach, wanting to know why his kid isn't playing more.

GARY ZARECKY, *basketball, Foothills Junior College, California:* They want control. They want to get beside the coach; they want favors, seats in the front row, or there's a friend of a friend whose kid plays ball and they'd like him scholarshiped. It's part of the game; you have to play. But it causes problems and *a lot* of stress.

KERRI HEFFERNAN, *Boston Beantown Women's Rugby Club:* The U.S. women's rugby team won the World Cup. No one in the States knew it. And you know what? That's nice. The players know that they do it for no greater glory than the love of the sport and to see how excellent they can be. It's why the obscure sports are kind of neat. Yes, it would be nice for someone to buy you a pair of warmups. But then someone else could lay claim to your victory. This way you don't have any crap hanging around. You can say, "I sacrificed all this—financially, physically, emotionally—just to see how far I could take it." There's a lot to be said for that on a personal and human level. That gets lost in a lot of other sports.

ED CHEFF, *baseball, Lewis-Clark State, Lewiston, Idaho:* We raise all of our own money for travel. Want to go to Hawaii for a tournament? Fine. Chop 120 cords of firewood and sell them around town. Football and basketball can end up leading the rest of the programs around by the nose. The other sports want what the money sports have in order to feel "equal." But it's the other programs that are better off. I guarantee it. They should be saying to those teams, "We're the one doing it right; you're the ones doing it wrong."

PAT GRIFFIN, *associate professor, social justice education program, University of Massachusetts, Amherst (former swim coach):* I remember when I was a high school coach we had a fund. We collected from all the students to pay for towels, and we used to raid that to pay for athletics. In college we had to drive ourselves to all our games; we didn't have uniforms. I remember once two players and I went down to the physical plant and talked some of the guys into coming up with a truckload of sod to cover the dirt spots on the lacrosse field. I would never want to go back to those days. But there was something about those days that was really special. There was a sense of . . . I don't know if you want to call it community, but it is completely missing now.

JOHN WOODEN, *basketball, UCLA (retired):* I've always felt the most difficult things with which to cope are too much or too little. Are we surprised that money rules everything? I thought that was true even before I retired. One of my teams was responsible for that—the game we played in the Astrodome against Houston. From that time on, television has had a tremendous impact.

I never wanted to play that game there. I thought it was making a spectacle out of the game. My coach at Perdue, Piggy Lambert, he felt that all games should be played on campus. I remember in 1940 Purdue won the Big 10 and was scheduled to play an NCAA game in Madison Square Garden, and he wouldn't go. [Wooden had graduated in 1932.] He stuck to his principles. He didn't like games in large, public places. He felt it was not in the best interests of intercollegiate sports. He thought that type of thing would bring problems, which it did.

JIM SATALIN, *basketball, Duquesne University (retired):* John Wooden was making thirty-two thousand dollars in 1973, after all his years as a coach. And they say maybe another eight thousand dollars in off-court stuff. You think about that and you say, "Jesus Christ!"

ROY CHIPMAN, *basketball, University of Pittsburgh (retired):* If coaches were still making that kind of money, they could walk away from the game. But there's a lot of money now. That has changed coaching tremendously. Coaches have sort of sold their souls to the devil. The more basketball games I win, the more companies want me to endorse their products. Advertising, television shows, radio shows. How do you walk away from a half a million dollars? I was lucky; I had an opportunity. Most guys don't.

What happens is, coaches are willing now to go over the edge. The president comes by and says, Here's the situation: We like you, blah–blah–blah. But you've got to win more games, you've got to sell more seats, you've got to get on national TV. That changes the focus. Now when somebody sells a recruit, I listen to this guy instead of saying, "Hit the road." Coaches are under tremendous influence to change their focus. You don't want to get fired. You can't *afford* to get fired.

CHUCK NOLL, *Pittsburgh Steelers (retired):* I enjoy football. I don't know how to do anything else. It's that simple. I have no alternative. Because if you have an alternative and you're in a tough profession, you end up choosing the alternative. So I tried not to have any alternatives. That was my choice.

I don't particularly like to be in the forefront, as far as media attention and that kind of thing. I don't think it serves the purpose that I want, and that is to have a winning football team. My goal has been to put a football team on the field, to help the players be the best they can be. The real thing is getting it done on the field, making it happen, and not necessarily talking about it.

[Noll never had a radio show or a TV show, and he rarely did commercial endorsements.] That was a conscious decision. If that would help us win a football game, then I'd do it. But that doesn't help us win football games, and that's my job. If money is your goal, then you do it. There are some people who come in and that's the only thing they're interested in—getting that money. God bless 'em. That's not me.

JIM SATALIN: I was a kid when I was hired at Bonaventure. Twenty-six years old and I'm the head coach. I didn't know any better. I was making twelve thousand dollars. It was a dream come true, the greatest job there could ever be.

I remember once I applied for a job at a Big East school. I can't remember the salary, but I do remember the coach with the lowest-paying sneaker contract in the Big East was making fifty thousand dollars. *The lowest.* When I went to Duquesne I got a ten-thousand-dollar shoe contract. Ten thousand dollars! But this—fifty grand! All of a sudden I saw coaching in a whole new way.

There are very few true coaches anymore. "True" in the sense that the coaching is done strictly for the love of the game. You're still seeing a great love for the game. But it's love for the game, *plus* a half a million dollars.

DR. GARY D. FUNK, *former coordinator, academic support center for intercollegiate athletics, Southwest Missouri State:* Kids are kids; they're pretty much going to live up to your expectations. What coaches get sick of is the middlemen. The sleaze factor. The "agents" you have to go through when recruiting. Remember when Syracuse was accused of working through an agent to get its players? Heck, 90 percent of Division I schools work through these guys.

They'll funnel kids to specific camps, get them identified as "Jim's kids," whoever, and the coaches have to deal with them. Coaches know these guys are sleazeballs, but if they want the quality players, those are the guys they've got to deal with. You've got to find the boosters to give the kids jobs. You've got to find the boosters to fly you all over the place. There's a lot of butt kissing.

ROY CHIPMAN: I've gone into homes, recruited kids. Go all the way through the process, and then all of a sudden, right when you think you're going to sign, some guy shows up you've never seen before. This is the guy who does the deal. Where the hell did this guy come from?

I used these guys. I've said to kids, you come with us and he can get you to the right camps, whatever. These guys have an influence they probably never started out to have. I think their intentions were good at the beginning. But do I think these guys are good for the game? No. They are another unfair influence on the kids. Another thing tugging the kids in a different direction. There are a lot of pimps.

KURT ASCHERMANN: I don't subscribe to the theory that sports is like life. Sports isn't like life. That's a bunch of crap. I have yet to conclude what sports *is* like, however.

TOM HOUSE: My dissertation was titled *Terminal Adolescence.* It became my book, *The Jock's Itch.* I am a terminal adolescent. I don't have an identity when I'm not in the game. The real world holds no fascination for me. Athletes are programmed to be dysfunctional. It's an itch you can't scratch in the real world.

Athletes work very well within their extended family, this closed environment called "sports." But they can't function in the real world. An athlete is asked to be responsible but not held accountable. He has status, but he doesn't have a role. He doesn't become a good brother, a good friend, a functional student.

I use the garbage-can analogy. Back when he was a little kid, on game day he wasn't expected to take out the garbage. On the professional level the athlete lives in this closed environment for much of his adult life. And for the most recent generation of athletes, sports has escalated financially into an even more protective existence, and they've closed ranks even more. Like in the '60s with the music business—they created self-sustaining pods that had no basis in reality.

The system perpetuates itself. It's only going to stop when we expect the seven-year-old T-ball whiz to be a human being and not just an "athlete." Reward him for being a person. If you feed him special meals, don't do it at the expense of his brothers and sisters. In the classroom, require him to pass the same classes, study just as hard. If he has a girlfriend, don't let the anger of the game affect his relationship with her. Make him take out the garbage.

NAN AIROLA, *volleyball, Providence Catholic High, New Lenox, Illinois:* You don't see the three-sport athlete anymore. Specialization is everything. It's scary. Here in Illinois, it's the open clubs. You have to try out, you have to have money to play. The girls who can afford it get the scholarships. The gifted athlete who can't play in an open club, she's only going to get so good just playing high school ball.

The goal has changed. It's not to win a state championship for your high school; it's to get yourself a college scholarship. The parents got involved. "How am I going to get my girl into college? Club volleyball!" You invest four, six, ten thousand dollars in high school to play club ball, you better get the payback in the end. But I don't see enough scholarships to go around anymore.

The worst thing is we're burning out the kids. They're starting in the third grade with this club business. They become so one-dimensional.

I've had kids come to me and say they're burned out, they need a break. The year we went downstate, we finished at midnight on Saturday. Sunday night all the clubs were having trials. They're producing great volleyball players, but they're not playing with much enthusiasm.

DR. GARY D. FUNK: I played tennis in college, then coached at the high school level. I finished up my graduate work and then began this academic coaching—I was referred to as the "academic coach." I got out in 1991. I looked at the job as a personal-growth thing: athletes fulfilling their potential. But most people saw it as a bottom-line thing: Do this, and player X stays eligible and we win twenty-three games.

There was never any overt pressure. But when I spoke to boosters, anybody, it was never "Hubert really has matured since he came here." It was always "Is Hubert eligible?" That was the only measure. I began to feel like a stranger in a strange land. I would see athletic personnel bring in athletes who had no business being here. They were going to be exploited, literally, because there was no way they were going to get a degree.

I didn't leave with any bitter feelings. Every year I became more removed from the academic coaching and more involved with the bureaucracy. And it wasn't supposed to be just for men's basketball. I'd say, "We have nineteen other sports with kids who need help." But they weren't revenue sports. I was always very up front about my priorities. We were successful in graduating some kids, and we were successful in keeping kids eligible. Because of that, I guess, they put up with my rumblings. Our program is not an outlaw program. Give the school credit: They provided good tutorial services and they gave kids the opportunity to stay in school after their eligibility was up.

All coaches would like their kids to do well in the classroom. But it isn't feasible. Unless you're a Duke, an Indiana, unless you're a coach at one of those top-flight schools, if you stress academics you're going to lose. Recruit fifteen kids who are capable students and make sure they graduate, and I guarantee that some north-central state is out there in junior-college land finding twelve athletes who are going to kick your butt. Do things the way the NCAA says in the public-service announcements and you lose. People do what it takes to win, because the winners get the dough.

Southwest Missouri is the kind of school that's made the NCAA what it is today. We've been in the tournament five of the last six years. We're one of those unknown little schools that nobody wants to play in the first or second round. We're the only show in the Ozarks. We've grown into this thing where the whole community lives and dies with the success of the basketball team.

It's a narcotic. We go to the tournament and we're flying out of the airport, and the TV cameras are there and there's a thousand people—it's a high. It is a bunch of fun. We'd always be the underdog, and we'd be scaring these big-name schools on national television. It was a big deal, a *big* deal. I started to wonder if in the long run maybe we weren't doing a real disservice. People want to know what's wrong with our educational system. Well, do we value the kids who are outstanding students, or would we rather have the local high school win the state championship?

JOHN WINKIN, *baseball, University of Maine:* Every dad thinks his kid is a million-dollar product, a six-figure bonus baby. Every dad wants that scholarship.

ABE LEMONS: They all say you've got to sell the mother. I think it was in Alabama where a mother slapped her son on a TV show because he announced he was going to one school and she wanted him to go to another.

JIM ZULLO, *basketball, Shenendehowa High, Clifton Park, New York:* I've had some good players. I had Greg Kubek, the captain at Duke; the captain of Dartmouth was mine. All college recruiters go through me. I insist. Recruiters eat kids up if you don't do it that way. It becomes a real mess.

Some recruiters recruit me: stroke, stroke, stroke to get to the kid. Some stroke the mother or father. Others go after the kid. Wherever they can get the in. They lie. Here's the typical statement: "We will not recruit another person at your position till you're a junior." The kid goes there and finds out they've recruited five others just like him. Don't pay any attention to what [recruiters] tell you. None of them. Some coaches play real games with kids' minds. "If you don't sign by tomorrow, we're not going to be here for you." I've had kids come out of meetings with college coaches crying—seventeen-year-old kids—because they had so much pressure put on them. A coach will run a respectable program, but when he needs somebody, he's going to do whatever it takes.

BILL WHITMORE, *athletic director, Concord school district, New Hampshire:* So many kids come with their hands out. A kid's on a campus visit, and you go to the bookstore and he says, "Boy, Coach, that's a nice-looking shirt." He's seventeen years old and he's going to make his choice because somebody gave him an extra sweatshirt?

JIM SATALIN: You put so much time and effort and money into recruiting. You can't ever say you had a bad year.

STAN MORRISON, *basketball, San Jose State:* A kid calls and says, "Coach, I'm going to . . . School B." You swallow hard, because recruiting is such an intimate, emotional experience. You just lost a son, right? And then you say, "That's a great decision. He's a wonderful coach. We're going to follow your career with great interest." Then you hang up and either break into tears or kick somebody. It's awful.

TOM BROSNIHAN: I was head coach at Creighton Prep for eight years. I left and became an assistant at Creighton University. I did the recruiting, and I loved it. I love Omaha. I loved Creighton. I loved the type of kid we could recruit. I think at one time we led the country in producing doctors or lawyers or teachers. We felt that if we could get that type of player we could be very competitive. We took De Paul to double overtime. We won the Missouri Valley; we beat Larry Bird.

That's what makes the Kevin Ross thing so ironic. I recruited Kevin Ross. He's the guy who wound up going to an elementary school in Chicago after he got out of Creighton because he couldn't read. When I was at Creighton, our graduation rate for basketball players was like 90 percent. We sent Kevin to that school in Chicago. We could have used up his eligibility, said bye-bye, and nobody would have ever heard of him again.

Thing is, we didn't have fifteen kids like Kevin, we had two. Both of them had the same background, inner-city kids with about the same

ACT scores. The other kid worked hard, got his degree, became a juvenile probation officer. Kevin, he went his own way. Two out of fifteen. One proved super; the other didn't. Not a bad percentage.

[Ross filed suit against Creighton in 1989 for negligent admission, educational malpractice, negligent infliction of emotional distress, and breach of contract. In 1990 the case was dismissed. In 1992 on appeal the court upheld the dismissal of all negligence but allowed for pursuit of breach of contract. Creighton, admitting no liability, settled with Ross in the amount of thirty-thousand dollars.]

BR. MIKE WILMOTT, S.J., *basketball, Creighton Prep, Omaha:* I went on sabbatical for a year and went to Marquette as a volunteer coach for Rick Majerus [now at Utah]. I couldn't go out and recruit, but I got a feel for what it's about. I would *never* want to get into that. Every day we'd have a meeting, and Rick would say, "Where are we with this kid? Who's seeing that kid?" You can never have enough good players.

When you get done recruiting one year, you're already planning next year. You're looking at high school juniors, high school sopho-mores—hell, college coaches have to know who the good high school freshmen are. They're always planning ahead, planning for tomorrow. They can't play for today. A college coach is never allowed to enjoy the day he's got and the kids he has.

GARY ZARECKY: One thing that always freaked me out at USIU [United State International University in San Diego] was that I had to be ten times more careful about what I did in regards to the NCAA rule book than the major schools had to be. Because I was at the kind of school that gets busted to set an example for the larger schools.

ANONYMOUS WOMAN, *Division I coach:* The big trick in women's recruiting is to tell a kid she doesn't want to go to a certain school because the coach is a lesbian.

PAT GRIFFIN: It's not unusual. "We don't have any lesbians; you'll be safe here." And it's not just the men who do it. Women do it. Sometimes lesbians do it. A self-protection camouflage.

ANONYMOUS MAN, *Division I coach:* They throw it out there, put the thought in people's heads. I'll be recruiting someone and he'll bring it up, tell me what another coach said. I've seen it from the coaches I respect the most. It's disappointing. Maybe they can't deal with the fact that a gay can coach as well they can.

AL BORGES, *offensive coordinator, Boise State, Idaho:* We had an opposing coach call up and cancel the return flight of one of our recruits who was visiting our campus. The kid comes to our school for the weekend, and on Sunday we drop him at the airport. He goes to the counter to get his return ticket. But there's no ticket. He spent the day at the airport. I really believe an opposing coach pulled that to make his trip miserable. We'd checked and rechecked that ticket. It's a very competitive world, and players are the coaches' blood.

WALTER LEWIS, *football assistant, University of Kentucky (retired):* I had a friend who was recruited. He was getting a lot of pressure from this one school. They drove him out into the woods somewhere and met up with another car. They'd flashed their headlights on him so he couldn't see. An individual got in the back seat. He still thinks it was the governor of the state.

JIM SATALIN: I heard a great story about a recruit who got a Jeep Cherokee from one school. He totaled it, so he signed with another school because they said they'd give him a car too. The first school couldn't say anything to anybody. It was all a wash, and the car was quietly delivered to car heaven.

RIC SCHAFER, *hockey, University of Notre Dame:* If a coach is driving himself to the airport and one of his players missed a bus to the airport, the coach can't give the player a ride. We can invite players over to our house for dinner, but we can't give them a ride to our house. It's ridiculous. But all the rules come from abuses. Some coach invited his guys for dinner and it turned out to be a banquet, and he picked them up in a limousine.

P. J. CARLESIMO, *basketball, Seton Hall:* You might as well have just one rule: You can't cheat. Who are we worried about? We're worried about the people who cheat. People who don't are the people who don't need rules in the first place. If a school's buying kids, giving them twenty-five thousand dollars, they aren't going to be awfully concerned about how many phone calls they can make to a kid in a seven-day period.

JOHN KEMMERER, *basketball, Riverdale High, Fort Myers, Florida (no longer coaching):* I got tired of banging my head against the wall. After a while you overlook things, because nothing happens anyway. A school was using two ineligible players. They were supposed to be playing for me but they couldn't because they were real attitudes. So they went to another school. One coach told me to let them play for half a season, *then* drop the dime and ruin their season. I turned them in right away. What about the other kids on the team?

Another time we had two brothers living in the same house playing for two different high schools. Explain that one.

A wrestling coach at one school was the biggest cheater in the world. He'd practice on Sundays, which is illegal. They flat out caught him and suspended him for a year. They got a new wrestling coach and made the other guy the assistant football coach. At the end of the year he's head wrestling man again. Big punishment.

ED O'BRIEN: The message kids get from that is "Whatever it takes." If you've got to play dirty, that's fine. If you have to break the rules, that's okay. Just win.

JOHN KEMMERER: Kids start to believe that stuff is okay. You catch a kid smoking dope and you report him. "Why'd you do that?" "Because it's my job. Because what you're doing is wrong." But the kid will look at you: "Why did you tell on me?" They don't understand that there's a reason, that it's illegal, that in the long run it's going to hurt them. That we did it for the right of it.

TRACY SUNDLUN, *track & field; executive director, Metropolitan Athletic Congress, New York City:* I was teaching a seventh-grade class, as a special guest, the year after Ben Johnson got caught. We were talking about drugs. The kids asked why it was bad. They wanted to know. They didn't understand. The ramifications of steroids run deep. Carl Lewis, and not Ben Johnson, won the gold medal and set the world record at the 1988 Olympics. There can be no greater accomplishment in sports than do something like that. But nobody in the class knew it—not even the teacher.

KEITH KEPHART, *former strength and conditioning coach at Iowa State, Kansas, South Carolina, and Texas A&M; no longer coaching:* If coaches feel they're playing against other coaches who are playing by the same rules, then they'll abide by any drug rules you want. All coaches want are the same rules, the same ball game, the same chance.

Coaches encourage steroids. A strength coach at one school had twenty kids benching over four hundred pounds. That got a strength coach at another school fired. I've had a coach tell me to put twenty pounds on every lineman before the season. He never said "steroids," but there's no other way to put on twenty pounds of muscle.

I had a kid come to me once. He was slightly built but an excellent athlete. He wanted to know what he could do. I said, "I can't get involved with that." I gave him the information, the pros and cons, what it's supposed to do, and how it could hurt you. He didn't get what he wanted from me, so apparently another coach set him up. The kid got bigger and stronger, and he played.

When a kid comes to you and asks about this stuff, he's putting you between a rock and a hard place. What am I supposed to do? Tell him where to go, what to take, how to do it? Or do I say, "Get out of my office"? Then he goes out to the streets and gets his information and maybe ends up dead or really screwed up. Either way, you lose. [At South Carolina in 1989, Kephart was indicted for purchasing steroids without a prescription, to be used, he says, for personal use. Two years later the indictment was dropped.]

BOB LUCEY, *football, Curtis High, Washington:* We heard a rumor— it was during the summer—that two of our players had tried steroids. When we confronted them, they admitted it. We're realistic enough to realize that those things do happen. But we were still surprised and shocked—it's something you'd just as soon never have to deal with.

Our policy was to treat it like any drug offense: Our kids were asked to go through a drug assessment and then were asked to follow up with it. One boy did. He had to go to weekly counseling and he missed a game, which follows our guidelines, and do some other things in order to be eligible for football. The other decided that football wasn't that important. I also tried to take advantage of it with the team. You know, "Is it worth it, doing what they did?"

I wonder, though, if the message is getting through. The message that kids are getting from a Ben Johnson or a Lyle Alzado is not "Don't take steroids"; it's "If you want to be successful. . . ." Ben Johnson still ran the fastest time ever clocked. Kids don't see Alzado's death, they don't see his cancer. They see his thirteen years in the NFL. It doesn't seem to hit home.

The thing I'm going to do is become more proactive. Do everything possible to keep my own gym open so my kids are lifting with *me* and not at some private gym. I'm also monitoring body weight. A kid gains forty pounds in seven months, I want to know why.

As a coach you encourage your kids to lift and work hard. What happens is that some of these athletes who get really involved, they become your hardest workers. It can be difficult to tell what's going on, because they're doing all the things you're asking of them and you've got to love how hard they're working. A coach can get blinded. You're a person with a mission; you're looking for results. And now here's someone who is really committed. You don't always see what you should. You need to decide what it is you really want. Is what you want really what you need? How big can these kids get? What's natural, what's not natural? How much weight can you put on a six-foot-six frame? Where does it stop?

TRACY SUNDLUN: Drugs in many respects ruined our sport. They've certainly hurt it greatly. If nothing else, just in public relations. Everybody gets painted as a druggie, and we think it's the end of the world, and our sport looks terrible.

Most of the records we now have were made while athletes were taking drugs. He or she just didn't get caught. Here's what I can say: Not all our best athletes are clean; not all our best athletes are dirty. What's happened, though, is the first question you hear when a new world record is set is, "Is he on drugs?"

There are performances that will never be broken without the aid of drugs. That's unfair to the sport; it's unfair to the kids coming up. It's unfair to everything. Ben Johnson ran a 9.79 hundred meters. An outrageous time, *untouchable.* Let's say he doesn't get caught. That becomes the time everyone has to beat. How do you beat it without drugs? You say, "Ben got caught." Fine. But he wasn't alone. A lot of others should have got caught, but they got lucky.

I've gotten very despondent about the whole thing. It's become quite hypocritical. I have virtually no interest in the elite levels of our sport anymore. [Sundlun has been a manager or coach at four Olympic Games and has coached Olympic athletes since 1972.] I believe that sports has marvelous benefits. Sports for sports' sake has little meaning, but for what sports can do for a society and for the impact it can have on somebody's life, sports can be great. Sports can keep your kids in school, teach them proper values. Success on the field can breed success off it.

But here's what happens: We encourage the kids to get involved, we hold out the carrot and get them believing in a Ben Johnson or a Katrin Krabbe [an East German world-champion sprinter banned from the 1992 Olympics], thinking they can be like them. They both got caught, but a lot of others haven't. So the kids stay with it, and sooner or later they're saying, "I was one of the best high school kids in the country; I've done well in college. How do I get to the next level?" Take drugs. And that blows the whole equation.

BRUCE WILHELM, *weight lifting and athletics; owner of an exercise-equipment shop in Daly City, California:* When I first started to compete in sports, I believed all the crap about how it's great for the body, it's great for the mind. In college, one of the coaches said, "You ought to take a look at this." I thought maybe I should, but I said, "I don't want to take anything that doesn't belong in the body." The real purist. I made the change when I saw my brother and another kid who was four years younger than me throwing the shot farther than me.

When I started, in 1969, this friend told me to take one tablet every other day. That was a joke. Five milligrams a day—the medicinal recommendation is ten. Each year I took a little more, and I noticed I was making good gains. It was no big deal; there were no rules against taking steroids. That's when I started injections. I didn't see any of the miraculous gains you hear about, but I noticed that I always felt like training. It puts you in second gear.

Everybody was doing it, and everybody knew it. The officials were going with what the AMA was saying, that steroids didn't enhance performance. It was even printed on the vials. But the athletes knew it worked. I got up to where I was taking sixty milligrams at the top of my cycle. Today that would be called "maintenance." These days an average load would be about 125 to 400 a day.

My turning point came in '77. I went to Stuttgart and took fourth in the World [weight-lifting] Championships. We heard that the Russians were taking some sort of stimulant; they were taking a new drug and they'd really increased the dosages. Every time I got close there was something new. I said it's just not worth it.

I got out when steroids were beginning to mushroom. They'd take different steroids, take them year-round, take animal steroids. It was unbelievable. It wasn't just weight lifting or track and field, it was all sports. Figure skating, speed skating, you name it. It's in all pro sports. Are you kidding me?

Some of these body builders, they're just off the wall. They're nuts. Hair loss, acne vulgaris. When women really load, the enlargement of the clitoris, the changing of the voice—and the voice never comes back. Men get "bitch tits," which have to be surgically removed. Athletes can't afford to stay on the programs they're on now, but they know there's a competitor who's taking more than they are.

We have to go to controlled usage. There's a way to take steroids and a way not to. Take enough but not too much. We could do that with controlled usage. Do profile tests before national championships and world championships or the Olympics. If an athlete's testosterone level goes over a predetermined level, pull his card. At least we'd have testing.

We're past the point where we can ask athletes to suddenly all come clean. We passed that point in 1980. What we could have done then was disqualify any athlete who was taking, suspend him for life. But we didn't, and it kept growing. More people got involved; more sports got involved.

I was becoming more involved in the other side of the Olympic movement then—the coaching part, the administration, the development. I used to get up at meetings and say, "We've got to do something for our athletes. They're the ones bringing us the glory, but they're also the ones taking the drugs." Everybody'd say, "American athletes don't take drugs." They'd get all incensed. But who were the first people to call me in August of 1983 when we had thirty-five, forty athletes haul ass from the Pan Am Games in Venezuela? I looked, and I gloated. I'd told these jerks what was happening, and nobody believed me. They had it coming.

Sport as we know it is no longer sport. There's no Olympics. The morals have changed with the money-making. Do well and cash in. You don't do it because you love it anymore. I slept on the floor so I could afford to compete in the Olympic Games. Today it's all money.

TWELVE

Dream Time

As a player, he knew the feeling. As a Boston Celtic during the late '60s, early '70s, not to have known it would have been impossible. Don Nelson owns five NBA championship rings from his playing days in Boston. In 1969 he made the shot that won the game and the championship series against the Los Angeles Lakers. It doesn't get better than that.

But now Don Nelson coaches the Golden State Warriors in the NBA. And as a coach, he wants the feeling again. "I'm searching for the big game," Don Nelson says. "I'll never feel I'm a total success if I don't get it. I'll still be a good coach, but it will separate me from the best."

Every coach, of every sport and at every level, dreams his own version of Don Nelson's dream. Some attain it. But one look at the numbers, and it becomes obvious that for most coaches it will remain a dream forever. Perhaps even for an acknowledged basketball genius like Don Nelson. There can be only one coach at a time immersed in "the feeling."

Still, they coach on, stalking the sidelines, ever hopeful. Along the way, in the absence of the big game, they busy themselves with other accumulations. There is only one Big Dream, but there are many little ones. The satisfaction of watching a player develop. The camaraderie of the locker room. The intensity of the game. Creating something of worth, perhaps even of lasting value. Finding a single moment to carry for the rest of their lives. Every coach harbors his own private destinies, searches to fulfill his own particular dreams. Taken together, perhaps they can surround the space that, in a more perfect world, would have been encircled by their championship ring.

FRANK LAYDEN, *Utah Jazz (retired):* It's a funny about that ring. Cliff Hagen told me that the first year he was in the league he won the ring with the St. Louis Hawks. He threw it in a drawer. Eight years later he took it out and put it on.

JOE NEWTON, *cross-country and track, York High, Oak Brook, Illinois:* The thrill never leaves. Once you go to the mountaintop, you want to stay there. You want to win that sucker every year. People ask me, "Doesn't it get to be old stuff?" It'll never be old because there are always new kids. I'm sixty-four. People say, "How can you be so enthusiastic?" Because I love my job. It's my passion. I can hardly wait to get to work every day. Most people hate their jobs. The people making all the money, they're worried about somebody stealing it or about making more. I don't have to worry. I don't have any money. I just have my team.

JOHN YOUNG, *founder and president of Reviving Baseball in Inner Cities (RBI) and scout for the Florida Marlins:* When I started scouting, in 1980, I'd watch the inner-city teams get hammered by the parochial schools, the small private schools. I saw the disparity in conditions.

When I signed [a professional contract] in '69, most of the players drafted were high school players. Now 81 percent are college kids. College coaches go get the best baseball player right now, with his present skills. That's why you're not seeing minority kids playing in college. The scouts, we talked about this all the time: "We got to get more black kids playing baseball, get more of them into college." That was the genesis of RBI.

We're not sociologists, but we're learning. Wanting to get more black kids to go to college and play baseball—well, that's one thing. But as we got into it, we learned. In the inner cities you've got kids dropping out of high school at a 58 percent rate. We've got to get kids through high school first.

You see so many kids walking around South Central [Los Angeles] with nothing to lose. You hear kids say, "Why should I go to school?" They see the dope pusher with a seventh-grade education with a nice car, the clothes, a lot of money. Kids at thirteen, they're impressionable. When you have nothing to lose, you are a very dangerous person. Inner-city kids have a better chance of going to jail than they do of going to college. That's a fact. You see kids rob people, beat people up, gang bang. Get arrested and be back on the street in two weeks. Nobody gives a damn.

We started RBI with twelve teams. We had no idea where the program was going. Right now we're working with a thousand kids in L.A. That's about seventy teams. We're in Kansas City now, St. Louis, New York. We're getting ready to have our Hall of Fame banquet, and we're going to honor this one kid. If ever there was a kid you'd say was going to fail, it was this kid. His mother is a druggie. He played baseball to get the hell out of the house. It had nothing to do with getting into college, getting drafted, being a major leaguer. None of that. He's the epitome of what RBI is supposed to be. Like I said, my goals were to have all the kids go to college, play pro baseball. People kept telling me, "If you save even one, it'll be worth it." Spend all that money? Put all that time in to save one kid? That's failure. But I see what they were saying now.

KATHY RUSH, *basketball, Immaculata College (retired)*: I graduated from West Chester [State, in Pennsylvania] in '68. I got married the following Saturday. My husband then was Ed Rush, the NBA referee. I was teaching at a local junior high school. I was going to do my three years and get pregnant. Then somebody mentioned there was this job open at Immaculata. I was twenty-two.

When I interviewed, I knew their gym had burned down, so I knew we wouldn't have any home games. There was a gym at the novitiate, where they trained girls to become nuns. That was our gym, real tiny, the walls right up to the out-of-bounds line. From 3 to 4 the novices had their recreation hour. We'd get there and there'd be eighteen, twenty-five novices playing volleyball or roller-skating, something. The roller-skating to me was the funniest thing, their habits flying.

There was no mandate from the school. Each game was a game unto itself. People ask me what Immaculata's record was before I got there. I don't know. I don't even know who the coach was. I just wanted to win. Do the best I could. We wore these tunics, a jumper with box pleats. They were wool, and you wore a blouse underneath and then bloomers. Very modest, very long, and very hot. I mean, it was funny.

We played local schools similar to Immaculata: Cabrini, Rosemont, Mercy Academy. And I find out we have people who can flat-out play. It was like this incredible miracle at Immaculata. Of course, the nuns knew that. They knew that God intended all of them to arrive at the same time. [The roster from 1972–74 included, among others, Rene Portland, now the coach at Penn State; Marianne Crawford Stanley (dismissed by USC in June 1993 in a salary dispute; she later filed a federal sex discrimination suit); Janet Young Eline, an assistant at Gettysburg; and Theresa Shank Grentz, the coach at Rutgers and the 1992 Olympic coach].

Theresa was a freshman [Rush's first year]. She was light years ahead of her time. Six feet tall, and if anybody pressed us she would bring the ball up. She was quick, an excellent athlete. She could jump and shoot. The whole package. In the national tournament in '73, we played four games and she averaged 24 points and 18 rebounds.

We had no idea what was out there. I had gone to West Chester and they're known as a P.E. school. Our schedule consisted of all these little places, so I talked to my athletic director and said, Let's play West Chester. They had a first and second team and a third and fourth team. They sent their third and fourth team. And we crushed them. That gave us the idea that we were pretty good.

In '69, '70, and '71 there had been an invitational women's tournament. In '72 they set it up like the men's NCAA. It was at Illinois State. There were sixteen teams, and they were the only people there. We beat West Chester, 54–48. When we flew home there were hundreds of people at the airport. It was overwhelming, what happened. Just incredible. The next year West Chester scheduled us during the season. They estimated there were forty-two hundred people at the game. In 1972, that's a lot of people. We beat them and people went crazy, hundreds of people on the court. And for the first time, there was press coverage at a women's game.

We caught the lightning and we rode it. We were on the East Coast, in a big media area. We were winning. In Theresa we had a dominant player. And we were a great story. The nuns came to our games and brought buckets and sticks and beat on them and cheered. The whole situation was unique.

And we won almost all of our close games. The most exciting game we ever had was in 1973, the semifinals of the national tournament against Southern Connecticut at Queens College. There's three minutes and twelve seconds to go and we're down twelve. I figure it's over. But we press, they turn the ball over and pretty soon we're up 1 and they call time-out. There's forty seconds to go. "Don't foul anybody. Don't foul *anybody.*"

Southern Connecticut dribbles over half court, and one of our players commits a foul. Why is it half the time players do the opposite of what you tell them? They miss the first and make the second. We call time-out. There's twenty-six seconds left. Women's basketball uses a thirty-second clock, but they forgot to turn it off. We start a play with ten seconds left. Only Marianne is looking at the thirty-second clock, which means there's only six seconds left. Everybody's yelling, "Shoot! Shoot!" Everything is breaking down. Marianne shoots and misses. Theresa comes out of absolute nowhere and taps at the ball, it bounces through, and the buzzer goes off. We win, 47–45. Just the way I diagramed it! I have pictures of the nuns running out of the stands, their habits flying. Pictures of priests standing on the floor hugging nuns, hugging the players. Everybody crying. It was just sensational.

We won [the national championship] in '72, '73, and '74. We were in the finals in '75 and '76. In '77 we lost in the semifinals. I went into that season with one senior, six or seven juniors, one sophomore, and one freshman. The handwriting was on the wall. Immaculata was not going to give scholarships. I was the head coach, and I was only making twelve hundred dollars. So at the beginning of that year, I said no matter what happens, whether we win it all or lose every game, I was leaving at the end of that season. In retrospect, Immaculata made the right decision [not to offer scholarships]. They were not going to compromise their standards to get students.

The era had passed. There was a definite realization on my part. But I don't think the whole community realized it yet. Without an infusion of talent, they were not going to be successful. The players were going to the places that offered money now. We were 27–5 my last year. The woman who came in, she went to maybe 16–16. People said, "It's not the same without you." Well, it wouldn't have been the same *with* me.

[Rush operates a summer basketball camp; she never coached again.]

HANK HAINES, *Blytheville Boxing Club, Arkansas (retired):* When

I was five my daddy brought home boxing gloves. That would have been about sixty years ago. I got swept up in it. I boxed a little as an amateur. I boxed a lot in the army; I boxed some in college, intramural stuff. And I boxed around at the gyms. One time when I was forty, there was this kid, and they asked me to spar with him. Kid almost wore me out.

I worked with a couple of amateur clubs. There was a Blytheville club in the '50s and I helped with that. There was another club in the '60s. But the only club I organized myself was back around 1974. I was newly divorced and looking for something to do. I was at a boxing match when this kid comes up to me and said he'd heard I was starting a boxing club. I said, "It's the first I heard about it." He said it was a Mr. James Long who told him to come see me. James Long, he had me figured—he'd sent along a nice-looking kid. He set me up. I told this kid to meet me down at the Blytheville YMCA on Monday and we'd see what he could do. Word got around down at the high school, and, Lord, next thing I knew, I had eighteen, twenty boys.

We fought at the Legion arena. It was a pretty good place. No, it wasn't, it was crummy. Hell, a boxing arena's supposed to be crummy. We drew pretty well. We fought on Friday or Saturday night. I wouldn't get back to my apartment until after midnight. I had to count the money, see who was hurt, put the gloves away, sweep up, turn out the lights, and lock the door. I loved it.

I don't consider myself a professional coach. But I did have success and I did care for the boys. There's something about a boy when he gets into that age from eleven to sixteen when they can go wrong as hell. The boys I had, they hadn't succeeded in any place in the world. They didn't even know they *could*. But they had good protoplasm. And boy, some of them just succeeded wildly. Every once in a while I'd ask one what he was doing being a boxer. It's a hell of a way to make a life. This one kid said he didn't want to be just another one of the kids down on Ash Street. It was straight out of *Rocky,* only the movie hadn't been made yet.

I'm not trying to portray myself as Father Kelly. But from time to time, some of these boys needed a little purpose, a little direction. It would really chagrin me when a parent would come in and say, "I didn't think he'd ever amount to nothin'." Well, Goddamn it, no wonder. I'd tell my boys, "You can be as good as you want to be." All I wanted was for them to get their feet underneath them, get their chins up, you know?

K. C. JONES, *Seattle Supersonics (retired):* Why does a CEO retire and then all of a sudden he's got this little business thing going down in Florida? It's the same thing for me and basketball. When I retired as coach of the Celtics, I thought I'd had my fill. But I'd been with the game since junior high, through college and the Olympics, then the Celtics. Without basketball I'd have been in trouble. Growing up a black teenager in the '40s in San Francisco, options were limited. It's one of those things where there's this cloud over you. Sitting in the back of the bus or up in the crow's nest at the movies—that hurts. I didn't have any other tools to work with besides basketball. That connection has never gone away.

KURT ASCHERMANN, *youth sports, Sparta, New Jersey; author of* **Coaching Kids in Baseball and Softball** *and* **Coaching Kids in Soccer:** The good thing about having lived in the same town now for over five years is that there's a whole bunch of kids on a lot of different baseball teams that I coached at one time or another. Being a coach gives me the chance to go to the park and spit sunflower seeds and shoot the breeze with a bunch of guys you've been with since spring. It's the joke about the snack bar being open and eating another "Ungerdog"—the field's called Unger Field, probably after a soldier who died in World War II. It's knowing you're going to have an "Ungerdog" for dinner and that come the third inning the kids will ask if they can go to the Dairy Queen after the game.

I like the look on a parent's face when we pull a double steal. I like it when a kid does something he didn't think he could do. Mostly, though, I enjoy watching these ten-, eleven-, twelve-year-olds progress. Watching them move from day to day, getting better and better. And it's the being there. At the park. To know you're still a part of it. I spent two years in the Cubs organization. Baseball got ahold of me. I love it. I've never made any bones about it.

BOB SIDDENS, *wrestling, West High, Waterloo, Iowa:* When I retired in 1991 after forty-one years [teaching; twenty-nine years as a coach], my wrestlers put together a reunion, a golf outing. Then they met in a social affair at the Sullivan in Waterloo. About three hundred of my wrestlers were there, from all over. Texas and New York and Okinawa and Seattle and Washington, D.C. They presented me with cuff links from President "Brush." Bush came to West High one time as vice president. Ten days before he arrived I go to the locker room, and these men are in there and they ask me what I was doing. I said, "I'm wondering what you're doing." Then it dawns on me: Secret Service! I say, "Oh yeah, a guy name of 'Brush' is comin'." They didn't think that was funny.

Anyway, there were maybe five hundred people at the Sullivan, what with the wives and family. I got to talking about my young men, my old wrestlers, and, well, that's when I lost it. I've always told them that they'd given me a whole lot more than I ever gave them. Now here they were. I was up on a little stage, looking down at all these guys, and it was like my whole life was sitting there right in front of me.

TINA SLOAN GREEN, *lacrosse, Temple (retired):* It's the process I'll miss. My husband, he remembers the scores and championships. For me it was always the getting them there, the people and the situations. It's watching kids grow up. Everything was special my last year. I knew I was going to retire, so I savored every moment. The last time down to Florida; beating Penn State, our big rival. The little things. My father had died the year before, and I felt the team had missed out on something from me, so I put everything I had into it. I think maybe the team noticed that I was more emotional. The tears would roll down my face.

GENE VOLLNOGLE, *football, Carson High School, Los Angeles:* [Vollnogle retired in 1991 as the winningest high school coach in California.] I've got a Toyota truck with a shell on it. It's all upholstered in the back: four inches of foam rubber and seats and everything covered with carpet. On Fridays, game day, I'd go out there after school and lie in the back and go over the game plan. The wind would blow through, and it would be nice and cool. I was away from the kids, too. No "Coach, I forgot my combination," or "Coach, where are my shoes?" I'd get away from everything for a little while. I'm gonna miss that.

JANET ELY LaGOURGUE, *diving, Mission Viejo Nadadores, California:* It's kind of magical what can happen when you work with these little athletes. How they really give themselves to you. If a coach is giving 100 percent, what you're doing is teaching an athlete to take 100 percent. There's such a trust and confidence between the coach and athlete. Sometimes I'll tell a kid, "If you want to reach where you're supposed to reach, become as good as you can become, then you have to go with what I'm telling you. Just go with it. Let go of your fear, stick it in the back seat, and come with me." There's not too many kids who can do that. To work with the kids who can, that's neat. It's scary and it's awesome.

I've got the kid on the board, and I'm going to take her someplace she's never been before. There's a high fear factor in diving. It's not natural to be tossed up and down, topsy-turvy, to free-fall from a high height. You have this natural instinct fighting against you when you coach this sport.

This one little girl, she's green but talented. She was learning a three-and-a-half tuck. I told her: "You're going to get scared up there, your heart's going to beat a million times a minute. You're going to walk to the end of the tower and think that what you're doing is crazy, and you're going to feel overwhelmed with fear. Push through it, just go beyond it. Turn that fear around. Know that this is your body's way of making everything very keen and acute. The adrenaline is going to make you strong; it's going to make your senses very keen. Don't react to it, that you're not ready, that you don't understand the action, or that you're blanked out. Just let it all go."

She did it, and she did it beautifully. I knew she was ready. That's the trick of coaching: knowing when they're ready and getting them to know it, too. Those moments are more rewarding than the big wins. When you have an athlete who gives herself to learning an action or gives herself to training, gives herself to an event, that's the rewarding thing, no matter the outcome. It's a giving. A coach can't take it, can't pull it out, can't kick it out. They've got to give it to you.

BILLY WILLIAMS, *coach assistant, Cleveland Indians:* In baseball, you try to beat the other team, sure, but you're competing against your territory and against the ball. I take an outfielder out to his position and

I tell him that. "This is your territory; this is your room. Nobody else comes in here and catches a ball."

There's an old saying, "When you can catch the wind, come talk to me." When I played, the wind knew when I caught it. It's when you're all out and you've got no more to give and you still get one. The ball burns the tip of the glove, and you bring it in for the catch. It's the ninety feet or the sixty, the one hundred or whatever you had to compete against to catch the ball. If you beat it, he's out and if you don't, he's safe. Damn.

The kids know I'm sincere. They know the things I'm telling them are right on. I don't bullshit them. And we work until we get it right. Then when it happens, we connect. I'm feeling what they're feeling; they're feeling what I'm feeling. Coach to player, you connect on that level.

Have you ever sat across the room from a person, your wife or your girlfriend, and you look at each other and you're right there with each other, thinking the same thing, feeling the same thing? That's what I'm talking about. Nobody experiences it but you and the outfielder. When he makes a good catch, that's an extension of me, that's a part of me, that's a part of baseball. I get fired up. I get cold chills running through me when he runs into the dugout and says, "Hey, Billy, right on!" Feel the wind blow, catch it in the air, and your hair flies. I still catch the wind. I catch it through my players.

CHUCK YATES, *Little League baseball, Bellevue, Nebraska:* We were practicing and I was pitching, and this little kid, Matt, was playing second base. One of the players hit a line drive, probably the best hit he had all year, and it hit Matt right in the chest. He kind of gave a yelp and a gasp, and by the time I got to him he pretty much went out right in my arms. Squirt ball's for seven- and eight-year-olds, but you can play up. Matt's only six. A real tough athletic guy. He'll put on his batting helmet and run and dive and flip over onto his feet. A little ball of fire.

At first I thought he was lying there taking the pain. His mom realized he wasn't breathing. His heart must have stopped immediately, at least that's the theory, because his eyes were steely and cold and staring off into space. I don't like to use the expression "dead in my hands," but he kind of melted right in my arms.

I remember I felt this incredible calmness and affirmative thing that everything was going to be okay. I had no doubts whatsoever; there was no screaming or being scared or anything like that. It wasn't until afterward when I came home and hit my knees in the living room and started wailing, "Oh, my God, this little boy!"

I had learned CPR back in 1968 but had never used it before. One of the other assistants checked Matt's pulse while I did about four or five rounds with the breathing and the chest pumps, and he came to. We have a volunteer fire department, so it took a few minutes for anybody to get there. By the time the rescue squad got there he was breathing on his own. They were concerned because you could see where the ball had hit him—this remarkable spot on his chest.

I understand a lot of kids don't come back when this happens. Oddly enough, the next night *20/20* did a story on Little League safety. They showed the same situation, the story of a little boy who didn't respond. Matt recovered immediately. Heck, he came over the next day with a heart monitor on, and he was fine. He's fine now. Everything's fine. We feel real fortunate.

We had a team meeting before the next game. Our team happened to be undefeated. I told them they sure had to realize there were other things more important than winning a baseball game. Then they went out and slaughtered the other team. It was like eleven runs in the first inning.

The kid who hit the ball, his dad handled it really well, explained and emphasized that it was an accident, that he had done nothing improper to cause the thing. None of the kids left the team; the parents have been great. If anything, there's more of a bond now. Matt's mother bought me a certificate to eat dinner at a restaurant. She's been very gracious. We don't talk about it that much. What more is there to say? You appreciate the fact that you were able to do something. It happened, and you kind of move on.

I don't consider myself to be any kind of hero. It was just something that needed to be done. It's humbling, I'll tell you. I see Matt all the time. He goes to school with my kids. We look at each other, and it's like we know there is something there. There's a bond. You're not going to get a six-year-old to articulate that in any way. We just kind of look at each other. And it's very interesting, this feeling that I get.

EDDIE TITUS, *one of four volunteer assistant football coaches at Santa Clara University; they each have been with the school at least twenty-five years:* This keeps me sane. I've worked in probation for twenty years. I deal with rapists, child molesters. I make recommendations that send people to prison. It's not about me being out on that field to do these kids some good. It's doing me a lot of good.

I used to be involved with the East-West [All-Star] Game. Coaching staffs from around the country would come out here to watch the players. It would be Christmastime, and there'd be all these coaches getting fired, looking for jobs. It was depressing: "Whose head's going to roll next? What have you heard?" I'd listen to that and think: I got a pretty good job.

JACK WHITE, *Pop Warner Football, Canton, Massachusetts:* [White coached for five years totally blind.] It was due to diabetic retinopathy. In 1985 I lost the vision in my right eye. In 1987 it affected my left. The periods of limited vision would last longer and be harsher each time. In 1989 I lost all my vision. There is no way to prepare for that. I needed a lot of anchors. I have a fantastic family—we have five children and a number of grandchildren. And my wife, Maureen, has been the biggest anchor.

And then there was football. Other than my family, football was the only thing I had. I made up mind that I couldn't coach anymore, but then I decided to ask my coaching staff. They're a good bunch of guys. They said, "Give it a try. Don't sit back and give it away."

It was a big experiment, and I made a lot of mistakes. There were a lot of things I could do, but there were also a lot of things I couldn't do. I got banged around, knocked down, got bumps and bruises. I'm always tripping over dummies. Sometimes you forget you're blind, you really do. You create a picture in your mind of what's around you based on what you know and can pull from your other senses. That works a great many times, except when there's a dummy lying in front of you. And I used to take a lot of balls in the face. We have this standing rule now: Nobody throw the ball to Coach White! The kids still forget. But I can laugh at myself. That takes the pressure off. Like when a kid runs into me—which has happened many times: "That's as hard as you can hit?"

There are some people who are intimidated by the fact that I'm blind. I can feel them looking at me, saying, "What the hell's this guy doing?" But they always give me a chance. What I've had to do is involve my other senses to keep myself in the game. I can tell during a blocking drill whether they're hitting low enough, just by where the noise is. The kids don't know I do this: I touch their shoulder pad when I'm talking to them. That way I know where the noise should be coming from. I know when they didn't do it properly. Some kids have actually accused me of faking being blind. "You can really see, can't you?" The coaches tell me I have this sixth sense. I don't know about that. It's experience. The game hasn't changed.

[Jack White died in September 1992; he was fifty-four.]

KURT ASCHERMANN: I had a high school baseball team my first year at Woodlands High School that went 3 and 18. People kept telling me that losing builds character, but by the time we got to 0 and 9 I had enough character. But it's those kids, and not the team that went like 17 and 6, who come back and see me. It was an awful year, but the strengths of our relationship were built in that adversity. You know what? Losing builds character.

Recently, one of the guys got married. I remember he was hitting .300 on his last at bat, and he asked me if he had to bat. I said of course. He grounded out to second base; ended up hitting .297. We've joked about that. I still think he's furious with me.

I got invited to his wedding and he put me at the table with a bunch of the guys from that team. We joked and talked about that team, about the time one kid went straight from the locker room into the gym without any clothes on. All the funny stories. The old coach with his guys. It was absolutely wonderful—to sit with those kids and reminisce about those 3-and-18 horrible times.

TOM McDONALD, *basketball, Ely High, Minnesota:* My dad's the winningest high school basketball coach in Minnesota. He got the record against me [612 wins against 217 losses]. He coaches at Chisholm High, and I'm here at Ely. There are six of us kids, four boys and two girls. Dad's a social studies teacher and a coach, and so are all of us. We got into basketball because of our dad.

I was water boy for him as a kid. I had a little suit, and I'd tag along. I got to see all the ins and outs. I loved to go with my dad on the bus and watch my brothers play. They were in three straight state tournaments, so I got to ride the vans down to Minneapolis. It was nice to be on the bench, to be around my dad, watching what he did. I think that's been a real help to me in terms of knowing how to coach and how to handle people.

The game when he got the record was kind of weird. It gave me goose pimples just to be on the same floor with him. I've always dreamed of it. Coaching in South Dakota for three years, I couldn't wait to get back into Minnesota. Just for the opportunity to be around northern Minnesota again and have a chance to play my dad. Going into the season, he needed twelve wins. The spring before, I said, "You'll probably get it against us." He laughed and said, "I'll be lucky to be 6–6 by then." He keeps knocking people off; I keep watching the papers. He loses one game. Sure enough, it comes down to he's got to play Ely to get the record. I think it must have been a pretty tough situation for my mother.

It was exciting to be part of history. I told my guys that I thought we could beat them. And we were up in the first quarter. The three networks from Duluth were there, and so were the papers. It was a big affair. It would have been something if we could have beat him—it would have spoiled a bunch of cake. We stayed with him until half-time, and then we faded. He beat us by 19.

After the game I gave him a big hug. There wasn't too much said. We have the kind of family that, once we get off the basketball floor, we don't talk about it much. I think that surprises people. For my dad it was just another game. There've been so many. I haven't really thought much about how much I want to beat him. It's not something I'm setting out as a goal. People ask me if, when my dad retires, would I take over his job. That's something to think about. It's the only place I'd think of moving to. But I don't know. There'd be a lot of big footsteps.

JOHN E. LEE, *football, Walpole High, Massachusetts:* Beating Brockton in the state championship, that's my greatest thrill. No one in his right mind picked us to win, playing Brockton, with almost four thousand students and Walpole's got seven hundred. They were the number one team in *USA Today,* and we won the game 6–2. And they left the ball on the one-inch line.

I celebrated by getting on an airplane and going to Arizona for a vacation. I'd booked way before the game. I owed my wife a vacation. I had never been to Arizona and I wanted to see the Grand Canyon. The next day I pick up the local paper, and see the state-championship football game is being played at the end of the week. My wife was great. She dropped me off and went shopping, I introduced myself to the coach and we hit it off real well for the whole week. It was a great vacation. Saw the Grand Canyon, too.

FRANK LAYDEN: I was already ready to gag it up. The funniest thing that ever happened to me was when Morganna the Kissing Bandit got me. I spun myself around and fell on the floor, spread-eagle, like I'd fainted. Another time at an away game I sent the ball boy to drink the water before I did in case it was poisoned. I'd play the buffoon, the guy who slipped on the banana peel. I mean, I'm so heavy I was seen as this comic figure anyway. Falstaff. It's got to be fun or what's the point?

But I wish I hadn't done it like that. When I first got to the Jazz I tried to do what Casey Stengel did with the Mets. Our team was not very good then, and I thought I could use my humor as a way of deflecting the criticism from my players. And it worked. But I don't think I ever got the respect for the coach I was. I think people looked at me as an aberration. If you were to ask my colleagues what kind of coach I was, I'd hope they'd say I was one of the good ones.

GARY ZARECKY, *basketball, Foothills Junior College, California:* One of the things I latched on to back in the early '70s was the fund-raising aspect of coaching. I built a program at Sweetwater High in San Diego, an inner-city school. By the time I left we'd generated close to one million dollars in goods, services, and cash. That attracted USIU [United States International University in San Diego]. They hired me to bring money into the school.

When I first came to USIU, the president called me into his office and said, "I don't care whether you win; your job is to take the guarantees and run." A lot of smaller schools think that way. I was trapped on the road. At USIU I did not have Division I talent; I was lucky if it was Division II. I had to find a way to recruit kids without any money, so I decided to develop a high-powered offense geared toward the press.

What I learned, after studying videos, talking to people, putting stuff through the computer, was that almost every great defensive coach is most likely a horrible offensive coach. My job was to get their teams out of that defensive mode. And I developed a system that did that. The first year at USIU we led the nation in scoring. Our record was 10–18. There was respect, there was notoriety—and there were jokes and ridicule. But when I left a gym and we were beat 130–115, I had something positive in my hand. We were no longer just getting thumped, we were one of the high-powered offensive teams in the country. We averaged 90 points a game. We gave up 101. That's no different than losing 60–49—which would have happened anyway. But we were causing the big boys fits, and they had to run with *us*.

I was getting secret calls from college coaches. I was getting high school and junior college coaches coming to my practices. We were getting front-page coverage. Attendance rose. We were in demand. Instead of the six-, eight-, ten-thousand-dollar guarantees, now we're up to twelve, fourteen thousand dollars. No-name schools don't put anybody in the arena. We did. We lit it up. Now I'm recruiting the entire country!

We were getting it going. But while I'm trying to build a program, stories started appearing about how the school was in financial trouble, which jeopardized accreditation. Apparently they were turning up stones with all kinds of debts underneath them. We'd go three, four months without a paycheck. I lost three starters; I lost three top recruits. I lost assistant coaches; I lost secretaries. We got evicted from our practice facility. We got a community center to give us a half court that we had to share with finger-painting and aerobics classes. I ended up with six players, kids I'd recruited. I could have walked, but my wife and I sat down and we said, I owe these kids something. We had to see the schedule through. We finished 2–24.

To this day, I think I could have done it at the Division I level if I'd been given the chance. But I've learned. There's a certain illness that comes with coaching at Division I. You become obsessed. I'm saying that with a smile on my face, because most coaches dream of Division I. I know I did.

BILL MUSSELMAN, *first coach of the Minnesota Timberwolves (now with a CBA team in Rochester, Minnesota):* When I was at Ashland

[College in Ohio], we lead the nation in defense. We gave up 33 points a game. We shut people *down*. But I wanted to win by a shutout. *That* was motivation.

I remember we had a game at Slippery Rock, and before our varsity game our freshman team was getting blown out. There was a full house and they're yelling, "You guys are number one?" Our club goes down to get dressed and I walk in and one of the players said, "You know that shutout you've been talking about, Coach? We're getting it tonight." I could have heard a pin drop.

The game starts, the ball's thrown up, and we score. Five minutes go by and they haven't scored, six minutes, eight minutes. We foul somebody about twelve minutes in, and they make one, and the place goes bananas. At halftime they had 3 points. What do you tell a team at halftime when you've given up 3 points? They went back out and *played*. In the second half I tried to put in the subs but they wouldn't go in. When they finally would, the starters had given up 11 points. We won 67–17. Their coach told me he never saw a team play so hard. They covered their man. It was perfection.

ANONYMOUS MAN, *Division I coach:* I sometimes worry that being gay is going to hold me back. I coach at a big sports institution where football is king. I've heard the comments "fags," "sissies." While I believe my boss knows, it's too risky for it to become common knowledge. I have goals beyond this—working at the national and international levels of my sport. This is where the fear lies—of having my career, which really has gone far at a young age, cut short.

I am not going to let them hold me back. In coaching, until you get to the ultimate job, you have to keep moving, increase your salary, increase your demand. I've made a couple moves already, and I can see myself making one or two more. There's risk in that. I could move to a better program and the boss knows and everything's fine. And then he's gone and there's a new boss. But that could happen here, too.

You've just got to deal with those things as they come. I could go crazy speculating. I've done well at each place I've been, and I plan to continue to do well. What can I do beyond that? There are things you can control and things you can't. The biggest thing for me is that I'm happy, and I plan to continue to be happy. I love coaching. That's what really matters to me.

CHARLIE THOMAS, *basketball, San Francisco State:* I was a tough player. I always played their best offensive player. I don't think that has ever ceased in me. I grew up in Harrisonburg, Virginia. I was good for my age, and I always played against the older kids. If I was better than they were, they beat me up. That made me tough. I'd go home crying, but I'd be there the next day.

[QUESTION: As a coach, are you still the little kid going against the big boys?] That's a good analogy. I want to go to a low Division I school that's not winning, and prove what I can do. [SFS is Division II.] Upset some big boys and put the school on the map. I've seen more than one guy do that. Go to like a Southwest Central State, and then all of a sudden you're 25 and 5, and you beat Texas and Missouri and you make it to the second round of the NCAAs and nobody's ever heard of you. That would elevate me into the spotlight and maybe get me to someplace else. That's what I'm hoping.

If I was starting out now, I'd have to do it a different way: get in as a grad assistant or a volunteer coach at the Division I level. But I'm not going to change. I'm going to make it on my own. Give me the same talent, the same players, give me a chance against the big boys, then see what I can do. That's it. It's the hard road, but I'm going to get there.

Someday I'll be in the Final Four. I just don't know yet who it will be with and who it will be against. I'd love to go against Bobby Knight. He's the best. I'm still using stuff that he was using back in '78. That would be a fitting end to my dream, to go against a coach I've respected and admired and looked up to all my life. To play Bobby Knight in the Final Four would be the ultimate. That's what I want.

TIM WILKE, *girls' basketball, Lowmira High, Wisconsin:* To go a long ways, you'd better have real drive. You've got to have fantastic self-esteem and self-confidence, because the odds are against you. If you don't believe 100 percent in yourself, you're not going to make it. You've got to be willing to keep pounding, keep pounding until you knock that door down. That's the only way you can become successful.

I have a plan. I guess all dreamers have a plan. I would like to win a state championship before I move on. If I got a great opportunity before that, I wouldn't pass it up. But if I can achieve a state championship, I'd know I'd be good enough to move to the next level. I need to learn more about the game, about the administration of the game, the responsibilities of the game before I can get to that next level. The timetable is hard to define. Part of it is instinct—you know you're there when you're there.

I work extremely hard at what I do, and I believe in myself. Actually, right now I'm not spending enough time on the basketball. I'm kind of anxious about that. I teach at an elementary school about fifteen miles from the school I coach at. I get to spend maybe fifteen hours a week in practice. I'll spend another twenty hours a week watching games and looking at videos. I'm not satisfied with that. I could lose myself in a basketball job.

The next step is to continue gaining knowledge. I'm twenty-nine; I'm still young. I feel good about myself as a game coach, but I need to learn how to break skills down and be able to teach them better. That comes with experience. I spend my summers at basketball camps. A friend of mine and me, we do our own for two weeks. And I go to Nelson-Sanders [Don Nelson and Satch Sanders] in New Hampshire for a couple of weeks. I pick everybody's brains. I come home with four, five new ideas from every basketball camp. I'm watching and stealing everything.

I believe things will take care of themselves. Life is a long process. Well, actually, it gets a lot shorter as you get older. I'm trying not to rush it, not be greedy. Winning a state championship, getting into college, winning a national championship, the NBA—that'd be perfect. At the same time, I don't expect any of those things to happen. I'm just going to do the best job I possibly can, keep believing in myself, and let the situation take care of itself. You've got to believe in God, too. I mean, in terms of accepting that things happen for a reason.

I was real disappointed when Don Nelson didn't get the [1992] Olympic [head coaching] job. If not *the* best NBA coach, then he's in the top three. Before the selection I asked him for a position, any position, on his Olympic staff if he got selected. I think he would have considered me. I don't know. But you've got to have that kind of gumption. If you don't, you're not going to get anywhere. You've got to have guts. You've got to stick your neck out, put it on the line. The way I figure it, the person you're asking, he's already done that, he's stuck out his own neck or he wouldn't be where he is now. He understands what you're doing.

BUTCH VAN BREDA KOLFF, *basketball, Hofstra University, Long Island:* I always wanted to kick a ball during a game. You know, really boot it. That's my dream, yeah. I was a soccer player when I was a kid, and I was pretty good.

I remember once when I was with the [Detroit] Pistons and we were playing the Bulls. Our guy went up for a shot and he got fouled and they goal-tended, so the basket was good and the foul was called, and while all this is happening there was a scuffle under the basket and the ball bounces over toward Dick Motta, the Bulls coach. And he drop-kicks it into the seats. I said, "Goddamn you, Motta! I always wanted to do that!" He didn't get a technical, nothing. The refs didn't even see it. I didn't even mind that he got away with it. I yell at the ref—it was Eddie Murphy—"Did you see what happened? Where's the ball?" And Murph is looking at me but like trying to look out the corner of his eye, looking for the ball. Meanwhile, some kid was trying to run away with it.

I always wanted to kick a ball. Still do. I had a chance once, in the ABA. I got four technicals in a game. I got one T early, and Eddie Rush, the ref, I knew he wanted to throw me out, so when he made another bad call, I said, "I'm going to be smart, I'm not going to yell." Instead, I walked over behind the bench. There were some friends there and I sat with them for three or four minutes to cool off.

When I'm coming back to the bench, Rush sees me and calls another T. "What's was that for?" I scream. He says, "You weren't on the bench." And I say, "There's nothin in the book that says I have to be on the bench." So Rush says, "You're out of here." I say, "I'm not leaving until I see it." I get a rule book and start looking through it— and I have no idea what I'm looking for. Rush comes up and says, "Every ten seconds it's another technical." So I go, "Beep! That's number three."

I know this is getting ridiculous, I know I don't know what I'm looking for, so I start to walk out. The guy's shooting the technicals and he misses one, and the ball bounces right over to me. Can you believe it? I could have let it roll right past me, but no, I pick it up. "Now what am I going to do with this?" It was right there! But I had loafers on—

this is going through my mind real quick—and I could see my shoe flying up in the air with the ball, and then I'd have to go up in the stands looking for my shoe. If only I'd had on sneakers! So I didn't do it. I didn't kick that ball. I gave Rush a little swoop and handed him the ball. That was T number four. It's always bothered me that I never kicked the ball. I could have really nailed that son of a bitch!

BILLY WILLIAMS: *[Played seventeen years in the minors through 1969; returned to baseball with the Cleveland Indians in 1989.]* I've lived my dream—part of it, anyway. My dad was a die-hard Dodger fan. He hated the Yankees. There's no way I can describe the feeling I have when I sit in the dugout now at Yankee Stadium. I feel the Phil Rizuttos, the Mickey Mantles, the Roger Marises. I feel all of that going through my body.

When I walked into the Stadium the first time [after becoming a coach with the Indians], we were having early BP. I picked up my glove and ran out to center field. The first ball came to me, a line drive, and I caught it. I hadn't thought about doing it in advance; it's just something I wanted to do when I walked out. Catch a ball in center field in Yankee Stadium! I ran back into the dugout and put down the glove and said, "That's it. I lived my dream."

GENE VOLNOGLE: My original goal when I started coaching was not winning all these city championships, not to be the winningest coach in California. My goal was to do the best I could. It wasn't until we'd won 250 games or whatever it was that it all kind of dawned on me. I saw it in print, that I'd won more games than anybody else, and my first thought was, "Heck, that's because I'm the oldest guy around."

I'd announced my retirement before the season started. There was a lot of publicity the whole year, and then the week before the city championships I was getting phone calls and letters from past players, that they're going to be at the game. It was a very emotional thing. We were also playing our arch-rival—Banning, where I'd started out—and the coach at Banning and I were tied at eight for most city championships.

I never broke down and cried, but I know I got tearful before the game in the locker room. I finally had to dismiss them, get them out on the field. To be honest, I got the kids up too high and we had way too many penalties. At half time I told them I could take defeat, but if we didn't play well and got defeated, that would bother me. It's what I'd always told the kids.

Anyway, we got things straightened out and we won 30 to . . . wait. It was about 27 to 13. Look at me: I'm having trouble remembering the last game I ever coached, but I can still remember getting beat 31 to nothing in 1955 when I was a B-team coach!

With the final few seconds ticking down all I could think was, "It's over. I won't be out here anymore." After the game I'm not sure there was a whole lot said. There was a lot of press and TV and our kids were milling around on the field. When I was able to make it into the locker room, they were all yelling and screaming and there was a lot of hugging. Thinking about it now, all I probably could have said anyway was, "Thanks. Thanks for a great season and thanks for a great career."

Roster of Coaches/Index

(Includes coaches interviewed who do not appear in this book)

NAN AIROLA, volleyball, Providence Catholic High, New Lenox, IL. Age 43; born in Joliet, IL. Has coached Providence to a 442–162 record since 1973; pp. 84, 115, 139, 153, 222–223.

KURT ASCHERMANN, youth league sports, Sparta, New Jersey. Author of *Coaching Kids to Play Baseball & Softball* and *Coaching Kids to Play Soccer.* Age 44; born in Ossining, NY. Founder of "Coaching the Coach Clinics" for volunteer youth coaches. Played baseball at Springfield College; played two years in the Chicago Cubs organization; pp. 24, 66–67, 171, 214–215, 221, 240, 246.

BOB ASHE, soccer, Catlin Gabel School, Portland, OR (retired). Grew up in Belfast, Northern Ireland, where he played rugby and soccer. Won five straight state championships and nearly three hundred games (against only fifty-four losses) during his career. National Soccer Coach of the Year in 1982. (AGC)★; pp. 15–16, 126–127.

★*America's Greatest Coaches* by Michael D. Koehler, Leisure Press, Champaign, IL, 1990.

DOUG BARFIELD, football, Opelika High, AL. Age 56; born in Castleberry, AL. Played football and baseball at the University of Southern Mississippi. Was head football coach at Auburn University from 1976 to 1983. Spent seven years away from coaching; has been coaching the Opelika Bulldogs for three years; pp. 42, 204–205.

BILLY BARNETT, six–man football, Dell City High, TX. Age 33; born in Iraan, TX. Attended Angelo State University, where he participated in football and track. Was at Christoval High for five years, with a 60–9 overall record. *San Angelo Standard Times* Coach of the Year 1988, 1989; pp. 25, 181.

LEE BATTAGLIA, Crystal Lake Gymnastics Training Center, IL. Coached Kurt Thomas, the 1978 world champion, in his comeback attempt to make the 1992 Olympic team. The 36-year-old Thomas finished sixteenth at the trials, making the national squad but not the Olympic team. Battaglia also coached 1992 Olympian Chris Waller. Has coached fourteen gymnasts to berths on U.S. junior and senior Olympic teams; pp. 172–173.

SALLY BAUM, tennis, Goucher College, Towson, MD. Age 36, born in Poolesville, MD. Played field hockey, basketball, volleyball, softball, and tennis at Poolesville High; field hockey and lacrosse at Slippery Rock University. Tennis coach at Goucher since 1979, with a 107–93–1 record and five conference championships. Elected to the Slippery Rock Hall of Fame in 1990; pp. 2, 111, 184–185.

NORMA BELLAMY, volleyball, Safford High, AZ.

WANDA BINGHAM, volleyball, Churchhill High, San Antonio. Age 42; raised in Uvalde, TX. Graduated from Southwest Texas State in San Marcos twenty years ago and has been at Churchill ever since. Has made playoffs sixteen times and regionals eight times, and at states finished third, second, and first two times each. Overall record is 546–134. (AGC); pp. 179–180.

GARY BLACKNEY, football, Bowling Green University. Spent twenty-one years as an assistant before being hired in 1991 as the head coach at Bowling Green, which was coming off a 3–5–2 season. In Blackney's rookie year the Falcons finished 10–1 and played in the California Raisin Bowl; pp. 200, 201.

DON BORDENAVE, volunteer assistant football coach, Santa Clara University.

AL BORGES, offensive coordinator, Boise State. Age 37; born in Salinas, CA. By the time he was 30 Borges had coached Pop Warner, at two California high schools, Diablo Valley J.C., the Oakland Invaders of the USFL, at Portland State at Division I–AA, and at Cal–Berkeley in Division I; pp. 2, 55, 57, 58, 161, 227.

JENNINGS BOYD, basketball, coached Northfork High in West Virginia to nine state titles, including a national-record eight in a row. Age 60; raised in Berwind, WV. Played basketball at Concord College in Athens, WV. Started as an assistant at Northfork in 1965. Won eight state titles from 1974 to 1991. Elected to the National High School Sports Hall of Fame in 1984. (AGC); pp. 82, 94, 208.

TOM BROSNIHAN, basketball assistant, West Side High, Omaha. Age 58; born in Omaha. Coach at Creighton Prep, 1960 to 1970. Assistant at Creighton University 1970 to 1982. Head coach at Dana College 1982 to 1986. Spent one year coaching the women's team at the College of St. Mary's, two years at Ralston, and one year back at Dana. A diabetic, he lost his left leg below the knee in 1992 and his right leg below the knee in 1993; pp. 3, 180, 215, 225–226.

HUBIE BROWN, New York Knicks (retired). Currently a basketball analyst on TNT's NBA telecast. Was an assistant coach with the Milwaukee Bucks (1972–74) and head coach of the Kentucky Colonels (1974–76) where he won the ABA championship in 1975. Was the head coach of the Atlanta Hawks in the NBA (1976–81) and the New York Knicks (1982–87). Selected NBA Coach of the Year in 1978; pp. 9, 15, 16, 18, 59, 60, 140, 148, 165, 182, 197.

OLLIE BUTLER, basketball assistant, Cal State University San Bernardino. Age 61; born in Bemis, TN. Played basketball at Oklahoma. Spent thirty-three years coaching high school teams in three states to an overall 605–251 record. Won fifteen league titles, including ten in a row, and nine coach of the year awards. Assistant at CSUSB for two years; pp. 4, 118, 161.

P. J. CARLESIMO, basketball, Seton Hall. Graduated from Fordham, where he played for Digger Phelps's 26–3 Ram team, then spent four years at Fordham as an assistant. Spent six years at Wagner as head coach before coming to Seton Hall, where he has been head coach for eleven years. The Hall has won two Big East titles and in 1989 came within an overtime basket of the NCAA Championship.

Coached the 1991 gold-medal U.S. World University Games team and was an assistant coach of the 1992 "Dream Team" U.S. Olympic basketball team; pp. 145–146, 167, 196, 227.

GREGORY P. CARPENTER, girls' basketball, St. Johnsbury Middle School, VT. Age 33; born in Norwich, CT. Played baseball at Plymouth State College in New Hampshire. Head coach of the girls' varsity at Concord High School in VT for six years. Has been at St. Johnsbury one year. Asked that his appearance in *Coach* be dedicated to his father, who died in March 1992; pp. 27, 74, 170.

ED CHEFF, baseball, Lewis–Clark State College, Lewiston, ID. Age 49; born in Butte, MT. Played football and baseball at Lewis and Clark College in Portland, OR. Coach of the Lewis–Clark Warriors for sixteen years, with an 802–205 record. NAIA National Champs 1984, '85, '87, '88, '89, '90, '91, '92. NAIA Coach of the Year 1986, '87, '91. (AGC); pp. 104, 108, 150–151, 218.

SANDRA CHILDERS, softball, Marion–Adams High, Sheridan, IN. Age 47; born in Lebanon, IN. Graduated from Indiana State; master's in elementary education from Butler. Teaches third grade at Marion Elementary School; pp. 47, 76, 170–171.

ROY CHIPMAN, basketball, University of Pittsburgh (retired). Age 54; born in Millbridge, ME. Started coaching in 1961 at Winthrop High in Maine. Took the Hartwick (NY) College Warriors to the Division II NCAA tournament nine times in ten seasons. Coached three years at Lafayette and six at Pittsburgh, where his teams made three NCAA and three NIT appearances; pp. 5, 6, 11, 78–79, 115, 140, 149–150, 161, 219–220, 221.

RICHARD CICIARELLI, baseball, Midlakes High, NY (retired). Age 47; born in Solvay, NY. Attended Clarkson College of Technology. Has coached bowling, junior high and varsity baseball, and football. Doesn't know his overall record because "I never kept track. In junior high wins and losses were not important"; pp. 171, 208.

PERRY CLARK, basketball, Tulane. Age 43; raised in Washington, DC. Played for and later coached under John Wooten at DeMatha High in DC. Attended Gettysburg College. An assistant at Penn State and Georgia Tech before moving to Tulane in 1988. As a head coach he is 63–55. Was 1992 National Coach of the Year; p. 57.

ART COLLINS, downhill skiing, Reno High, NV. Age 47; born in

Hollywood, CA. Attended Glendale High in California; threw the javelin for the L.A. Striders. Spent three years in Vietnam. Attended the Univesity of Nevada–Reno; stripped elbow ligaments ended javelin career. Coach at Reno since 1979. The girls' team has won fourteen straight titles; the boys' won thirteen before losing in 1993; pp. 44–45, 153.

BOBBY CREMINS, basketball, Georgia Tech. Age 46; born in The Bronx, NY. Played in an ACC championship game as a player at South Carolina and later coached in two ACC championship games at Tech. Started coaching in 1971 at Point Park College in Pittsburgh, then spent two years as an assistant at South Carolina before becoming head coach at Appalachia State for seven years. Head coach at Tech since 1981, where he has won two ACC championships and been to one NCAA Final Four. Overall record: 321–194; record at Tech: 221–124; pp. 55–56, 143–144.

JIM CRINER, football, Sacramento Surge of the World Football League (league suspended). Age 52, born in Lurton, AR. Owner of Bud Lilly's Trout Shop in West Yellowstone, MT, and an outfitter for Yellowstone National Park. Made assistant or head coaching stops at Claremont High School (CA), Clovis High School (CA), University of Utah, Elk Grove High School (CA), California State, BYU, UCLA, Boise State, Iowa State, and the Surge. These teams produced nine championships, one Rose Bowl win (UCLA), one national championship (Boise State), and one World Bowl championship (Surge); pp. 157, 201, 202–204.

BILL CURRY, football, University of Kentucky. Age 50; born in Atlanta. Played football at Georgia Tech and spent ten years in the NFL, where he played in the first Super Bowl. Head coach at Georgia Tech from 1980 to 1986 and was ACC Coach of the Year in 1985. From 1987 to 1989 he was 26–10 at Alabama. In 1989 the Crimson Tide was 10–1, shared the Southeastern Conference title, and appeared in the Sugar Bowl. He was SEC Coach of the Year in 1987 and 1989. At Kentucky since 1990; pp. 14, 31, 103, 168, 169–170.

CHARLOTTE DAVIS, synchronized swimming, national head coach since 1985. Age 42, born in Seattle. Founder and coach of the Seattle Aqua Club, 1971; pp. 119–120.

RON DICKERSON, defensive coordinator, Clemson University (now head coach at Temple). Age 45. Over seventeen years made assistant stops at Kansas State, Penn State, Colorado, and Clemson before being named head coach at Temple in November 1992. A past president of the Black Coaches Association; pp. 27, 41–42, 51.

DAVE DOLCH, football, Morningside College, Sioux City, IA. Age 38; born in Baltimore. First head job was in 1986 at Bowie State. Was 0–9 his first year, was 9–2–1 two years later and in the NCAA Division II playoffs. Moved to Morningside in 1990; turned a 2–9 team his first year into a 7–4 team his second year; p. 52.

W. S. DONALD, football and track & field, Wooddale High, Memphis. Age 65; born in Sallis, MS. Won five straight track & field state titles at Horn Lake High in MS. At Trezevant High won a cross-country state title in 1966. Track coach at Wooddale since 1967; won state titles in '73, '86, '87, and '88. Head coach of Wooddale football since 1985; has a 135–75 record. (AGC); pp. 9, 17, 106.

ANSON DORRANCE, women's soccer, University of North Carolina and head coach 1991 Women's U.S. World Cup champions. Dorrance was born in Bombay and lived in Calcutta, Nairobi, Addis Abbaba, Singapore, and Brussels. Attended high school in Switzerland and college at the University of North Carolina. Head coach of UNC men's team from 1976 to 1989 and head coach of the women's team from 1979. His women's teams have won eleven of the twelve national collegiate titles contested in women's soccer; pp. 2, 43, 95–96, 123–124, 125–126, 154–156, 215–216.

BOBBY DOUGLAS, wrestling, 1992 Olympic coach and Iowa State head coach. Spent eighteen years as the head coach at Arizona State. His teams posted a 225–77–6 dual-meet record. In 1988 the Sun Devils won the NCAA team title and Douglas was coach of the year. Named the Iowa State coach in 1992. As the 1992 Olympic coach, he placed all ten U.S. wrestlers in the top ten of their weight classes, a U.S. Olympic first. Excluding 1984, when the Eastern Block nations didn't compete, the three golds by the U.S. in 1992 tie the record for most ever by the U.S. Head coach of the 1989 World Championship team, and in 1988 he guided the U.S. to a 7–3 dual-meet victory over the Soviets at the Sunkist/Fiesta Bowl; pp. 3, 21–22, 91–92, 119.

DOROTHEA EDWARDS, field hockey, Casady High, Oklahoma City. (AGC).

JANET ELY–LaGOURGE, diving, Mission Viejo Nadadores. Age 39; born in Albuquerque. Competed in the 1972 and '76 Olympics; world platform champion in 1975. Attended the University of Michigan and SMU; started coaching nineteen years ago while still in college. Coached Olympic and world medalist Wendy Williams, and was coach of the 1991 U.S. Junior Olympics; pp. 98–99, 242.

ED ETZEL, psychologist and assistant professor, West Virginia University school of physical education. Age 40; born in North Haven, CT. Coached the Mountaineers' rifle teams from 1976 to 1989 and won five NCAA championships. Individual gold medalist in rifle at the 1984 Olympics; pp. 213–214.

VIRGIL FLETCHER, basketball, Collinsville High, IL. (AGC)

JO FOWLER, girls' track & field, Owensboro High, KY (retired). Age 67; born in Blackey, KY. Attended Berea College and the University of Kentucky. Played AAU basketball and tennis. Won a state track and field championship in 1967; p. 173.

DR. GARY D. FUNK, Director of the Southwest Missouri State University/Southwestern Bell Telephone Literacy Center, formerly the coordinator of the Academic Support Center for Intercollegiate Athletics at SMSU. Age 35; born in Decatur, IL. Attended Kickapoo High School in Springfield, MO; Southwest Missouri State; and Oklahoma State. Author of *Major Violation;* pp. 221, 223–224.

CLARENCE "BIG HOUSE" GAINES, basketball, Winston-Salem University, NC. (AGC).

STEPHANIE VANDERSLICE GAITLEY, basketball, St. Joseph's University, Philadelphia. Age 33; born in Ocean City, NJ. Attended Villanova University and made the AIAW Final Four. Head coach at Richmond University at age 25, where she won two Colonial Athletic Association Championships and was coach of the year in 1990. In two years at St. Joe's has won two Big Five Championships and been named Big 5 Coach of the Year. Overall record is 154–83; pp. 31, 79, 80, 137, 185–187.

MIKE GEAR, football, Sidney High, MT. Age 46; born in Dickenson, ND. Is 124–38 and has won eight Class A state titles in seventeen years; p. 6.

DICK GRAY, basketball, Benson High, Portland, OR (retired).

TINA SLOAN GREEN, lacrosse, Temple (retired). Age 49; born in

Philadelphia. Graduated from West Chester State, where she played lacrosse, field hockey, and badminton. An All–American in lacrosse, she then played on the U.S. National Team. In seventeen seasons with the Owls won three national titles, becoming the first African-American to coach a team to a national championship. Her record was 196–57–4. Founder of the Inner–City Field Hockey and Lacrosse Program; served as program director for the National Youth Sports Program; pp. 5, 21, 51–52, 111, 112, 115, 241.

RON GREENE, basketball, Caloway County High, Murray, KY. Spent twenty-three years coaching college, first as assistant at Murray State and Loyola–New Orleans, then as head man at LSU–New Orleans, Mississippi State, Murray State, and Indiana State. Coach of the year in Southeastern and Ohio Valley conferences; pp. 27–29, 42, 167.

PAT GRIFFIN, associate professor of social justice education, University of Massachusets–Amherst (and former swim coach). Age 47; born in Washington, DC. Played basketball and field hockey and swam at Maryland. Coached field hockey and basketball in high school. Holds a Ph.D. in education from U–Mass. Competed in the triathlon at the 1990 Gay Games; pp. 17, 47, 205, 209, 219, 226.

BILL GUTHRIDGE, basketball assistant, University of North Carolina. Played at Kansas State in the late '50s for Tex Winter. Has been Dean Smith's lead assistant at UNC for twenty-six years. In that time the Tar Heels have won two NCAA titles and made the Final Four eight times. An assistant to Smith's gold–medal-winning 1976 U.S. Olympic team and head coach of the 1968 Puerto Rican team; pp. 58–59.

HANK HAINES, founder and manager of the Blytheville Boxing Club in AK (retired): Age 66; born in Blytheville. Currently lives in Murfreesboro, TN. Attended the University of North Carolina. Boxed in the service; pp. 25–26, 116, 238–240.

DORIS HARDY, athletic director at Riverside–Brookfield High in Riverside, IL. She retired from coaching in 1991. Came to Riverside in 1964. Her first coaching assignment was synchronized swimming, but, as a one–woman athletic department, she "coached everything at one time or the other"; pp. 39–40, 173–174, 185.

KERRI HEFFERNAN, Boston Beantown Women's Rugby Club (retired). Age 35; raised in Altomonte Springs, FL. Ran track at

Florida State; holds a master's in education from Boston University Played on three undefeated U.S. international sides; coached Beantown to a national club title her first year; pp. 74–75, 162, 218.

STEVE HODGIN, football, Western Carolina University. Age 45; born in Greensboro, NC. Played football at the University of North Carolina. Coached for eight years at Tuscola High in Waynesville, NC, and fourteen years at Western Carolina. The Catamounts' head coach four years; pp. 38–39.

GAYLE HOOVER, basketball, Parker High, SD. Age 57; born in Ocheydon, IA. Played basketball at Sioux Falls College and is still the leading collegiate career scorer in the state. Retired after thirty-four years at Parker High. His 577–217 record is most wins of any high school coach in the state. Has won twelve conference, twelve district, and eight regional championships and has made eight trips to States; p. 9.

KATIE HORSTMAN, track & field, Minster High, OH. Age 58; born in Minster. Played four years in the All-America Girls Professional Baseball League and barnstormed for three more years in the 1950s. Coach at Minster for twenty-two years, has won eight state championships in girls' track and one cross–country title, and was a runner–up in volleyball. First woman elected to the Ohio Track Hall of Fame, in 1986. In 1993 played for the Dayton Cardinals women's softball team that won a bronze medal at the Senior Olympics. (AGC); pp. 33–34.

TOM HOUSE, assistant to the general manager (and former pitching coach), Texas Rangers. Age 46; born in Seattle. Played nine years in the major leagues as a relief pitcher. Began coaching with the Houston Astros in 1980, moved to the San Diego Padres in 1982 and to the Rangers in 1985. Holds a Ph.D. and is author of *The Jock's Itch.* pp. 101–102, 161, 162, 162–163, 197, 217, 221–222.

KEN HOUSTON, defensive backfield, University of Houston (retired), now a counselor at Terrell Alternative Middle School in Houston. Played fourteen years in the NFL with the Oilers and Redskins and played in twelve Pro Bowls. Selected to the *Sports Illustrated* pro football "Dream Team" as strong safety. Coached with the Oilers and at Wheatley, Westberry, and Sterling High Schools in Houston; pp. 34, 114–115.

NICK HYDER, football, Valdosta High, GA. Age 57; born in Eliza-
bethton, TN. Head coach at Valdosta for nineteen years. Has won
fifteen regionals, nine sectionals, seven South Georgia championships,
six state championships, and two *USA Today*/National Sports News
Service national championships. Coached at West Rome High School
from 1958 to 1973. Lifetime record is 264–40–5; p. 141.

WILLARD IKOLA, hockey, Edina High, MN (retired). Age 61;
born in Eveleth, MN. Played in goal on three undefeated Eveleth
High state-championship teams in 1948, 1949, and 1950, then tended
goal at the University of Michigan, where the Wolverines won two
NCAA titles. In 1956 he won a silver medal on the U.S Olympic
hockey team. Took over Edina in 1958 and stayed thirty-four seasons,
running his record to 600–148–38. The Hornets won eight state
titles; pp. 22–23.

RANDY JABLONIC, rowing, University of Wisconsin. Age 57; born
in Waukegan, IL. Member of the 1959 eight–oared Wisconsin crew
that won the intercollegiate championship; member of the 1960
team that finished eleventh. Spent thirty-four years coaching Wisconsin, twenty-six years as head coach. National coach in 1981,
'82, and '83; pp. 19, 76–77, 104, 107, 123.

BARBARA JEAN JACKET, coach of the 1992 U.S. Olympic
women's track & field team. Age 57; born in Port Arthur, TX.
Graduated from Tuskegee Institute in 1958. Came to Prairie View
A&M in 1964 as the women's track coach, retired in 1991. Won
twenty national titles and twelve indoor Southwestern Athletic
Conference titles, seven consecutively. Second African-American
woman to be named head Olympic track coach; pp. 3, 52–53,
100–101, 134.

SID JAMIESON, lacrosse, Bucknell University; original coach and
executive director of the Iroquois Nationals Lacrosse Team. Played
football and lacrosse at the State University of New York–Cortland,
where he graduated in 1964. Became the lacrosse coach at Bucknell
the next year. Coached the Iroquois Nationals, a lacrosse team com-
posed of Native Americans, for six years and served as executive
director for eight; pp. 77–78.

SHERYL JOHNSON, field hockey, Stanford University. Born in
Stanford, CA. Participated in field hockey, basketball, softball, track,

gymnastics, and volleyball in high school; field hockey, basketball and softball at Cal–Berkeley. A fourteen-year member of the U.S. women's field hockey team, won a bronze medal at the 1984 Olympics. Coach of the Cardinals for ten years, has been ranked as high as number five in the nation—with a complete walk-on team; pp. 211–212.

K. C. JONES, Seattle Supersonics (retired). Won two NCAA championships at the University of San Francisco in 1955 and 1956 and a gold medal on the '56 U.S. Olympic team. Played nine years with the Boston Celtics, from 1959 to 1967, and won eight championship rings. Head coach at Brandeis 1969–71, the ABA San Diego Conquistadors in 1972–73, and the NBA Washington Bullets 1974–76. After one year as an assistant with the Bucks and five with the Celtics, was Celtics head coach from 1984 to 1988, where he won two championships in four trips to the finals. Coached Seattle all of the 1990–91 season and part of the 1991–92 season. (AGC); pp. 8, 54, 105–106, 197–198, 240.

CHUCK JORDAN, football, Conway High, South Carolina. Played football at Presbyterian College in Clinton, SC, then coached there for two years. Moved to Conway in 1983. Ten-year record is 76–41; his 1985 team was ranked number one in the state; pp. 16–17, 81, 164, 174–175.

REGGIE JOULES lives in Kotzebue, AK, about fifty miles north of the Arctic Circle. He is 40 years old and has long championed the Eskimo–Indian games indigenous to the Inupiak people; pp. 130–132.

GEORGE KARL, Seattle Supersonics. Coached the Cleveland Cavaliers and the Golden State Warrior in the NBA and the Albany Patroons and Real Madrid before landing back in the NBA with the Sonics in February 1992. While with Albany his team set a professional basketball record when it won all its home games in one season; pp. 10, 14, 50, 147–148.

TOM KEESEY, St. Mary's CYO basketball, York, PA (retired).

JOHN KEMMERER, basketball, Riverdale High, Fort Myers, FL (no longer coaching). Age 45; born in Kingsport, TN. Coached fifteen years at the high school varsity level. Now a phys-ed teacher at Sun Coast Middle School in North Fort Myers; pp. 84, 85, 148, 149, 150, 180, 228.

KEITH KEPHART spent twenty years as a strength and conditioning coach at Iowa State, the Universities of Kansas and South Carolina, and Texas A&M. Age 49; born in Iowa City. While at South Carolina was indicted for purchasing steroids without a prescription for, he says, personal use. Two years later the indictment was dropped. Currently employed as a land developer; pp. 58, 229.

DERRIL KIPP, girls' basketball, Maine West High, Des Plaines, IL. Age 48; born in Moline, IL. Warriors coach for twelve years, has won 328 games and lost 49. Won states in 1988, and has finished second once, third twice, and fourth once. Holds current longest win streak in IL at 65; pp. 118, 142–143.

DARLENE KLUKA, Ph.D., assistant professor in health, counseling, and kinesiology at the University of Alabama at Birmingham and retired volleyball coach. Graduated from Illinois State and holds her Ph.D. from the Texas Woman's University in Denton. Coached seven years at New Trier High School in Winnetka, IL, and two years at Bradley University. Member of the board of directors of the U.S. Volleyball Association; pp. 82, 183.

DONNA KRIEGER, volleyball assistant, California Baptist College.

GENE KRIEGER, volleyball, California Baptist College. Age 36; born in Long Beach, CA. Has coached at Cal–Baptist for five years, where he is 85–31. In 1992 his team was national runner–up and he was National Coach of the Year. He has coached at six other colleges and high schools and has an overall record of 297–97; pp. 7, 35–36.

DAVE LAFFERTY, girls' basketball, Vinson High, Huntington, WV; boys' basketball, Ceredo–Kenova High, Kenova, WV. Age 52; born in Huntington. Graduated from West Virginia Tech in Montgomery and holds his master's from Marshall. Coached the Vinson girls until 1991, the C–K boys until 1992. "It was time to coach in a different place." Presently exploring new coaching possibilities; pp. 85–86, 141.

BARRY LAMB, defensive coordinator, San Diego State. Age 27; born in Santa Barbara, CA. Began as a student assistant at Oregon in 1977. Has coached at Oregon, Arizona State, UNLV, Idaho, and San Diego; pp. 8, 13, 14, 50–51, 93.

TONY LaRUSSA, Oakland Athletics. Age 48; born in Tampa. Played sixteen years of professional baseball, but never spent an entire season at the major league level. Began his managerial career in 1978 when he took over the White Sox double-A team in Knoxville. Promoted to the big club in 1979 and stayed through 1986. In 1983 the White Sox won the American League West. Moved to the Athletics midway through the 1986 season. Between 1988 and 1990 the A's won three American League West titles, three American League pennants, and one World Series; pp. 4, 168, 199–200.

FRANK LAYDEN, Utah Jazz (retired). Coached Calvin Murphy at Niagara—his alma mater—and took them to the 1973 NIT final. Has been with the Jazz since they moved from New Orleans to Salt Lake City. Coach of the Western Conference All-Star team and NBA Coach of the Year in 1984, the year the Jazz won the Midwest Division. Retired as coach seventeen games into the 1987–88 season. Is currently president of the Jazz; pp. 7, 17, 87–88, 90, 93, 104–105, 110, 123, 124, 140, 148, 158, 161–162, 176–177, 197, 235, 248.

LINDA LEAVER, coach of Brian Boitano, the 1988 Olympic figure-skating gold medalist, since he was 8 years old. Boitano, 30, has been reinstated as an amateur and is planning to compete at the Olympics again, in 1994. Leaver remained his coach during his post-1988-Olympic touring and professional career, and will be his coach again in Lillihammer, Norway, in 1994; pp. 1–2, 29–30, 81–82.

ANN LEBEDEFF, tennis, Cal–Poly Pomona. Age 41; Oceanside, CA. Played tennis, basketball, volleyball, field hockey, and badminton at both San Marcos High School and San Diego State. Coached one year at San Diego City College, then spent ten years at the University of Arizona before moving to Cal–Poly. Won back-to-back national championships in 1991–92. Wilson Coach of the Year in 1991; pp. 116–117.

JOHN E. LEE, football, Walpole High, MA. Age 60; born in Newton, MA. Retired after the 1992 season after twenty-five years with a 212–33–6 record, the highest winning percentage of any high school coach in Massachusetts. Won twelve league titles, played in five state championship games, and won three; pp. 2, 73, 74, 207, 247–248.

ABE LEMONS, basketball, Oklahoma City University (retired). Lemons started coaching at Oklahoma City College in 1955, where he established his reputation with seven NCAA appearances. Part of his reputation was his willingness to travel—OCC played in thirty-nine states, including Alaska. In 1973 he moved to Pan American and won fifty-five games and lost sixteen. In 1976 he moved to the University of

Texas. He won the NIT in 1978 and had Texas ranked fourth in the nation in 1982 when his star player was hurt. Let go at the end of that season, Lemons returned a year later to OCU, now an NAIA team, and stayed until his retirement in 1990; pp. 8, 14, 88–89, 119, 159–160, 207, 218, 224.

CARLTON LEWIS, coach of high school football in West Point, GA, for twenty-four years. He played basketball and baseball at Georgia Tech. At West Point he won three state titles, finished second three other times, and compiled a 185–71–4 record. He retired from coaching in 1971; pp. 26–27, 182–183.

WALTER LEWIS, former football assistant, University of Kentucky, now a public financial analyst for the Central Bank of the South in Birmingham, AL. Age 33. Played at Alabama from 1980 to 1983; played two years in the USFL and one year each in the CFL and NFL. Coached with Bill Curry at Alabama in 1989; moved with Curry to UK, where he coached for two more years; pp. 32–33, 227.

FAITH LITTLEFIELD, field hockey, Bonny Eagle High, Buxton, ME. (AGC).

JOHN LIPON, roving instructor, Detroit Tigers. Age 70; born in Martins Ferry, OH. Played in the majors from 1940 to 1954. Was a minor league manager for thirty-three years with the Tigers, Indians, and Pirates organizations. Lifetime record of 2,187 wins and 1,970 losses. Managed the Cleveland Indians for two months in 1971. Crowned "King of Baseball" at the 1992 winter baseball meetings; pp. 2, 53–54.

ROBERT LUCEY, football, Curtis High, Tacoma, WA. Age 44; born in Tacoma. Played football and wrestled at the University of Puget Sound. Has been the head coach of the Vikings for twenty-two years. Has won two AA state championships and two AAA titles at Curtis. Washington State Football Coach of the Year in 1990–91 and the *Tacoma News Tribune* Coach of the Year in 1989. An overall record of 110–55; pp. 9, 133, 167, 171, 229–230.

PAT MANCUSO, football, Princeton High, Cincinatti. Age 64; born in Leetonia. Played and then coached for one year at Mt. Union College in Alliance, OH. Was head coach at Leetonia High for five years before moving to Princeton thirty-three years ago. Has won three state championships, including the first-ever Ohio state title in 1972; pp. 5, 6, 20–21, 207.

MIKE MARCOULIS, JR., basketball and baseball, Freemont High, Oakland, CA. Now a basketball assistant at Cal-State Hayward. Coached baseball for fourteen years and basketball for eight years at Freemont. Won three city basketball championships and made four state-tourney appearances; 285–105 overall record. Won one baseball city title; pp. 10, 88, 109, 120–121, 134, 149, 150, 208–209.

DICK MacPHERSON, New England Patriots (retired). Started in 1959 as the freshman coach at the University of Massachusetts. Made assistant-coaching stops at Cincinatti and Maryland and in the NFL with the Denver Broncos and the Cleveland Browns. Head coach at U–Mass from 1971 to 1977, where he won four Yankee Conference titles. From 1981 to 1990 his record at Syracuse was 66–46–4. Spent 1991 and 1992 as head coach with the Patriots. During the 1992 season, with the Patriots on the way to a 2–14 season, he was hospitalized and later let go by the Patriots; pp. 8, 140–141.

NICHOLAS MARIOLIS, basketball, St. Nicholas Newark Greek Orthodox Youth Association. Age 32; born in East Orange, NJ. Has coached at the Newark G.O.Y.A. since 1979. A volunteer women's assistant at Essex County College in Newark; p. 58.

GLEN MASON, football, Kansas. Grew up in Toledo, OH, and played football at Ohio State under Woody Hayes. Started his coaching career at Ball State in 1972 and made assistant stops at Allegheny, Iowa State, Illinois, and Ohio State before landing the head job at Kent State in 1986, where he was MAC Coach of the Year in 1987. Moved to Kansas in 1988. His first year the Jayhawks were 1–10; in 1992 they were 7–4; pp. 93, 111, 165–166.

SUZIE McCONNELL, basketball, Oakland Catholic High, Pittsburgh. Age 27; born in Pittsburgh. Played at Penn State and was a member of the 1988 U.S. Olympic women's gold-medal basketball team and a member of the 1992 bronze-medal team. Took over at Oakland in 1990 when she was 23. Won a state title in 1993 and was women's co-coach of the year; pp. 18, 75–76, 138–139.

PAT McCRACKIN, badminton, Miller Place High, Long Island.

TOM McDONALD, basketball, Ely High, MN. Age 30; born in Chisolm, MN. Played at SD State and coached for three years at Lymen High School in SD, where he won a state title in 1990. Moved back to Ely High in 1991; pp. 246–247.

JOHN B. McLENDON, JR, basketball. Age 78; born in Hiawatha, KS. Attended Kansas State, where he apprenticed under Dr. James Naismith. Coached thirty-four years at North Carolina Central, Hampton, Tennessee State, Kentucky State, Cleveland State, the Cleveland Pipers in the AAU and the ABL, and the Denver Rockets in the ABA. At Tennessee State was the first coach ever to win three straight national titles, when he won the NAIA in 1956, '57, and '58. Member of two Olympic coaching staffs and author of three books; pp. 68–72.

MIKE MESSERE, lacrosse, West Genesee High, Camillus New York. Age 48; born in Syracuse. The Wildcats head coach for seventeen years, he has amassed a 351–18 record. Has won sixteen league, eleven sectional, eleven regional, and ten upstate championships, and has had seven undefeated state-championship teams. In 1983–84 his teams won ninety-one consecutive games. A *USA Today* Coach of the Year in 1991; pp. 4, 172.

RON MODESTE has been a volunteer football coach at Santa Clara University for thirty-one years. He is a principal at St. Lawrence Academy in Santa Clara, CA; p. 5.

STAN MORRISON, basketball, San Jose State University. Age 53; born in Lynwood, CA. Member of the 1959 University of California team that won the NCAA championship under coach Pete Newell. Head coach at the University of the Pacific from 1972 to 1979; head coach at USC from 1979 to 1986. Pac-10 Coach of the Year in 1985, when the Trojans were co-Pac-10 champs. Spent three years as the athletic director at the University of California, Santa Barbara. Head coach at San Jose since 1989; pp. 3, 4, 9, 12, 17, 109–110, 111, 122–123, 140, 141, 201, 225.

BILL MUSSELMAN, coached as a grad assistant at Kent State, then moved to Ashland College where he compiled a 120–30 record. In four years at the University of Minnesota he won a Big 10 championship and was twice ranked in the final-season Top 10. Since then he has made coaching stops with the ABA, the short-lived Western League, the Cleveland Cavaliers, and in the CBA, where he won four straight titles. He was the first coach of the expansion Minnesota Timberwolves in the NBA; pp. 13, 16, 24, 65–66, 90, 100, 136–137, 160–161, 209, 249–251.

DON NELSON, Golden State Warriors. Age 53. A two-time All-American at Iowa. Played fourteen years in the NBA—two years with the Los Angeles Lakers, twelve with the Boston Celtics. Owns five championship rings from his years with the Celtics. Coached from 1976 to 1987 with the Milwaukee Bucks. After one year as just the general manager of the Warriors he moved to the bench in 1988 and has been there ever since. A three-time NBA Coach of the Year; pp. 2, 24, 43, 90, 125, 147, 148, 153–154, 166, 169, 178, 234–235.

JOE NEWTON, cross-country and track, York High, Oak Brook, IL. Age 64; born in Chicago. Cross-country coach at York for thirty-seven years. From 1962 to 1992 his teams won seventeen state titles and sixteen national cross-country titles. His track and cross-country teams have won a total of 1,650 dual meets, for a 92 percent winning mark. Only high school coach ever named an assistant manager of the U.S. Olympic track & field team (1988); pp. 34, 59–60, 100, 217, 235.

JOHN NICKS, Olympic-level figure skating. Coached Tai Babalonia and Randy Gardner, Tiffany Chin, and Christopher Bowman, among others. Has been the figure-skating director at the Ice Chalet in Costa Mesa, CA, the past ten years; pp. 48–49, 162.

CHUCK NOLL, Pittsburgh Steelers (retired). Age 61; born in Cleveland, OH. Played seven years for the Cleveland Browns after being selected in the twenty-first round out of Dayton. Started coaching in 1960 under Sid Gillman with the Los Angeles Chargers. In 1966 he moved to the Baltimore Colts under Don Shula and was named head coach of the Pittsburgh Steelers in 1969. Won four Super Bowls in the 1970s and coached through the 1991 season. Elected to the Football Hall of Fame in 1993. (AGC); pp. 94, 134, 220.

WANDA ANITA OATES, boys' basketball, Frank W. Ballou High, Washington, DC. Graduated from Howard University in 1965 and has been at Ballou ever since. Has coached girls' basketball, boys' soccer, girls' softball, and indoor track. Moved to boys' basketball in 1988. Named the Inter High East *Washington Post* Coach of the Year in 1991; pp. 21, 49, 152.

ED O'BRIEN, basketball, Bishop Verot High, Fort Myers, FL. Age 46; born in Camden, NJ. Started his coaching career in 1968 at St. Catherine of Siena Grade School in Horsham, PA. Head coach at Verot for five years. Coached the Vikings to their first-ever twenty-win season and a district championship in 1991. Coach of the year in Southwest Florida in 1991 and 1993; pp. 13, 18, 218, 228.

RON O'BRIEN, diving, Swimming Hall of Fame Aquatic Complex, Fort Lauderdale, Florida (coached Greg Louganis for ten years). Age 55; born in Pittsburgh. Three-time NCAA diving All-American at Ohio State. Head coach at the University of Minnesota, Ohio State, the Mission Viejo Nadadadores in CA, and Mission Bay Aquatic Center in Boca Raton, FL; pp. 127–129.

JACK PARDEE, Houston Oilers. Age 63; raised in Christoval, TX, where he played six-man high school football. Played for Bear Bryant at Texas A&M. Played fifteen years in the NFL with the Los Angeles Rams and the Washington Redskins. Has been the head coach of the Florida Blazers in the WFL, the Chicago Bears, the Washington Redskins, and the Houston Gamblers in the USFL, and with the University of Houston and the Houston Oilers. Took the Blazers to the World Bowl game in 1974, and was NFC Coach of the Year in 1976 and NFL Coach of the Year in 1979; p. 12.

BUTCH PASTORINI has been a volunteer football coach at Santa Clara University since 1968. He also played for the Broncos, in the early 1960s, and was named to the Little All-American Team; pp. 102–103.

TED PETERSEN, football, Trinity High, Washington, PA. Age 37; born in Kankakee, IL. Played nine years in the NFL, the first seven with the Steelers, where he won two Super Bowl rings. Spent one year as an assistant at Canon McMillrow and then one year as the head coach before moving to the Trinity High "Killer Gorillas" in 1990; pp. 37, 99–100.

WADE PHILLIPS, named head coach of the Denver Broncos before the 1993 season, after having been the team's defensive coordinator. Phillips joined the NFL as a coach with the Houston Oilers when he was 28, after coaching stints in Texas high schools and at the University of Houston; pp. 8, 23, 76, 81.

JERRY POPP, boys' and girls' cross-country, Bowman High School, ND. Age 40; born in Royalton, MI. Has coached the Bulldogs for eighteen years. Won twenty-four boys' and girls' state cross-country championships, including twelve consecutive girls' titles—a national record. Has also won six track state titles; pp. 24, 85, 180.

MIKE PRICE, football, Washington State. Age 47; born in Denver. Made assistant-coaching stops at Washington State, the University of Puget Sound, and the University of Missouri before getting the head job at Weber State in 1981. Moved to the head slot at Washington State in 1989. Took the 1992 Cougars to a 9–3 record and a 31–28 Copper Bowl victory over Utah; pp. 7, 14, 107, 108, 163.

JOE RAMSEY, basketball, Millikin University, Decatur, IL. Age 49; born in Monticello, KY. Coached Robert Morris Junior College to a third-place national finish in 1969 and 1971. Assistant coach at Oklahoma 1971 to 1973 and head coach 1973 to 1975. At Millikin for seventeen years. Conference champions in 1983 and 1989 and in the NCAA Division III tournament in 1983, 1988, and 1989. Record at Millikin is 241–201; overall record is 397–247; pp. 10, 165, 177–178.

JAMES REYNOLDS, JR., football, Martin Luther King, Jr., High, Detroit. Age 47; born in Colombus, GA. Graduated from Tuskeegee University in 1968. Head coach at King for nineteen years, with a 118–60 record. State regional champ three times and the East Side champ twelve times. Coach of the year eight times; pp. 11, 80–81.

JERRY REYNOLDS, coach turned general manager, Sacramento Kings. Grew up in French Lick, IN, before Larry Bird. An assistant at Vincennes J.C. and West Georgia. Head coach for nine years at Rockhurst College in Kansas City, MO, and for one year at Pittsburg State in KS. Joined the Kings in 1985 as an assistant. Has been interim and head coach with the Kings, and director of player personnel; pp. 3, 89–90, 147, 150, 151, 163.

DR. DOROTHY L. RICHEY, track & field, Chicago State University (retired). Currently an assistant professor of physical education and athletic administration at Slippery Rock University in PA. Coached at Indiana State 1967 to 1972, and Chicago State 1972 to 1978, where she was one of the first woman ADs for both men's and women's programs; pp. 97–98.

MARGE RICKER, 69, founded the Orlando Rebels, a women's fast-pitch softball team, in 1954, and coached until the team disbanded in 1985. Ricker figures the Rebels played at least 2,000 games and won at least 1,500 in their travels around the country in search of games. Ricker had only one losing season. In 1981 the Rebels won the national championship; pp. 62–63, 209–10.

JEANE ROISE, basketball, University of North Dakota, Williston. Age 32; born in Minot, ND. Coached the Grand Forks/Red River High Roughriders for ten years. Won a State Class A championship in 1988 and was coach of the year; pp. 5, 79, 81–82, 153.

ALAN ROWAN, track & field, Punahou School, Honolulu, HI (retired). Age 65; born in Paia, Maui, HI. Head coach at Punahou from 1954 to 1992. Won over four hundred dual meets and thirty league and twenty-one state championships. National high school track and field coach of the year in 1986. (AGC); pp. 121–122.

KATHY RUSH, basketball, Immaculata College (retired). Age 46; born in Atlantic City, NJ. Rush coached Immaculata from 1972 to 1977, where in 1972 the Philadelphia school won the first-ever women's intercollegiate national championship. Immaculata also won in 1973 and 1974. Retired in 1977 and never coached again. Director of Future Stars International basketball camps at Swarthmore and Delaware Valley Colleges in PA and SUNY-Oneonta in NY; pp. 188, 236–238.

SAM RUTIGLIANO, football, Liberty University, Lynchburg, VA. Age 59; born in Brooklyn, NY. An NFL assistant at Denver, New England, the New York Jets, and New Orleans before spending seven years as the head coach of the Cleveland Browns, where he was twice named AFC Coach of the Year; pp. 158, 159, 178, 181, 182, 196, 200, 201, 206.

JIM SATALIN, basketball, Duquesne University (retired). Age 46; born in Syracuse. Won a 1977 NIT championship while at St. Bonaventure. Coached seven years at Duquesne until 1989, then spent one year as a volunteer assistant at West Virginia. Worked in the private sector until 1993; currently pursuing a career as a TV basketball commentator; pp. 6, 118, 188–189, 197, 198–199, 219, 220–221, 225, 227.

RIC SCHAFER, hockey, University of Notre Dame. Age 42; born in Minneapolis. Played hockey and graduated from Notre Dame in 1974. A Fighting Irish assistant for five years before taking over a new hockey program at the University of Alaska-Fairbanks. Returned to his alma mater in 1987 as head hockey coach; pp. 148–149, 166–167, 170, 227–228.

BOBBIE SCHULTZ, field hockey, Shawnee High, Medford, NJ. Age 46; born in Passaic, NJ. Head coach since 1968; 338 wins, 55 losses, 55 ties. Has won thirteen league championships and seven state titles. National High School Federation Outstanding High School Coaching award in 1987; p. 133.

ROSE MISURACA SCOTT, softball coach at Andrew Jackson High in Challmette, LA, for twenty-two years, until the school became a magnet school and teams sports were dropped. Her teams were in the state playoffs nineteen of those twenty-two years. They won eight state titles and were runners-up twice. She has been the athletic director since 1974. (AGC); pp. 195–196.

PAT WARD SEIB, track, basketball, and volleyball, Gibson Southern High, Evansville, IN. Age 43; born in Owensboro, KY. Coached basketball eight years, volleyball nineteen years, track and field twenty-two years; pp. 63–64.

JIM SHORT, wrestling, Simley High, Inver Grove Heights, MI. Age 45; born in St. Paul. Founded the Simley wrestling program twenty-two years ago. Has won four state team championships since 1987 and has coached eleven individual state champions. State coach of the year in 1987 and selected the USA/Minnesota Man of the Year in 1985. Has a twenty-two-year record of 264–120–5; a 170–21–1 record the last nine; pp. 74, 136, 141–142.

BOB SIDDENS, wrestling, West High, Waterloo, IA (retired). Age 68; born in Council Bluffs, IA. Spent twenty-nine years at West, where he coached Dan Gable, America's greatest wrestler. (AGC); pp. 113–114, 240–241.

LARRY SMITH, football, most recently the head coach at USC (1987–92) until he was forced to resign. Started coaching in 1962 at Lima Shawnee High in OH. Made assistant-coaching stops at Miami, Ohio, Michigan, and Arizona. Has also been head coach at Tulane (1976–79) and Arizona (1980–86); pp. 6, 42, 92.

STAN SMITH, Director of Coaching for the USTA.

JOHN STERNER, wrestling, Southwest State, Marshall, MN.

MIKE STERNER, wrestling, Moorhead University, MN.

CLEVELAND STROUD, basketball, Rockdale High, GA. Age 54; born in Atlanta. Graduated from Morehouse College and became the junior varsity coach at Rockdale in 1971. Took over the varsity team in 1976. Won a state championship that was taken away when he volunteered information that he had inadvertently played an ineligible player for forty-five seconds in a 20-point win. Georgia Coach of the Year in 1987, Jack Kennedy U.S. Olympic Award winner in 1988, Georgian of the Year in 1989; pp. 47–48, 151–152.

PAT HEAD SUMMITT, basketball, University of Tennessee. Age 41; born in Ashley City, TN. Member of the silver-medal U.S. women's Olympic basaketball team in 1976. Lady Volunteer head coach since 1974. Has been to the Final Four twelve times and has won three NCAA titles. Her overall record is 562–128. National Coach of the Year in 1987 and 1989. Coached the U.S. women's Olympic team to a gold medal in 1984. (AGC); pp. 10, 144–145.

TRACY SUNDLUN, former coach of track & field at Georgetown, USC, and the University of Colorado, as well as for the D.C. Striders and San Luis Obispo track clubs. Since 1970 he has coached over one hundred athletes who have represented their countries in Olympic and international competitions. His runners have been ranked in the top ten in virtually every event from the one-hundred-meter dash to the marathon. He is president of the New York Amateur Sports Alliance; pp. 228, 230–231.

CHARLIE THOMAS, basketball, San Francisco State. Age 41; born in Harrisonburg, VA. Played on the NIT Champion Virginia Tech team in 1974 and played professionally in Luxembourg and Venezuela. Was head coach at Emory and Henry College in VA and Bristol College in TN before becoming head coach at SFSU in 1988; pp. 15, 49–50, 109, 159, 251.

EDDIE TITUS, probation officer, also a volunteer coach at Santa Clara University for twenty years, where he coaches the defensive backfield. Played football at Oakland City College and had a tryout with the San Diego Chargers; p. 245.

JOE TORRE, St. Louis Cardinals. Age 53; born in Brooklyn, NY. Played in the National League for seventeen years; named MVP in 1971 with the Cardinals. Began managing with the New York Mets in 1977. Took over the Atlanta Braves in 1982 and won a West Division Title and manager of the year honors. Spent six years as a broadcaster for the California Angels before becoming the Cardinals' manager in 1990; pp. 12, 105, 179, 197, 207–208.

CHUCK TRUBY, wrestling assistant, Chicago Vocational High. Age 27; born in Chicago. Attended Thornton Fractional South in Lansing,

IL, and Chicago State. An assistant coach at Lew Wallace High in Gary, IN, and Carver Area High in Chicago; pp. 12, 13, 26, 43.

BUTCH VAN BREDA KOLFF, basketball, Hofstra University. Age 70. Coaching for forty years. Coached the Lakers, Pistons, Suns, and Jazz in the NBA, the Memphis Tams in the ABA, and the New Orleans Pride in the Women's Professional Basketball League. Coached at Lafayette from 1952 to 1955 and again from 1984 to 1988; coached at Hofstra from 1955 to 1961 and again since 1988. Coached at Princeton from 1963 to 1967. Spent 1983 at Picayune High School in Mississippi; pp. 56–57, 159, 168, 183–184, 202, 253–254.

HARRY VANDERSLICE, Little League baseball, Ocean City, NJ. Age 69; born in Philadelphia. Coached Little League in Ocean City for thirty-two years. Won the city championship four times. Named Ocean City's Sportsman of the Decade for the 1980s; pp. 12, 60, 83–84, 142, 182.

JIM VAN HORN, for seven years a volunteer assistant at Allentown College of St. Francis DeSales and Lafayette College, both in PA. Owns a sports-marketing company, Van Horn Associates, in Allentown, PA. (Coached the author's senior year at Allentown in 1973–74); pp. 56, 57, 135–136.

DICK VERMEIL, Philadelphia Eagles (retired). From 1976 to 1983 coached the Eagles to a 54–45 record, four playoff appearances, and one trip to the Super Bowl, in 1980. NFL Coach of the Year in 1979. Coached UCLA for two years to a 15–5–3 record, a PAC–10 conference title, and an upset of Ohio State in the 1976 Rose Bowl. An ABC–TV football analyst, he has been nominated for two Emmys; pp. 3, 93, 134–135, 146–147, 162, 163, 167, 169, 206–207.

GENE VOLLNOGLE, football, Carson High, Los Angeles (retired). Age 62; born in Freemont, CA. Won two city championships and compiled a 75–10 record at Banning High School from 1953 to 1962. Moved to Carson in 1963, where he won 235 games, lost 66, and tied 1 before retiring in 1991. His Carson teams won eight city championships and were runners-up eight more times. One of only six coaches at any level to win 300 or more games; pp. 18, 150, 216, 241, 254.

LINDA WELLS, softball, Arizona State. Coached at the University of Minnesota for eighteen years before moving to ASU in 1989. An assistant coach of the gold-medal-winning 1987 Pan Am team and coach of the U.S. gold-medal-winning South Pacific Classic team. An inaugural member of the National Softball Coaches Hall of Fame, 1991; pp. 61–62.

JACK WHITE, a Pop Warner football coach in Canton, MA. Interviewed in April 1991, he died of leukemia at age 54 in September 1992. Coached Pop Warner for twenty-five years. The last five years he coached he was totally blind; pp. 91, 216–217, 245–246.

BILL WHITMORE, head basketball coach of the University of Vermont for five years. Age 41; born in Red Bank, NJ. Attended Alabama for one year, transferred to St. Bonaventure's, where he played one year of basketball and two years of soccer. The year after he graduated he took Rushford High in upstate NY to a state title; pp. 30, 86, 87, 139, 189, 205–206, 225.

BRUCE WILHELM, weight lifting and shot put. Age 48. Finished fifth in the super-heavyweight division at the 1976 Olympics. He placed second behind the legendary Vassily Alexeyev in the snatch and was fifth in the jerk. He tied for third in the final standings, where the bronze medal was determined on the basis of body weight. In 1977 and 1978 he was crowned "The World's Strongest Man" on the CBS made-for-television competition. He was also nationally ranked in the shot put; pp. 36, 231–233.

TIM WILKE, girls' basketball, Lowmira High, WI. Age 31; born in Marshfield, WI. Coached one year of boys' freshmen basketball before moving to the girls' varsity in 1990. In three years he has a 50–19 record; lost in the state semifinals in 1993; pp. 137, 251–253.

BILLY WILLIAMS, now in his sixth year as a coach in the Cleveland Indians organization. He is currently an outfield instructor in the club's minor league system. He spent seventeen years in the minors, from 1952 to 1969, and ten days with the Seattle Pilots in the majors. He returned to baseball after seventeen years in the haberdashery business; pp. 36, 65, 111, 242–243, 254.

BR. MIKE WILMOTT, S.J., attended Marquette High in Milwaukee and entered the Jesuits as a brother in 1958. Went to Creighton Prep in 1964, where he started as an assistant track coach. Became head basketball coach in 1970. Has coached the Blue Jays to ten state tournaments and to championships in 1976 and 1981. Coached track until 1987 and has been the defensive coordinator of the football team for twenty years; pp. 11, 35, 226.

LADONNA WILSON, basketball, Austin Peay State University, TN. Age 27; born in Grovette, AR. Played basketball at Missouri Southern State College. Head coach of the Governors at 24; pp. 79–80, 169.

WALTER WILSON, basketball, Haskell Junior College. Age 45; born in Idabel, OK. Coached four years at Baptiste High in Oklahoma before coming to Haskell, where he has been head coach for thirteen years. Graduated from and earned his post-grad degree at Southeastern Oklahoma State, where he spent two years as a graduate-assistant coach; pp. 60–61, 79–80.

JOHN WINKIN, baseball, University of Maine. Age 73; born in New York City. First coaching job was with the Englewood, NJ, American Legion baseball team. In his nineteen years at Maine he has taken the Black Bears to the College World Series in Omaha six times. A member of the American Baseball Coaches Hall of Fame; pp. 90, 147, 224.

SR. LYNN WINSOR, B.V.M., CAA, golf, Xavier Prep, Phoenix. Age 50; born in Fond du Lac, WI. Entered the Sisters of the Blessed Virgin Mary out of Dubuque two years after graduating from Arizona State. Returned to her high school alma mater in 1974. Has coached basketball and softball in addition to golf. Has won thirteen consecutive state golf titles, a national record for boys or girls; pp. 69, 101, 178–179.

BOB WOOD, tennis, University Liggett School, Grosse Pointe Woods, MI. Age 52; born in Jackson, MI. Won the 1965 NCAA small college singles and doubles crown at St. Lawrence College in Canton, NY. Spent four years coaching at Harrisburg (PA) Academy; has been at Liggett for twenty-eight. Won twenty boys' state titles at Liggett, including a then-record thirteen in a row from 1972 to 1984. Coached the girls for five years and won four state titles. (AGC); pp. 83, 109, 164.

PAUL WOODALL, track and field, Bryan Station High, Lexington, KY.

JOHN WOODEN, basketball, UCLA (retired). Coached at UCLA from 1948 to 1975, where he won 620 games and lost 147. From 1964 to 1975 the Bruins won ten NCAA championships, including seven in a row. Also coached at Dayton High in Kentucky and Central

High in Indiana, compiling a 218–42 record. He was also 47–14 at Indiana State. An All-American at Perdue, he is the only person inducted into the Basketball Hall of Fame as both a player and a coach. (AGC); pp. 2, 59, 106, 118, 119, 164–165, 167, 209, 219.

CHUCK YATES, Little League Baseball, Bellevue, NE. Age 44; born in Red Oak, IA. Works the 7-to-midnight shift at KEZO AM/FM Z–92 in Omaha; pp. 243–244.

JOHN YOUNG, founder and president, Reviving Baseball in Inner Cities (RBI); scout for the Florida Marlins. Played professional baseball from 1969 to 1977, including a four-at-bat stint with the Tigers in 1971. Was a player coach for the Arkansas Travelers, a double-A team, in 1977. Played one year in the Mexican league, then began scouting, first with the Tigers, then the Padres, Rangers, and now the Marlins. Started RBI in 1989; pp. 30, 36–37, 235–236.

GARY ZARECKY, basketball, Foothills J.C., Los Altos Hills, CA. Age 48; grew up in Sacramento. Coached at Sweetwater High in San Diego for fifteen years, was nationally ranked by *Basketball Weekly* three of his last five years. In 1984 became first coach to take a high school team to Yugoslavia. Coached at United States International University in San Diego for six years. In 1992 Freemont averaged 103.6 points per game, second highest in the nation; pp. 44–45, 166, 218, 226, 248–249.

JIM ZULLO, basketball, Shenendehowa High, Clifton Park, NY. Played basketball and graduated from the University of Connecticut in 1965. Has been at Shenendehowa since 1973, where his record is 348–149. Has won nine Suburban (Albany) Council League Championships, five sectionals, and one New York State Championship. State coach of the year in 1986; pp. 15, 137–138, 224–225.